THE

MAILBOX
CONSPIRACY

THE

MAILBOX
CONSPIRACY

The Inside Story
of the Greatest Corruption Case
in Hawai'i History

Alexander Silvert

WATERMARK
PUBLISHING

ISBN: 978-1-948011-63-1

Library of Congress Control Number: 2021945786

Photos and artwork used with permission:
Puana family photos (pp. 20, 231),
Honolulu Star-Advertiser (p. 180),
Dannah Mari Hidalgo (p. 191),
all others courtesy Hawaii News Now

Design and production
Angela Wu-Ki

Watermark Publishing
1000 Bishop St., Ste. 806
Honolulu, HI 96813
Telephone 1-808-587-7766
Toll-free 1-866-900-BOOK
sales@bookshawaii.net
www.bookshawaii.net

10 9 8 7 6 5 4 3 2 1

Printed in Korea

E Hoʻomau

To all state and federal public defenders who fight every day
for justice and fairness against overwhelming bias and inequity
in our criminal justice system.

And to my sons, Kal and Che, and my wife, Diana,
who through thick and thin supported me in my own small efforts
to fight injustice. We did it together as a family.

Hoʻomau is the Hawaiian value of perseverance and persistence.
In practicing this value we become more tenacious and resilient,
and thus more courageous. Hoʻomau also means to perpetuate,
and to continue in a way that causes good to be long-lasting.

Contents

Preface

This is an important book. It's the story of a public defender who, in the course of defending his client, ended up defending all of us. It's the story of a public defender who, even after he had found the evidence needed to acquit his client, brought that evidence to the United States Attorney's Office and to the Federal Bureau of Investigation, in hopes that they would see that a criminal conspiracy to frame an innocent man was occurring at the highest levels of law enforcement in Honolulu.

Federal public defender Alexander Silvert's investigation revealed the unthinkable—that Honolulu chief of police Louis Kealoha and his wife, deputy prosecuting attorney Katherine Kealoha, had choreographed an extraordinary and elaborate conspiracy to frame Katherine's uncle in order to cover up financial crimes against her own family, crimes committed to sustain the Kealohas' luxurious lifestyle. Loyal police officers, all members of a secretive black ops unit within the Honolulu Police Department, executed their scheme and later destroyed evidence as Silvert dug deeper. His investigation, further developed and prosecuted by a special prosecutor appointed by the United States attorney general, resulted in criminal convictions and lengthy prison sentences for Chief

Kealoha, Katherine Kealoha and two police officers. And at this writing, the federal investigation is still ongoing, with FBI target letters outstanding against major political players in Honolulu's government.

This book is also a cautionary tale, a warning against willful blindness to police corruption. When the federal investigation became public, many in Honolulu simply could not believe that a police chief, a deputy prosecuting attorney and police officers would conspire to violate the very laws they had sworn to uphold. Most believed that Silvert was grandstanding without any solid evidence. The Honolulu Police Commission, designed to provide civilian oversight over the police chief, was in such a state of denial that it allowed Chief Kealoha to resign in good standing, handing him a check for $250,000 as he took early retirement.

Congressman John Lewis once said, "When you see something that is not right, not fair, not just, you have to speak up. You have to say something; you have to do something." This book shows us what is possible when we heed Lewis's words.

—*Loretta Sheehan, Former Chair, Honolulu Police Commission*

ACT I

CHAPTER 1

"I Didn't Do It!"

"**I** didn't do it," my client said. "I'm being framed."

"I understand," I responded. But really I didn't. I'd heard these words from clients before, and they had been neither framed nor innocent. But they were insistent despite, in most cases, the overwhelming amount of evidence against them. I sighed. It appeared he was going to be a difficult client to handle. He was charged with destruction of letter boxes or mail, a federal crime punishable by up to three years in jail. It was alleged that my client had stolen a mailbox from a residence in the affluent suburb of Kāhala in Honolulu. It was certainly not the most serious of crimes, but it was a felony, nonetheless. Besides facing possible jail time, a person convicted of a felony loses valuable civil rights, like the right to ever own or possess a firearm and, sometimes, the right to vote. But who steals an entire mailbox? Mail, yes. Thieves steal mail to get credit cards or gift money sent by Grandma. But stealing the *entire* mailbox? No, I hadn't seen that one before.

Although my client had originally been arrested by the Honolulu Police Department and charged with the state crime of felony theft, the case had then been picked up by the United States postal inspector and charged in federal court by the United States Attorney's Office. Why this particular case had been accepted by the United States Attorney's Office was unclear. There are serious crimes in the Aloha State. Cases concerning large quantities of drugs or violent crimes brought originally in state court are sometimes taken over by the feds because federal sentencing laws are generally much more severe than state sentencing laws. Unlike under state law, there is no parole when serving a federal sentence, and except for the possibility of getting about two months off per year for good behavior, a defendant serves the entire sentence imposed by the court. But I had never seen this type of low-level case come into federal court. Why was the United States Attorney's Office interested in this case? It was, to say the least, very unusual.

It's very expensive to hire an attorney when charged with a federal crime. I've heard of fees of up to $25,000 just to plead someone guilty, with expenses of well over $100,000 if a case goes to trial. Not many people, even those with full-time jobs, can afford to hire a private attorney in federal court. As a result, the Office of the Federal Defender for the District of Hawai'i, which provides representation to indigent defendants, has at times represented over 80 percent of all defendants charged in federal court. Because my client in this case could not afford to pay for his own attorney, we were appointed to represent him.

On July 1, 2013, after my client's initial appearance in court, I assigned the case to myself. As first assistant, I was in charge of assigning all cases that came into the office. In my twenty-five-plus years of practicing as a federal public defender, no such case had ever come into my office. It was a novelty. My usual caseload was a steady diet of serious drug offenses, mostly methamphetamine; bank robberies; gun cases; and large-scale white-collar fraud cases, all of which carry hefty jail time if the client is convicted. A simple theft of a mailbox piqued my curiosity. But what really caught my attention were the owners of the residence, where now only the pedestal to the mailbox remained. They were none other than Louis Kealoha, the chief of police of the Honolulu Police Department—the twentieth-largest metropolitan police department in the United States with over 1,800 officers—and his wife, Katherine Kealoha, who was the third-highest-ranking prosecutor in the City and County of Honolulu's prosecuting attorney's office and the head of its Career Offender Unit.

HPD police chief Louis Kealoha and his wife,
deputy prosecuting attorney Katherine Kealoha

Looking at the criminal complaint, which specified the charge and contained a brief statement of the facts in the form of an affidavit from the postal inspector, I learned that on June 21, 2013, at around 11:20 p.m., several surveillance cameras captured images of a white car with a sunroof driving up to the Kealoha residence on a semi-deserted street in the upscale suburb of Kāhala on Oʻahu's southern shore. In the footage, the car stops in front of the white mailbox outside of the Kealohas' home. A man wearing khaki shorts, white socks, sneakers and a baseball-style cap exits the driver's door of the vehicle, strides up to the mailbox and, after several attempts, yanks the entire mailbox off its pedestal. The man then carries the mailbox away, like a loaf of bread, back to the vehicle, places it in the passenger rear seat and drives away. No license plate number is visible due to the glare from the streetlights. The make and model of the vehicle itself is difficult if not impossible to determine. The entire theft as captured on the video takes less than thirty seconds.

The following day two Honolulu Police officers, beat cops, responded to a 911 call made by Katherine Kealoha. Katherine told the officers that her mailbox was stolen the night before. Her statement was taken, the crime scene processed, numerous photographs shot, schematics drawn and official HPD reports filed. Several days later, two homicide detectives from the Honolulu Police Department's Criminal Investigative Division (CID) were assigned to investigate the theft. On the eighth day after the theft, on June 29 at 5:00 p.m., Katherine Kealoha, for the very first time, positively identified the "thief" from the surveillance video. It was Gerard Puana, her fifty-three-year-old uncle. Her father's youngest brother. Ten minutes later Gerard was arrested as he drove into his church's parking lot with his girlfriend.

Gerard, the man sitting uncomfortably before me, was not initially accused of having committed any federal crime. He was initially charged under Hawaiʻi state law for theft in the second degree, a felony offense. But two days later, after being held in a cell in the basement of the Honolulu Police Department, the state charges were dismissed and the case was turned over to federal postal authorities. Gerard was transferred into federal custody and charged with the federal crime of destruction of letter boxes or mail, a felony offense. Subsequently, on July 1, he was released on a $25,000 unsecured bond, which meant that he didn't have to put up any money but could be held liable for $25,000 were he not to show up for court hearings.

And now here he sat in my office, nervously rubbing his legs and moving around in his chair. Although we'd just met, I could see he was anxious and couldn't wait to tell me his side of the story. I wasn't surprised by his behavior. Some clients don't want to tell you anything. Others are eager to give their side of the story, and like an out-of-control firehose spray information at you. There is usually nothing in between. Almost immediately, Gerard burst forth with a stream of words so fast that I could not understand everything he was saying. But I got the gist. He was repeatedly telling me he was totally innocent and was being framed. Framed because he had filed a civil complaint against his niece, Katherine Kealoha, and this was her way of retaliating against him.

I listened and didn't interrupt, even though much of what he was saying came across to me as nothing more than disjointed bits and pieces of information. Not knowing anything about what had led up to this point in his life, I was not able to follow along with his story. Having just met him, I had no idea who most of the people he was talking about were nor how they related to him. I didn't know anything about the events he was describing to me, nor could I put them in any context. But I could tell he needed the release. He believed, after all, that he was speaking to a sympathetic ear. His defense attorney.

But in my mind, I was thinking, *Really? Who frames someone for stealing a mailbox? Certainly not the chief of police and his prosecutor wife, an attorney.* Even more unlikely when the entire crime, all thirty seconds of it, was caught on surveillance video. Reaching for my yellow legal pad, I let out a deep sigh.

After a while I tried to regain control of the meeting so that I could explain to Gerard the intricacies of the federal criminal process. But every time I thought he was done talking, Gerard couldn't contain himself, and another burst of his story was hurled at me. A story I could not hope to fully understand yet, but he couldn't help himself. Finally, like a squeezed-out sponge, he was done. He looked down, exhausted, and slumped in his chair. I waited a few seconds, letting the silence serve as a break in our conversation. I told Gerard, to his obvious dismay, that I didn't want to talk about the facts of his case during this first meeting. But not to worry, I hurriedly added, there would be plenty of time for that later. He gave me a blank stare. I told him before he started to protest that it was not because I wasn't interested, no, not at all, but we were going to take things slowly, orderly and with purpose.

I've learned over the years that first explaining the federal criminal process to a client, without any discussion of the particular facts of their case, helps to develop a rapport without having to jump to any conclusion as to guilt or innocence. Talking about the court process is an entirely neutral topic. This would allow us to learn about one another without the pressure to make any decisions, and it also afforded me the opportunity to demonstrate my knowledge and experience of criminal law to him. Gerard had never met me before, and he didn't know or trust me yet. I'm a federal public defender; Gerard wasn't paying for my services. He didn't choose me to be his attorney. So why should he trust me at all? I got it. Many of my clients don't even believe public defenders have a legitimate law license, let alone that they've won a single case. If we were any good, many sincerely believe, we'd be in private practice. They also believe we work for "the government."

I completely understand these preconceived notions of what a public defender is and don't take any personal offense. But such assumptions could not be further from the truth. Not only are federal public defenders committed to the work we all do, but because the entirety of our practice is criminal defense in federal court, the Federal Public Defender office (and this is particularly true of my Honolulu office) is often referred to by members of the private criminal defense bar as the "best law firm no one can hire." But my clients are not part of that fraternity. To most of them I'm just some government lawyer who is overworked and only paid enough to plead them guilty and move on to the next case. Gerard, I had no doubt, was having some of these same thoughts as he sat before me. The most important task I had to accomplish as I started to represent Gerard was to get him to trust me.

* * *

For me, being a public defender is more of a calling. Like a rebel *with* a cause. But I'm not what some would call a "true believer." Most people charged with a federal crime are guilty. They did in fact commit the crime they are charged with. But the criminal justice system can be unfair and unjust. It's as simple as that. Anyone who works in the federal criminal justice system knows this fact.

I was raised in a liberal household on the East Coast. Both my parents were college professors. In the late '60s and early '70s my mother would take me to demonstrations to protest against the Vietnam War or Richard Nixon. The first time I was involved in a demonstration, or should I say, taken to a demonstration, I held my mother's hand as she and those around me shouted, "Hey hey. Ho ho. Richard Nixon has got to go!" I joined in. Why not? It was like singing in school. I was nine years old when my mother dragged me out of bed at ten at night, in my pajamas, and took me to a rally that was being held against George Wallace. He had come to Dartmouth College in New Hampshire to give a speech when he was running for president in 1967. My mother, a professor at Dartmouth, organized students to heckle him during his speech, and it got a little out of control. I don't exactly know what she thought I was going to do at the age of nine, and in my pajamas, but I was there and that's all that mattered. I had no idea what was going on, but it was exciting.

When I was thirteen years old my mother took me to Washington, DC, to participate in my first big demonstration. We were part of a group that was tear-gassed as we marched down Constitution Avenue. Not a pleasant experience for anyone, at any age. I certainly didn't feel like a "radical hippie," as we were portrayed in the national newspapers the next day. My mother tried to shield me as we dodged tear gas canisters that were being fired directly into the crowd by police dressed in full battle gear, with armored personnel carriers blocking the street. I'll never forget the irony of a national guardsman, who just moments earlier had fired tear gas canisters at us, now allowing us safe passage through the line of officers and vehicles, as all around us other officers continued to lob canisters into the crowd.

Gerard didn't know that the lawyer sitting in front of him had never even wanted to be an attorney. After graduating from UCLA and driving a cab in New York City for a year, I enrolled in New York University to obtain my PhD in political science. I wanted to become a college professor like my parents. After my first year of postgraduate courses, I went to study law at Boston College Law School in Newton, Massachusetts, but I never went intending to become an attorney. I fully intended to return to NYU and obtain my PhD.

During my second year of law school, I enrolled in a clinical program that provided free legal counseling and representation to indigent people in civil matters. At the time I was in law school, the early 1980s, these types of clinical programs were relatively new and were considered outlier courses, particularly at Boston College Law School, which billed itself as a business law school. In the civil law clinic, under the supervision of a licensed attorney and professor, I worked on divorce cases or disputes for nonpayment of electricity or water bills and represented families of children with special educational needs in disputes with the Department of Education. I learned very quickly that while I liked the hands-on feel of working on an active case, civil litigation was not for me. Too messy. The cases never ended. One problem only led to another problem, which led to some crisis that never seemed to end. But I loved the work and I loved helping people.

In my third year I took a criminal law clinical where students represented indigent people accused of petty crimes, like small retail theft cases and first offense drunk driving charges. Cases where the stakes were small and no real harm could be done to a defendant who accepted our representation. I immediately fell in love with the entire criminal process. The sights and even the smells of walking into a grimy police station's cell room at eight o'clock in the morning. Helping new arrestees get released on bail and hopefully back to their families. Each case presented a different problem, and there was always something new to learn about. But most importantly to me, I found the battle in the courtroom exhilarating. I knew after my first courtroom experience that this was what I wanted to do. I would not be going back to get my PhD. I could always go back later, I thought, but I never did. I was hooked for life.

After graduation, I became a state public defender and then a federal public defender in Philadelphia. It was grueling work. My day often started at 6:00 a.m. and ended after midnight when I had finished prepping for the forty to sixty cases I would handle the next day. I was in court every single day, learning my craft. Every day, hearing after hearing, trial after trial, I was learning from my mistakes, trying new approaches to cross-examination and figuring out how to make a persuasive argument. It was an exhausting but exhilarating time in my life. Federal court practice was very different from state court practice, and I had to learn an entirely new skill set, requiring a lot more legal research and writing. While the courtroom action was the same, the consequences for my clients were normally much, much higher.

I met my future wife during our last year in law school. She was from Hawai'i. Her father had chosen to retire on O'ahu after serving in WWII, Korea and Vietnam. He had met his wife in Japan while serving as part of the American occupation force, and Hawai'i was a great place for her to live as well. After my wife served as a clerk for a year for a Hawai'i Supreme Court justice, she moved to Philadelphia. She already had a clerkship with a federal judge in Hawai'i lined up "just in case it didn't work out." We might have been in love, but she was no dummy. The first day she was in Philadelphia, her car, which we had driven cross-country and which still had Hawai'i license plates on it, was spray-painted. Welcome to the City of Brotherly Love! She stayed nevertheless and landed a job working for the Third Circuit Court of Appeals. We married two years later in Hawai'i on Waimānalo Beach. When our first son was three weeks old, we moved to Hawai'i and I began my job at the Office of the Federal Defender for the District of Hawai'i in 1989. After two years I was chosen to be the first assistant federal defender, a position I still held when I took on Gerard's case in 2013.

In 2000, I was named Federal Defender of the Year, along with several other federal defenders from offices around the country, for the work I had done on several high-publicity and first-of-their kind cases. My friend and co-worker, Charlie Rose, a Hawaiian activist, former Big Island cop and the first investigator I ever worked with in Hawai'i, often told me that "we were the last hope for the hopeless." He was absolutely right, and I took what he said to heart. I approached every case with this thought in mind.

*   *   *

But Gerard, sitting impatiently, waiting for his turn to talk, didn't know who I was or why I do the job I do. He couldn't care less. The emotions of his arrest and the days sitting in jail before his release made it too difficult for us to have any meaningful discussion. I know from years of experience that trust must be built slowly and patiently, brick by brick, before a client will talk candidly with me about what occurred. Even then, more often than not, my clients never tell me the whole truth. Bits and pieces, but never everything.

Many attorneys rush criminal defendants to make a decision about their case, which is usually to plead guilty. Defendants call these types of attorneys "dump trucks." Very few cases charged in federal court go to trial. About 90 percent of all cases brought in federal court result in a guilty plea. Advising a client to plead guilty is not unusual. But this moniker is reserved for attorneys who seem uninterested in doing the work, who don't fully read police reports or take the time to hear their clients' stories before telling defendants they must plead guilty. I'm not a dump truck. I fully realize and appreciate that after all is said and done I'll be going home at the end of the day, but my client may be going to prison for years. Taken away from his family, his friends, everything he knows, to sit in some jail cell on the Mainland, as there are no long-term federal prison facilities on the Islands. I told Gerard that I could only go home at the end of his case if I had a clear conscience that I had done everything I could for him. This meant that he had to work with us, learn to trust me and my staff and above all else have patience as we gathered evidence.

Gerard was having none of it. He didn't want to hear my interesting and scholarly discussion of the federal criminal judicial system. He didn't care who I was or why he should come to trust me. No. There would be time for that later, he told me, parroting my words back to me. He just wanted me to know two things. One, he was innocent. Two, he was framed. At that moment I had no idea whether Gerard was telling me the truth, but he was already setting the bar higher than it needed to be. Being found not guilty simply means that the government doesn't have enough evidence to convict you. It doesn't mean you didn't commit the crime. Being actually innocent is an entirely different matter altogether—it means you did not commit the crime at all. At trial I would not have to prove Gerard was innocent; I would only have to convince the jury that the government failed to present sufficient evidence of his guilt. But to Gerard, apparently, this wouldn't be enough. I sighed again, this time with the understanding that I might not be able to meet his high expectations. That could make our relationship difficult. ❖

CHAPTER 2

The Iceberg

Gerard was formally indicted by a federal grand jury on July 11, 2013. Eight days later we received our first batch of discovery documents from the government. Federal Rules of Criminal Procedure 16 dictates what evidence the government and the defense are required to share with one another prior to trial. Unlike civil cases, where the exchange of evidence and documents is expansive, in criminal cases, to many people's surprise, discovery is extremely limited. Even though a person's liberty is at stake, the law allows the government to keep much of its evidence secret. Witness names are not required to be disclosed until the weekend before trial. Full police reports are not turned over. And only in rare circumstances are depositions, the formal taking of a witness's statement prior to trial, allowed. While a prosecutor can elect to turn over more evidence than is legally required, no court can order them to hand it over if not otherwise required by law. Many prosecutors therefore opt not to turn much evidence over to the defense. This is why criminal trials are often referred to as "trial by ambush."

I met with Gerard and gave him copies of what we had received. I once again told him we would not be discussing the facts of his case, since we both needed time to look over the documents the government had just given us. It was better, I told him, to discuss his case when we had a better understanding of the evidence the government had against him. Although I could tell he was less anxious than when we had first met and more willing to hear me out, the look on his face screamed impatience. But I needed Gerard to be patient. I needed time to build trust between us. Gerard was the one person I had on my side of the ledger who could give me firsthand information, but I needed that information to be truthful or it would be of no use to me.

I told Gerard to visualize Rule 16 as an iceberg floating in the ocean.

The iceberg represents all the evidence the government has in its possession. But we only see one-tenth of the iceberg floating above the surface; the other nine-tenths lies hidden below the ocean waves. It is that one-tenth of the evidence the government has that they are required to disclose to us. Nothing more. I told Gerald to envision the iceberg that sank the *Titanic*. Gerard didn't like what I told him next: "You are the *Titanic*." I didn't tell him this analogy to dishearten him. I didn't tell him this to make him want to plead guilty. No one wants to compare their situation to that of the *Titanic*, but when you get charged with a federal crime, it's best to understand that things aren't looking up for you. Gerard needed to fully understand the gravity of his situation. I wasn't going to lie to him to ingratiate myself to him. I don't lie to my clients, period. Good news or bad news, they're going to hear it from me straight, and that process started for Gerard right then and there. He slumped back in his chair, but the fire in his eyes didn't lessen for an instant.

While the evidence disclosed to us by the government was bad enough, I was more worried about the evidence the government had not given us, that nine-tenths of the iceberg hidden below the waterline. I told Gerard that in order for me to provide him with the best possible defense, I needed to know what that evidence might be. While I could take an educated guess at the types of evidence the government might have acquired during its investigation—like DNA, fingerprints and statements from still unknown adverse witnesses—we wouldn't know what this undisclosed information was until trial, and by then it might well be too late. Gerard himself, I told him, was my key to understanding what evidence lay concealed. I could almost hear him thinking that this couldn't really be how the American criminal justice system works. Wasn't he entitled to a fair fight?

After this reality check, I now needed to build Gerard's hopes back up and, by doing so, get him to believe in me, my office and our dedication to his defense. "The *Titanic* didn't have to sink," I told Gerard. "It could have been avoided." If we worked together, we could change the course of *his* history. Not, I emphasized, as a lawyer and a defendant, but as a team. All that was required was his trust and his honesty. I, in turn, promised Gerard I would do everything I could to defend him. Gerard did not look all that convinced. I told him that we too had some weapons on our side. I had three highly skilled investigators who could track down and interview witnesses and obtain documents. But, unlike the government, we couldn't compel them. If a witness did not want to voluntarily cooperate with us, they could simply walk away. Most people, when confronted by a law enforcement officer with a badge, are more than willing to make a statement to a government agent. And even if a witness does not want to talk to an agent, the government has the power to force them to answer questions by putting them before a grand jury where they have little or no choice but to answer their questions or be held in contempt of court if they refuse.

We had no such power. No right to make anyone talk to us. Which is why, I explained to Gerard, my investigators were trained to get a person talking. In Hawai'i, we call it "talk story." While we had the ability through court-ordered subpoenas to obtain documents and records we believed might be helpful to our defense, like bank records, state administrative records or medical reports, we could not make anyone talk to us. Law enforcement officers knew this and routinely never agreed to speak with us prior to taking the stand at trial and often told civilian government witnesses to do the same.

My most important resource for obtaining information, I told Gerard, was himself—who better to tell me what did or did not happen? I acknowledged that I understood he barely knew me, so why should he be open and honest with me? The law, I explained, provides a legal protection which allows a defendant and their attorney to freely talk to one another without fear that what is discussed will be disclosed to anyone else, including the prosecution. This "attorney–client privilege," I explained, belonged exclusively to him. I could not breach it without his express permission, absent one notable exception. If he were to tell me he was going to kill or seriously injure another person or witness, I would then have a duty to disclose that to the court. This attorney–client privilege did not mean he had to like me, I told Gerard, but he did have to trust my legal abilities and my desire to help him.

It didn't matter to me if he were guilty, I explained. I was not his confessional. I was not his priest, rabbi or minister. It would make no difference to me in terms of how hard we would work on his case. It was the government that had to prove he was guilty beyond a reasonable doubt. We did not have to prove he was innocent. A jury doesn't ever actually decide if a person is innocent. A jury only decides if the government has or has not met its burden to prove a person's guilt beyond a reasonable doubt. I told Gerard he would never hear the word "innocence" come out of my mouth again.

Gerard quickly leaned forward, placing both hands firmly on my desk, making sure I was looking squarely into his eyes, and said, "But I am innocent, and I want you to prove that I am innocent."

Again, I thought to myself, he was setting the bar too high. "I understand," I told him, adding, "We can have this conversation later after we've looked through the evidence." I, for one, was not going to commit to proving his innocence. I didn't even know if we could convince a jury he was not guilty.

We initially received eighty pages of discovery. We were given most of the Honolulu Police Department reports, in full, and a United States postal inspector memorandum about the investigation. We had also received a copy of the video surveillance footage allegedly showing the theft of the mailbox. I was grateful. This was a lot more than was required to be disclosed. The principal document provided to us was lead HPD detective Dru Akagi's CID closing report, dated July 2, 2013, which consisted of six pages summarizing his entire investigation. This was the only report Detective Akagi wrote. Attached to his report were several reports prepared by other officers related to their activities in the investigation. It was obvious to me why assistant US attorney Les Osborne, the assigned prosecutor and supervisor of the entire criminal division of the Hawai'i United States Attorney's Office, had given us this evidence. It was not out of a sense of justice or fairness, but rather because a good prosecutor knows that providing some, but not all, of their strongest evidence up front often convinces a defense attorney to advise their client to throw in the towel quickly and plead guilty before the situation gets any worse. Charging defendants with additional and possibly more serious offenses is a common practice in federal court if a defendant doesn't plead guilty fast enough to suit a prosecutor.

The good news was that, overall, a lot of information had been disclosed and there was much to process in these combined reports. The bad news was that, at first glance, it did not look good for Gerard. There was no question that the mailbox had been stolen. We could see that in the videotape. A crime had certainly been committed. And, to make matters worse, at least two individuals, both of whom had known Gerard for years, one a family member and a highly respected prosecutor, the other related by marriage and a trained police officer, claimed they could identify Gerard as the person in the video. Not good. This wasn't a case where witnesses were identifying a total stranger. They were identifying Gerard because they knew him. They knew what he looked like. How he walked. What clothes he wore. No, not good at all.

The only piece of good news was that the mailbox and any mail that might have been in it had not been located. Nothing had been found in Gerard's possession, in his vehicle or his residence. At least, not yet. Despite Gerard's protestations as to his innocence, I could see why the government thought it had an open-and-shut case. They wanted a quick resolution. It looked like a slam dunk to them, and they expected that I would convince Gerard to plead guilty in the face of this overwhelming evidence. But they did not know Gerard. It was never going to happen.

At the end of our meeting, we shook hands and I escorted Gerard to the door. He looked a little numbed by our conversation. I told him to go home, that we'd talk again after we both had thoroughly gone through the material given to us by the government. I still had not sat down with Gerard and really heard and understood his story. I wanted to do that after we had reviewed the government's evidence, as that would help me formulate questions and guide our discussion. I was having a hard time seeing how we were going to prove Gerard was not guilty, much less innocent. But first impressions are often wrong.

After Gerard left, I gave a copy of the police reports to Brian Wise, one of my office's investigators. "Another client saying he's innocent," I told him. We exchanged a knowing look. No words needed to be spoken. We'd both been down this path before. I asked him to look at the surveillance tape first. No need to waste our time going through the rest of the police reports if the person on the tape was clearly Gerard. Gerard could say he was innocent all he wanted, but the proof in this case was in the pudding. And the pudding was the videotape. ❖

CHAPTER 3

A Tale of Two Mailboxes

When is a mailbox not a mailbox? When it's not *the* mailbox. When Gerard returned to my office a few days later, we had our first conversation about who he was and his side of the case. But we didn't have a detailed conversation about every aspect of the case. In every case, getting information from a defendant is an ongoing process. A client may forget to tell you something important initially but remember it days or weeks later. In many cases, it's not readily apparent at the outset what facts or events are important. As I learn more about a case, either from our own investigation or from further discovery provided by the government, facts or events I never thought relevant become significant. It's a dynamic process, and it requires that I be flexible in my understanding of the case and in my willingness to hear and consider new information. And that includes new information from my client. I also don't want to lock my client into a story at a point when we don't have many of the facts from the government. It makes it that much harder for me to learn the truth when new facts emerge if a client feels wedded to a particular story told in haste, fear and distrust.

I like having short meetings with a client, keeping them to an hour or so. I find that after an hour either my client or I start to lose focus. I'd rather have several meetings or even short phone calls to talk about specific facts than a long meeting where information becomes nothing more than a stream of consciousness. This was the process I undertook with Gerard. Over the course of months we had many, many conversations that eventually led to the whole picture coming together. If something came up, we met, or I had my investigator call Gerard. A need-to-know kind of approach. New information brought new questions, and new questions often elicited new information.

This visit, I wanted to know more about Gerard as a person. Most people like to talk about themselves, and I find it a useful way to get a client talking and putting them at ease without going directly into what happened in a case. Gerard, now more relaxed and comfortable in his chair, told me he was the youngest of nine children. He was named "Gerard" after his mother, Florence, prayed to Saint Gerard to have another son. Florence had had two miscarriages before Gerard was born. Katherine Kealoha's father, Rudolph, or Rudy for short, was the second child born to Florence and was twenty years older than Gerard.

Florence and Gerard Puana

In 1956 Florence and her husband, John Kenalio Puana, moved into the home they had built at 3934 Nioi Place on Wilhelmina Rise in Honolulu. Gerard and Florence were extremely close, he being the youngest. He considered her not only his mother but also his friend. When Gerard's father passed away, he promised him he would take care of Florence. And he had. After graduating from Kalani High School, Gerard landed a job at the Pearl Harbor shipyard as a marine pipefitter. Unfortunately, he was seriously injured in a work accident and had surgery to repair herniated disks in his back. Gerard was told he might never walk again, but after months and years of rehabilitation, he regained his ability to walk. For years, however, he used a cane and still had a slight hitch in his step. Even now he couldn't feel much in his legs and often had sharp pains, "like pins and needles," running up and down in his legs. Because of his injuries, however, he received monthly disability insurance payments, which he was able to save up because he didn't have many expenses while living at home. A few years later, he got a job as a security guard for a private security agency and eventually became a co-owner. But after 9/11, when more well-funded and larger security firms came into existence, he couldn't compete, and he and his partner closed down their business. Gerard had been unemployed since then but made extra money by buying vintage cars, refurbishing and selling them.

I paid careful attention to Gerard's explanation of his injury and how it affected his ability to walk because Katherine and Louis both claimed that they could identify Gerard as the thief due, in part, by the way the person in the surveillance video walked. We had Gerard walk up and down the hallway so we could observe his walk for ourselves.

Now that we had the videotape surveillance footage, Brian, Gerard and I reviewed the video, which consisted of half an hour before and after the theft. The videotape footage consisted of six different camera angles, but only three had caught portions of the theft. To our surprise, it wasn't at all clear that the person seen stealing the mailbox was Gerard. No matter how many times we looked at it, we just couldn't say it was him. I brought in other members of my office to look at it, and they all agreed it wasn't clear enough to make out who the person was in the video, much less that it was Gerard. My administrative assistant, Lynelle Oshita, reviewed the tape. Over the years I had come to trust her opinions to be unbiased and unfiltered. She would tell me exactly what she thought, regardless of what I wanted to hear. If she didn't think the person in the videotape was Gerard, I could bank on that. She agreed. The person in the videotape was not Gerard. I let out a sigh of relief. The videotape was not conclusive. Now we could turn our attention to the other evidence we had been given.

The mailbox at the entry to the Kealohas' Kāhala residence

We started by reviewing the police report of the first officers on the scene. On June 22, 2013, at 1:35 p.m., five minutes after Katherine Kealoha called 911 to report that her mailbox had been stolen the previous night, beat police officers Frederick Rosskopf and Carl Jurison arrived at the Kealohas' Kāhala residence. As the first police officers on the scene, Officers Rosskopf and Jurison processed the crime scene for evidence. Officer Rosskopf photographed the mailbox pedestal, which was all that remained of the mailbox assembly. Officer Rosskopf took a statement from Katherine Kealoha on a standard HPD-252 witness statement form. This form allows a witness to state what occurred in their own words and in their own handwriting. At the end of the document, a typed section verifies that the statement is a true and accurate rendition of what the witness told police.

> I have read this statement prepared by _____ which consists of this typed/handwritten page and _____ continuation page(s), and have been given the opportunity to make corrections thereon. I attest that this statement is true and correct to the best of my knowledge, and that I gave this statement freely and voluntarily without coercion or promise of reward.
>
> Signature_____
> Date: _____ Time: _____
>
> Investigator's Signature _____
> Date: _____ Time: _____

Katherine Kealoha confirmed that she had prepared the statement by writing her name in the blank section of the first line and by signing the form acknowledging that her statement was true and correct.

According to Katherine, sometime between "6/21/13 around 6pm and 6/22/13 at around 5:30am someone stole our mailbox." She described the mailbox as "18 inches x 18 inches by a foot long approximately, with a white shingled roof, approx. value of $380.00." Katherine Kealoha did not state the brand name of the mailbox. She concluded her statement by saying "at this time there is *sic* no known suspects."

Three days later, on June 25, 2013, Detective Dru Akagi and his partner, Detective Greg McCormick, were assigned to investigate the case. Both were from the specialized Criminal Investigation Division (CID) of HPD, which is principally assigned to investigate homicides. Why, we immediately wondered, were homicide detectives assigned to investigate a petty mailbox theft? As one reporter would later comment, as far as he knew, "no mailbox was killed in the commission of this offense."

Detective Akagi's six-page CID closing report, dated July 2, 2013, stated that the mailbox had been purchased in 2005 for about $380. Akagi wrote in his report that "the mailbox was described by [Katherine] Kealoha as":

Gaines brand Classic Locking Mailbox
with pedestal
White with Satin and Nickel finish
Address Plaque
Security lock
Item #GMPCL
Mailbox and 2 keys
50¼" H x 15" W x 10" D
Incoming Mail Slot
2⅞" H x 10" W
Locking Access Door
4" H x 10½" W
Gaines Manufacturing

Lead HPD detective
Dru Akagi

Following standard HPD protocol, another CID detective, Michael Garcia, was brought in as a trained and qualified police officer to provide an independent appraisal of the value of the mailbox. Detective Garcia confirmed, in his report dated June 30, 2013, that the stolen mailbox was made by Gaines Manufacturing, and he appraised the fair market value of the mailbox, used, to be $375. Detective Garcia stated his appraisal was done "sight unseen," but in reliance upon "a photograph of the scene and the initial police reports," which included Katherine Kealoha's statement. He described the mailbox as being a "Gaines Classic Top GMPCL Cast Aluminum, white w/Satin Nickel Accents, Address Plaque and Security Option Lock—Paid."

Having grown up in New York City, I wasn't familiar with the concept of high-end mailboxes. I was used to the simple slot-in-the-front-door variety of Manhattan's brownstone houses or, if one lived in an apartment building, the small mailbox receptacles built into a wall in the entrance to the building. Even when I lived in more suburban areas in Vermont and Hawai'i, my experience with mailboxes were of the $30 garden-variety type bought from the local hardware store. As far as I was concerned, you simply screwed the mailbox onto a wooden post you'd hammered into the ground and presto, your mailbox was ready to receive all the junk mail you never wanted. The idea that someone would pay $380 for a mailbox was a foreign concept to me.

In my initial conversations with Gerard there had been no reason to question the description and value assigned to the mailbox. We had never really discussed anything about the mailbox itself other than Gerard having told me that he had helped install it years earlier by laying the concrete with Rudy Puana, his brother and Katherine's father. Katherine's description of the mailbox was not suspicious in and of itself, particularly given that it was certified as true and correct by Detectives Akagi and Garcia. But our approach to investigating the case had now changed once we had viewed the videotape surveillance evidence and determined that the person captured on the tape did not appear to be Gerard. It certainly seemed more likely that we were headed for a trial, particularly since Gerard continued to maintain he was innocent. This meant investigating every single piece of evidence, regardless of how trivial that piece of evidence might be or how fruitless our efforts could prove. We knew we were going to have to dot our i's and cross our t's.

Brian got to work and contacted Gaines Manufacturing to verify the make and value of the mailbox as described by Katherine and Detectives Akagi and Garcia. It was an easy effort, and we expected nothing more than a simple confirmation. Brian faxed a copy of the crime scene photograph of the pedestal taken by Officer Rosskopf to Mr. Grady Slaugh, a representative of Gaines Manufacturing, and waited for a response. Once we confirmed this small and seemingly insignificant fact, we would move on to more complex and important matters.

"No way! You gotta be fucking kidding me," I exclaimed. Brian had just told me that the mailbox in front of the Kealoha residence could not have been the make and model that Katherine and the Honolulu Police Department's detectives claimed it to be. Only minutes after sending the fax, Brian had received a call from Mr. Slaugh. He told Brian that whatever mailbox had been stolen, it was not a Gaines mailbox because the pedestal in the photo was not one of theirs and could not have been used to secure any of their mailboxes. He explained that every pedestal and corresponding mailbox unit are unique and made to fit one another with securing mechanisms designed specifically for each system. The pedestal in the photograph was not manufactured by Gaines; thus, the mailbox wasn't manufactured by Gaines either. Mr. Slaugh had one more bit of useful information. From the depiction of the pedestal in the crime scene photograph, he was also able to discern which company had actually made the mailbox pedestal: Solar Group, also known as Gibraltar Mailboxes, a competitor.

Brian immediately contacted Mr. Derrick Dryer, a representative of the Solar Group, and sent him the same HPD photograph of the pedestal we had sent Mr. Slaugh. We waited anxiously to learn if he would confirm that the pedestal was made by his company. If he did, this would be our first compelling piece of physical evidence that Katherine and at least two HPD detectives were lying. At this very early stage of our investigation, this was a critical moment. Were we going down a rabbit hole, or was there really something more nefarious going on? The answer came back swiftly. Mr. Dryer confirmed that not only was the pedestal manufactured by his company; it was specifically built for their version of an aluminum pedestal/mailbox system, model number PEDW. The specs for this particular mailbox, manufactured by the Solar Group, were 17" H x 18" W x 12½" D, made of aluminum, weighing thirty-one pounds. The Gaines Manufacturing mailbox Katherine claimed to have had stolen, on the other hand, was 18¾" H x 15" W x 10" D, and made of cast aluminum, weighing forty-one pounds. Additionally, the Solar Group mailbox, model number PEDW, consisted of one solid color with a red flag, while the Gaines mailbox was two-toned and had a gray-colored flag. The shapes of the roofs of each mailbox were also different. While both were shaped like pagodas, one roof was much more pointed than the other, making the difference in the shape between the two roofs easily distinguishable. Given all these differences, there was little chance anyone could confuse the two mailboxes. Particularly not a trained appraiser such as Detective Garcia.

But we still were not done. Now that we knew that the mailbox was not the one claimed to have been stolen, we needed to gather evidence to prove it to a jury. I recalled that Gerard had said he had helped install the mailbox, but I doubted he had paid attention to the make and model of it at the time. We called him and asked him to find out if he or his family had any photographs taken of the front of the Kealohas' house that might depict the mailbox in the background. Luckily, while I was still stuck in the pre-Internet way of thinking, my investigators were not. Adam Choka, who took over the investigation from Brian, who was moving back to the Mainland, came into my office with Brian and plopped several photos on my desk. Google Maps photos. Adam and Brian had gone to Google Maps and simply typed in the address of the Kealohas' residence and zoomed in on the front driveway. And there it was, in full color, plain for all to see, the pedestal and mailbox. The mailbox, painted in all white with a red flag, sat tall and true on top of the same pedestal depicted in the crime scene photograph. The Solar Group mailbox. Model PEDW. No doubt about it. You gotta love modern technology!

I asked Adam to make me "twenty-seven 8 x 10 color glossy pictures" of each Google Map photo. He looked at me quizzically, wondering why I would need so many copies. I told him, "Never mind," realizing that I seemed to be the only one in the room old enough to enjoy my reference to the song "Alice's Restaurant." Sometimes you just have to amuse yourself.

Gerard confirmed our findings by providing us with several family photographs of the front of the Kealohas' residence, which all depicted the Solar Group mailbox in the images. We would later issue subpoenas to Mr. Dryer and Mr. Slaugh to be witnesses at trial. Now we had compelling and irrefutable evidence from multiple different sources that would prove what we later came to call "the lie." There would be no wiggle room. No room for doubt when we went to trial and proved to the jury that the HPD detectives and Katherine had outright lied about the make and model of the mailbox. We were growing in confidence that we were on our way to convincing a jury that the government could not prove beyond a reasonable doubt that Gerard had stolen the Kealohas' mailbox...either of them. Not necessarily that he was innocent, or had been framed, as Gerard claimed, but we were on our way to sowing reasonable doubt.

But why, we asked ourselves, lie about the type of mailbox that had been stolen? Peter Wolff, the head of my office, supplied the answer. Mr. Dryer confirmed that the value of a brand-new Solar Group mailbox was approximately $180. Not used, but brand new. Katherine and Detectives Akagi and Garcia stated that the value of the "used" Gaines mailbox they claimed was stolen was $375 to $380. Was this difference in value significant? You bet it was.

We knew that the case against Gerard had originally intended to be brought and litigated in the Hawai'i state court system under Hawai'i state criminal law. Gerard had originally been arrested and charged under state law with theft of private property, a felony offense. Peter Wolff realized that under then existing state law, a theft of an item with a value *over* $300 was a felony. A theft of an item with a value *under* $300 was a misdemeanor. Thus, the value of the mailbox was critical under Hawai'i state law. A felony offense is a much more serious crime, with more serious ramifications than a misdemeanor offense. Plus, a felony conviction can sometimes be used in other court proceedings to discredit the credibility of a person, who because of it, in the eyes of the law, would be seen as less likely to tell the truth.

Katherine, a high-ranking and longtime City and County prosecutor, and her husband, the chief of police, as well as Detectives Akagi and Garcia, all would know like the back of their hand that the value of the stolen property was a critical factor in determining whether the crime was a felony or a misdemeanor. They arrested and charged people with theft on a daily basis. They would know that the critical threshold was $300. It had taken us a little while to figure this out, but we got there. Now, not only could we prove that they had lied about the make, model and value of the mailbox that had been stolen; we could also prove why. Juries always want to know the "why."

Having found this crack in the government's case, we were determined to pry it open as far as we could. Once we were in trial, we would need to drive it home to the jury in a way they would not forget. To burn this lie into their brain. A lie, a big enough one, an important enough one, can often raise a reasonable doubt. So, we purchased both mailboxes and their respective pedestals. We could now introduce them as exhibits during the trial, confront the witnesses with the two mailboxes standing side by side and, as the jury compared the two mailboxes themselves, destroy the credibility of these witnesses. While this might appear a bit theatrical, a trial is, in part, a staged production for the benefit of the jury. And we were bringing props.

We assembled the two mailboxes and placed them on their pedestals, standing tall next to one another in our office. They were quite a sight. The differences between the two were readily apparent. And while no mail was ever going to be delivered to or stolen from them, they stood as sentinels of "the lie." It would be difficult, if not impossible, for the jury to ignore the truth that these two mailboxes represented. They would ensure that the jury never forgot, never forgave, the lie.

The rules of criminal procedure required us to notify the prosecution that we had physical evidence, the mailboxes, which we intended to introduce at trial. On November 24, 2014, I sent a transmittal letter to the government stating that we had a tangible item, a mailbox, which we intended to use at trial and invited the government to "contact us when and if you wish to view the item." I intentionally did not say we had "two mailboxes" because it was not clear under the law that I had to show them the one mailbox we were going to use to impeach the witnesses, but I had made the decision, out of an abundance of caution, to show them both when they came to take a look at our evidence. But no one ever came. There was, in fact, no response to my letter at all. No call or inquiry. No visit. Nothing. Utter indifference from the government.

Whatever the reason, we held our collective breath, hoping to spring the mailboxes on the witnesses at trial in total surprise. But the lie that had been made up about the mailbox's make, model and value had one more secret to reveal. It was the "why why." The "why" behind the "why." ❖

The difference between the two mailboxes was readily apparent.

CHAPTER 4

"I Was Being Watched."

Gerard pulled his cell phone out and waved it in the air, repeatedly saying, "I was being watched. I swear." Gerard claimed that in the days immediately prior to his arrest he'd been under police surveillance and had seen unmarked police cars following him on several occasions. He was insistent on this. Over the years, many of my clients have made similar allegations, claiming they were subject to illicit surveillance by unknown but very secretive government agencies. Almost all of these claims had either been paranoid delusions, or surveillance was actually occurring as part of perfectly legitimate undercover police operations. In Gerard's case, however, Detective Akagi's closing report specifically stated that the police had no suspect until Gerard was identified by Katherine on June 29, 2013, at 5:00 p.m. There was no mention whatsoever in Akagi's closing report of any surveillance being conducted on Gerard. But if we could prove Gerard had been under surveillance *prior* to his identification as a suspect on June 29, it would go a long way to support our now blossoming theory that he was framed. After all, why would a person be under surveillance if they hadn't even been identified as a suspect yet?

In the early stages of our relationship, Gerard would continually make these types of claims. My years of built-up cynicism told me I might have another mental case on my hands, but I put those thoughts into the back of my brain and listened. As we verified more and more of Gerard's story, I learned to take things Gerard said more seriously.

Gerard had once worked in private security. He'd learned a thing or two in that job about how to conduct surveillance and, more importantly, to make sure he had proof. Gerard tapped on his cell phone and said he had photographs of the surveillance vehicles he'd seen. He'd taken these pictures by photographing the cars in his rearview or side-view mirrors while he was driving. Really? Photos? If we could make out the license plate numbers, we could subpoena records from the state's motor vehicle division to match the vehicle to the registered owner. If it turned out the cars weren't registered to either HPD or to a police officer, the photos would be of no use, nothing more than snapshots of random cars taken by a paranoid individual, and we'd be breaking out the tinfoil hats. But what if they were, in fact, registered to HPD or a police officer?

Gerard insisted they were unmarked police cars and that on one occasion he had even been followed into a local diner by the occupants of two of the surveillance vehicles. They were cops. "No," he said, "they didn't have any uniforms on," but he could tell they were cops. He was certain. He'd been around enough cops, particularly at his fitness center and dojo where he worked out with off-duty police officers, to know whether a person was a cop or not. But a person's intuition, even if accurate, isn't evidence. We'd need something just a little bit more concrete than his hunch.

In addition to his photos, Gerard said he'd also written down license plate numbers of several of the vehicles he believed were following him or that he had seen parked in his neighborhood watching his residence. Gerard had photographed four distinct vehicles following him and had written down their license plate numbers: two vehicles on June 27 that had followed him from his residence down to the Mānoa Marketplace, a third vehicle the next day near his residence and a fourth vehicle on June 29 just several hours before his arrest. Using his photos, we obtained and filed multiple subpoenas to the state of Hawaiʻi motor vehicle division to ascertain the names of the registered owners. Several weeks passed before we received the returns on the subpoenas, but it was well worth the wait. The results were astounding.

HPD authorizes three types of vehicles for police work: regular marked patrol cars (blue and whites), subsidized unmarked personal vehicles and divisional undercover vehicles. The subpoena returns proved that three of the vehicles Gerard had photographed were registered to HPD officers. All three were subsidized unmarked personal vehicles. Vehicle number one, photographed on June 27, was a silver Toyota 4Runner registered to a Sergeant Michael Cusumano. Sergeant Cusumano was one of two supervising sergeants assigned to the District 6 Crime Reduction Unit (CRU), the unit that was involved in the arrest of Gerard on June 29. CRU consists of specialized plainclothes officers who assist regular patrol officers in their daily activities. Each CRU covers a specific geographical area but can assist with investigations and arrests outside such boundaries. CRU District 6 arrested Gerard on June 29, even though it was not within their normal designated geographical area. The crime had occurred in CRU District 1 geographical territory. The arrest of Gerard occurred in a geographical area normally under the control of CRU District 7. No member of either unit was involved in his arrest or the investigation of Gerard. Not one. There was no evidence that CRU District 7 had even been informed that there was a "planned" arrest of a suspect in their patrol area, completely violating HPD protocols. This fact was, in and of itself, revealing. It raised red flags as to what was really going on within HPD regarding how the investigation of the theft of the mailbox was being conducted and by whom.

Reports filed by members of the CRU District 6 arrest team showed they had been briefed about the possibility of the arrest of Gerard at "1630 hours," or 4:30 p.m. This fact raised even more red flags. Red flag number one was that the arrest team was briefed more than a half hour *before* Akagi claimed Katherine first identified Gerard as a suspect at 5:00 p.m. Red flag number two was that CRU District 6 was involved in the case, although the crime and arrest occurred in other CRU areas. Red flag number three was that Akagi's closing report contained no mention of any involvement of Sergeant Cusumano in the case whatsoever. What, exactly, then, was Sergeant Cusumano doing on June 27 when Gerard spotted him following him two days *before* Gerard was identified as a suspect and two days *before* CRU District 6 was briefed on his arrest? Whatever the answers, red flags were flying high.

Sergeant
Michael Cusumano

The second vehicle, another unmarked subsidized car, was a black Nissan four-door truck belonging to a Corporal Landon Tafaoa. Gerard had spotted and identified this vehicle following him on June 27. Corporal Tafaoa was not a member of CID, like Akagi. He was not a member of CRU District 6, like Sergeant Cusumano. Corporal Tafaoa was a member of the Criminal Intelligence Unit, commonly referred to as CIU. CIU was a secretive investigative unit whose members were exclusively selected by chief of police Louis Kealoha and reported only to him. CIU officers did not write reports, rendering their work essentially untraceable. For all intents and purposes, CIU operated as a black ops unit existing within the police department, responsible only to the chief. We were informed that the commanding officers of CIU were all allegedly close friends of Chief Kealoha. If all this sounds a bit scary, it is. Not surprisingly, we discovered that CIU had a well-documented check-ered history going back years to several highly publicized corruption and abuse of power scandals. CIU's involvement in Gerard's case indicated that Louis might have been more actively involved in the investigation of Gerard than we'd previously thought. It was strange enough that a CID homicide detective was investigating a mailbox theft, but now we had the possible involvement of the chief's very own black ops unit. And Akagi had made no direct mention of CIU's involvement in the investigation of Gerard in his report other than the recovery of a hard drive by CIU officer Niall Silva. Without Gerard's photographs, we would never have known that CIU had taken an active role in the investigation of his case.

We knew one other CIU officer was a witness in the case, Officer Bobby Nguyen. But this was purely in his personal capacity, in that he would identify Gerard as being the person in the surveillance footage stealing the mailbox. Bobby was married to Katherine's niece. He had lived for a short time in a cottage at the Kealohas' residence. He knew Gerard from having seen him around the house. Bobby, we learned, was the youngest and the lowest-ranking member of CIU. Normally, only graded officers were assigned to CIU. Bobby was only a foot officer. Akagi's report did not mention Bobby as playing any part in the investi-gation, not even that he was going to be an identification witness. It was not until the feds took over the case that United States postal inspector Brian Shaughnessy noted, in his report dated July 5, 2013, that Bobby had positively identified Gerard from the video surveillance footage due to Gerard's "very unique strut."

The third car Gerard photographed was another silver Toyota 4Runner truck belonging, incredibly enough, to Akagi himself. This photograph was taken on June 28 near Gerard's residence, a day before his identification as a suspect and arrest. Gerard told us that he took the photograph because he was being followed, not that he had simply seen the vehicle in the area. Once again, Akagi's report was silent as to any surveillance he himself might have conducted on Gerard on June 28. It was one thing to omit information related to what other police officers had done, but quite another thing to omit your own investigative activi-ties. Another red flag.

The fourth and final vehicle we were able to identify was again driven by CIU Corporal Tafaoa, but he did not own it. It was this vehicle that was the most significant to us. Gerard snapped a photograph of this car on June 29 near his residence, about an hour or two before he was arrested. However, it took a bit more effort to identify Corporal Tafaoa as the driver, because the registration did not list him as the owner. But we were able to determine that the vehicle was purchased by HPD from a US marshal's sale and had become an undercover vehicle assigned to CIU. CIU acting captain Derek Hahn, in response to one of our subpoenas, confirmed that the vehicle was assigned to CIU and that Corporal Tafaoa was "responsible for ensuring the maintenance and repair of this vehicle, and also ha[d] access to this vehicle encompassing the date in question." We could now demonstrate, beyond any doubt, the direct involvement of CIU in the investigation of Gerard through Corporal Tafaoa's use of this CIU unmarked undercover vehicle, even though Akagi had made no mention of it. And that again pointed to the direct involvement of Louis Kealoha.

We now understood how Gerard had been located and arrested less than ten minutes after Katherine identified him as the person in the videotape, a piece of police work that in and of itself would have been astonishing even under normal circumstances. Gerard had been arrested in record time because HPD knew exactly where he was…because his exact whereabouts were known to HPD long before he was officially declared a suspect in the case. Gerard's claim that he was being framed was coming more and more into focus. But Gerard had still more to give. I was listening. He had my full attention.

*　*　*

Two days before his arrest, on June 27, Gerard had called 911 to report that his residence was under surveillance by unknown persons. Two officers responded and took a statement from Gerard. Gerard told us that he called 911 because, by then, "I was really getting freaked out." He didn't know why he was being followed nor why anyone would stake out his house. Our immediate thought was that if Gerard had really stolen the mailbox, why would he call police and draw attention to himself? Wouldn't he be hiding in some deep dark hole hoping no one came knocking on his front door, rather than inviting them in? If we could prove he called 911, this would further bolster Gerard's credibility to a jury and add more substance to our conspiracy theory.

According to Gerard, HPD officer Chad Gibo and his partner responded to his 911 call. Gerard told Officer Gibo of his suspicions and gave him the license plate numbers and descriptions of the two vehicles he believed were conducting surveillance of his residence. He also showed him several photographs he had taken of the vehicles. These were the same photos Gerard had shown us. Gerard wrote down Gibo's name and the HPD incident report number Gibo provided to him, 13-233884. This number would correspond with the police incident report Gibo told Gerard he'd be filing.

After Gibo received this information, he left Gerard's presence, but Gerard could hear him speaking into his police radio. Rather than seeking any information on the vehicles, he was asking for a criminal record check…on Gerard! When Gibo returned, he told Gerard it was all just coincidental and not to worry, and then he left. Gerard did not see Gibo or his partner do anything to determine whether his story was true. They didn't look around his house. They didn't check up and down his street. Nothing. I initially sympathized with Gibo. How many of these types of calls did he have to respond to in a month? But given what we had learned so far, his actions seemed suspicious.

Gerard, to his credit, had saved the notepad that he had shown to Gibo that night, which had the license plates and vehicle descriptions written on it. For us, this was yet another important piece of physical evidence that helped prove Gerard was telling the truth and that called HPD's investigation further into question. Gerard was turning out to be a treasure trove of information and evidence. I no longer envisioned him in my mind's eye with tinfoil on his head. Gibo's police report would be the next piece of tangible evidence to confirm this part of Gerard's story. Confirming that Gerard had called 911 and invited police into his house at the time when he had allegedly stolen the mailbox would go a long way towards convincing a jury that he hadn't committed any crime. We contacted HPD and asked for a copy of Gibo's report. There was no need to go through the formal subpoena process because we had Gerard's consent to obtain the police report he had made. We thought that obtaining this report would be a relatively straightforward matter. We were wrong.

HPD informed us that no report existed under that incident number. While I couldn't confirm the accuracy of Gerard's version of events, I did not for a moment think he had simply made everything up, including a fictitious police report number.

We didn't give up. We were now far from believing anything HPD told us. HPD's claim that no report existed was not an official response, since we hadn't issued them a subpoena. If they were going to deny that Gerard had called 911, if they were going to deny that officers had responded, if they were going to deny any police report existed, we needed it to be official. On October 14, 2014, we sent HPD a court-issued subpoena requesting any and all documents related to the preparation and filing of incident report number 13-233884. This time we did receive documents in response. They were, to say the least, confusing and contradictory,

One document we received, dated October 3, 2014, was an email from Sergeant Kevin Oshiro to Officer Gibo. The subject line stated: "Chief Kealoha's Mother in laws house on Noio Pl. Rpt # 13-233884." The email read:

> Chad, The Federal Public Defender, Adam CHOKA is representing PUANA in the Chief's Mailbox theft case tried to get this report from records, but…no mo. Can you type one and call him [ ] to let him know that he can go to records for a copy.

We wondered how Sergeant Oshiro knew that the report had anything to do with Chief Kealoha's mother-in-law's house if no report existed? We certainly had never told HPD that the report was about an incident at Louis's mother-in-law's house. And could it really be proper police procedure to instruct an officer to simply "type one" up more than a year and a half after an incident had occurred? It appeared to us that Sergeant Oshiro was asking Gibo to simply take his best shot at dummying up a report. All this lent further support to our argument that HPD was conducting an improper investigation when it came to all things Gerard.

The second document was Gibo's report itself, which reflected a filing date of "10-6-2014," not "06-27-13." Apparently Gibo had done as he was instructed, but he claimed that he had indeed written and filed his report on June 27, 2013. As Gibo explained it in an email, the problem was that he had initially filed it under the wrong incident report number by mistake, so it had been rejected by the police computer data entry system. He hadn't ever noticed his error until we had inquired about the report, more than a year later. So, he'd simply refiled it under the correct incident report number.

Regarding his encounter with Gerard, Gibo's newly filed report stated:

PUANA said two trucks were following him at various places & times. He stated they "just drive by me" and he is paranoid about it. He showed me a photo of a SUV (RWD707) and a black truck with illegible plates. I assured him its just coincidental but he wanted to document for peace of mind. DISP: RECORDS

The good news was that Gibo's report confirmed that Gerard had in fact called HPD on June 27 to report his belief that he was under surveillance. We could now present this second piece of tangible evidence to the jury to bolster Gerard's credibility. The report also confirmed that Gerard reported that two vehicles were following him and had shown him photographs, but Gibo only listed the license plate number of one of the two vehicles. Gerard, on the other hand, had told us he gave Gibo both license plate numbers as written on his notepad. There was also nothing in Gibo's report to show that he had made any effort to run the license plate number or do any routine investigation to verify Gerard's claim his house was under surveillance. Had he run this license plate number, Gibo would have learned the vehicle belonged to Sergeant Cusumano of CRU District 6. And had he written down the license plate number of the second vehicle Gerard had seen, Gibo would have learned it belonged to CIU Officer Tafaoa. Perhaps, we thought, Gibo had failed to mention this second license plate number because he had, in fact, run it and was not going to put in his report any activity connected to a CIU officer. We'd be sure to point all these facts out to the jury.

But Gerard was not done telling his story of all the strange events leading up to his arrest on the 29th. During the evening of June 28, after Gerard had during that day photographed another vehicle he believed was following him, which we discovered was registered to Detective Akagi, Gerard once again suspected his house was under surveillance. Gerard turned off all of the lights in his house so his eyes could adjust to night vision to get a better view outside. He admitted he didn't see anything suspicious. Nevertheless, he called his brother-in-law, Rick Hartsell, and asked him to come over. Rick Hartsell had worked as a law enforcement investigator with the county prosecutor's office in Hilo for over fifteen years and later as a probation officer before moving from the Big Island to Honolulu. Gerard trusted that Rick would know how to conduct countersurveillance and could help him figure out what was really happening. But Rick also did not see anything suspicious. Gerard was not satisfied. He wanted to know for sure. So, they got into Gerard's car and drove down the street to see if anyone followed them, and sure enough, several cars immediately pulled out behind them. Gerard gunned his engine and quickly drove into a side street, pulled into an empty parking space and turned off his lights.

I was beginning to think Gerard had watched way, way too many movies. This type of thing might happen on *Magnum, P.I.* or *Hawaii Five-0*, but not in real life and certainly not to a guy who might or might not have stolen…a mailbox. But, according to Gerard, the cars following him whizzed past him on the main street. A few minutes later, he could see several cars slowly driving up and down streets, searching. Gerard turned his lights back on and pulled back out onto the street. But before he could pull out onto the main road, he was stopped and surrounded by vehicles. A plainclothes HPD officer walked up and asked Gerard for his identification and driver's license. Gerard provided his name but said he didn't have his license or any other form of identification with him. Gerard asked the officer why he had been stopped. The officer replied that there had been reports of burglaries in the neighborhood and the entire area was under surveillance. According to the officer, Gerard's vehicle was stopped because he had been driving erratically. A plausible explanation, but for the fact that Gerard claimed the unmarked police cars had specifically followed him *from* his residence. No tickets or citations were issued, and Gerard and Rick were allowed to drive away.

If Rick could corroborate Gerard's account, that would tell us if Gerard was being truthful. And if it was true, we might also be able to obtain police records of the event. We could use yet another provable encounter with police, whether routine or not, to further bolster Gerard's credibility with a jury. We knew that if the jury had not already been convinced by all our other evidence, they would have to believe Gerard if we were to have any chance of success.

Thankfully, Rick confirmed Gerard's story in its entirety. As a result of his law enforcement experience, Rick was convinced Gerard was under surveillance that evening. Rick's testimony would be important, as we now had an independent witness to back up Gerard's story. We were making progress.

Armed with Rick's information, we issued subpoenas for any and all records from HPD that might have been generated by such a vehicle stop. There are usually records of most routine traffic stops, if nothing more than logs of a police officer calling in to make a vehicle registration and driver's license check. There were none. Not a single report could be found referring to this traffic stop. Three or more unmarked HPD police vehicles had chased them down, surrounded them and questioned them, but according to HPD, not a single shred of paperwork existed to document this event. No radio calls. Nada. This didn't jive with what we understood of standard HPD protocol. But the fact that HPD claimed there were no records fit nicely into our argument that something was amiss with the department's investigation of Gerard and supported our position that HPD was dealing from the bottom of the deck.

It can be difficult to prove a conspiracy, much less a conspiracy to frame an innocent man by law enforcement officers. It is particularly difficult to prove a conspiracy through circumstantial evidence alone. In most cases, when the government alleges a conspiracy, the prosecution has successfully turned a defendant, commonly referred to as a snitch or rat, who testifies to the existence of the conspiracy and the members in it. Then, when the government introduces the circumstantial evidence that matches up with what the snitch has already testified to, the conspiracy can be fully understood and believed by the jury. We had no snitch. No HPD officer was coming forward to admit to us that they had conspired with the Kealohas to frame Gerard. Yes, we had circumstantial evidence, a lot of it, but that was it. We were building a case to argue that members of HPD were working to frame Gerard, including the chief of police and his prosecutor wife. That was going to be a tall order to sell to a jury through circumstantial evidence alone. But my gut told me we were right. There were too many inconsistencies, too many critical facts omitted from police reports, and just too many coincidences.

It was now November of 2013, more than five months since I had first met Gerard. I was beginning to believe we could win. And winning, to me, still simply meant getting a not guilty verdict. We hoped and began to believe the jury would agree and say "No mo." ❖

CHAPTER 5

"0859 Hours"

Among the documents we received from the government were two HPD reports filled out by CIU officer Niall Silva. He was a technician assigned to CIU, overseeing the use and maintenance of CIU's surveillance equipment. This assignment included making sure that video or electronic evidence was properly seized and preserved for use in court. All physical evidence seized by police must have a complete record, called a "chain of custody" report, of who handled or accessed it from the moment it is seized until its use in court to ensure the evidence has not been tampered with or altered in any manner. One of Silva's principal responsibilities was to prepare chain of custody report and maintain and ensure proper custody of seized evidence.

A chain of custody report is like bookkeeping on steroids. It absolutely must be properly done, or critical evidence can be lost to the prosecution. It is meant to prove that the piece of seized evidence has not been altered. Evidence is kept in a secure cabinet or vault, sealed and labeled, and a running log is kept as to exactly who has handled it and when. How many and which people have handled evidence can be just as critical as the evidence itself, or how and where it was seized. To fully

CIU officer
Niall Silva

appreciate this fact, just recall the O. J. Simpson case, where an officer with alleged racist tendencies had access to a critical piece of evidence, in that case blood evidence, and as a result that evidence was no longer considered reliable by the jury. Normally, a quick glance at one of these reports is all that's necessary to determine that a piece of evidence has been handled properly before you move on to more important things. But not in this case.

Officer Silva had prepared two reports regarding the seizure of the videotape evidence that allegedly showed Gerard stealing the mailbox. The first was the Evidence or Property Report, HPD-192A (Evidence Form). This was the chain of custody report for the videotape footage obtained from the surveillance cameras at the Kealohas' residence. The second was a one-page report entitled HPD follow-up report. Each page of the reports was signed by Silva and included the date and time he prepared the report, which was not June 22, when the evidence had been seized, but July 1, more than a week later. Thus, there was a gap of more than a week from when the videotape had been seized by Silva to when it was officially placed into evidence. There was no record of where it had been, how it had been handled nor who had it in their possession for eight days.

But it was the HPD Follow-Up Report that caught our attention. This was a one-page preprinted standardized form that simply required Officer Silva to fill in blank spaces. Silva had done so by typing in his responses. The form attested that the video consisted of "true and accurate depictions" of the events on "6-21-13 at approximately 2331 hours [f]rom 1018 Kealaolu Avenue." The form further stated that Silva "recovered footage on 06-22-13 at about 0859 hours." According to Silva's report, "On 07-01-13, I [Officer Silva] released 1 original and/or 1 copy of surveillance photographs videos." Silva certified that he had checked the surveillance equipment and that it was functioning properly. Detective Akagi, in his CID closing report under the heading "Evidence," wrote that "[t]he home surveillance footage was recovered from the residence of 1018 Kealaolu Avenue by Officer Niall SILVA. For further facts and circumstances, refer to follow up report submitted under this report number." This confirmed that Silva had himself gone to the Kealoha residence and retrieved the surveillance footage.

Katherine claimed she called 911 to report the theft at 1:29 p.m. on the afternoon of the 22nd. That was when two beat officers had responded and taken her statement. When asked about the videotape surveillance footage, according to Officer Rosskopf's official report, Katherine replied that "she has security camera in the area, but she has not reviewed it at this time until a relative retrieved it for her to review. She will call HPD if anything shows up and submit the DVD." She repeated this claim in her signed, under oath statement that she had written herself: "At this time there is no known suspects, but we will be reviewing our security camera and will give that information to the police when it becomes available."

But Officer Silva's police report stated that he had retrieved the videotape surveillance footage at "0859 hours," which meant that he had seized the surveillance evidence more than four and a half hours *before* Katherine first reported the crime by calling 911. Why call 911 at all at 1:29 p.m. if CIU, and thus HPD, was already involved in the case? There was not a word in Detective Akagi's report that HPD was aware of the crime until Katherine called 911, so how was it possible Silva had seized the evidence at 8:59 in the morning? At that time, by all reports, HPD didn't even know a crime had been committed at the Kealoha residence. And Silva hadn't just seized the evidence according to his report, he went to the house and made sure that the surveillance recording equipment was functioning properly and watched it, all before returning to his office at CIU with the hard drive.

Yet Katherine called 911 at 1:29 that afternoon and acted like this was the first contact with HPD regarding the theft of her mailbox. And, when directly asked about the surveillance footage by Officer Rosskopf, Katherine stated that a relative had the footage and that once she had reviewed it, she would notify HPD. Katherine never stated that HPD, in the form of CIU officer Silva, had already been to the house and that the footage was already in the hands of HPD—surely facts one would expect a prosecutor to tell a police officer she had summoned by making a 911 call. Akagi had obviously read Silva's reports himself, given that he directly referred to them in his own CID closing report and had attached them to his final report, saying nothing about this time discrepancy, let alone making any attempt to explain it away. Akagi was the lead detective; it was his responsibility to make sure everything about the investigation added up and made sense. We doubted that Akagi, a homicide detective, would have failed to notice this discrepancy. Nor did Akagi pay any attention to Katherine's sworn statement that "a relative" had the videotape and would turn it over to HPD later in the day. This statement was made at 1:30 p.m., long after Akagi was aware that Silva had already seized that same videotape at 8:59 that morning. None of this made sense, unless....

In our opinion, it was simply not possible for the videotape to have been seized by Silva at 8:59 a.m. Given Silva's version of events as compared with Katherine's version, and the timing of her call to 911 as recorded by Officer Rosskopf, something nefarious was going on. This was the icing on the cake in support of our argument that Gerard was being framed. We added Officer Rosskopf's name to our growing list of defense witnesses. We believed his testimony would be deemed credible by a jury, as he was just the 911 beat officer who responded to a call for police assistance. His entire report read like he was the first responder. He had absolutely no reason to lie about anything. And he couldn't be mistaken about what Katherine had told him regarding where the videotape footage was because Katherine had written the same information down in her own handwriting. This, we believed, was damning evidence. Very damning. But there was more.

Although we had received Silva's two HPD reports from the government as part of discovery, we had independently subpoenaed HPD for all of their reports related to the theft in the simple belief that there might be additional documents that HPD had either hidden or refused to turn over to the federal prosecutor. By this point, we were operating under the assumption that members of HPD were out-and-out lying to the government in aid of their boss, the chief.

In response, we received copies of Silva's two reports. But to our surprise, the copy of Silva's HPD follow-up report we received from HPD was different than the one we had been given by the government. Where Silva had typed in the number "1" in the space saying how many originals and copies he had made and released, the report we received from HPD had the number "4" handwritten in both spaces. It looked like the "1" was changed into a "4" in ink, not by being typed in on a computer. All other aspects of the report, including the date and time the report was created, and his supervising officer's signature, were identical. While a report can be amended with new or updated information, the proper procedure to change information on an official report is to create a new or supplemental report and date it accordingly, with the supervisor re-signing. It is not proper to Wite-Out, delete or write over an original report. This could only mean that at some point Silva had, for whatever reason, altered the form and done so improperly. And the fact that more people had access to the videotape, "4" rather than "1," raised questions as to whether the videotape might have been altered, which is why noting and limiting the number of people who have access to evidence is so important in maintaining the integrity of a piece of evidence.

If Silva had in fact made four copies of the video and released them to four people as this new form indicated, then this was the true and correct chain of custody form that should have been turned over to the government for use at trial. A report of any kind that we could actually prove was altered was exactly what we had been hoping for. While we had proof that many HPD reports contained false information or omitted critically important information, we now had a form that had been improperly altered. And perhaps even more importantly, an altered form that was hidden from the federal prosecutor by HPD. This was like blue lettering on the icing on top of a cake. To us, it spelled out "frame-up." ❖

CHAPTER 6

Lies, Lies and a Polygraph

At 11:28 p.m. on the evening of June 21, 2013, a car was captured on video surveillance slowly driving up to the Kealoha residence in Kāhala. The streetlights blur out the details of the vehicle and its driver. Investigators Adam, Brian and I repeatedly watched the surveillance footage hoping to see something, anything, that would help us identify the vehicle or its driver. No matter how hard we tried, even using image enhancement technology, it was impossible to decipher the make and model of the vehicle or clearly see the driver. The license plate number could not be read. Nor could we see any wording or symbols on the vehicle to indicate what make of car it was.

But some details could be made out. The car was white or light colored. It had a sunroof. It had four doors. The grille on the front of the vehicle could be seen to a degree. But no other distinguishing features could be made out because of where the vehicle was parked, the position of the cameras, and the blurring streetlights. Had we been able to see the license plate number, we could have issued a subpoena to determine the vehicle's registered owner. Had we been able to determine the make and model of the car, we could have at least figured out if it was a type of vehicle owned by Gerard or one that he could have had access to. Had the driver stopped a little nearer or further ahead of the mailbox, we might have been able to gather more details. It raised the question as to whether the driver of the vehicle had stopped where he did intentionally. It certainly appeared as if the thief knew exactly where to position the car to get the most glare.

Detective Akagi either had better eyes or better image enhancement equipment than we did. "Possible Suspect Vehicle Located: 2003 Acura/4 door sedan/white," he wrote in his report. Gerard told us that he hadn't driven his car that night and had stayed home all evening. Gerard's car was silver-colored, not white, as Detective Akagi claimed. But Gerard didn't have an ironclad alibi that we could prove because the only other person with him that evening was a friend visiting from out of town. He'd slept in the upstairs bedroom and couldn't vouch for Gerard's where-abouts. Gerard also pointed out that from what could be seen of the front grille of the car and where the license plate was located, the car could not have been an Acura as Detective Akagi suspected, but resembled a Lexus.

But not only had Akagi determined that the vehicle in the videotape was an Acura; he said it was a 2003 Acura. And it just so happened that Detective Akagi found just such a vehicle parked very near to Gerard's home. The registered owner of this "suspect vehicle" was a woman named Carrie Arakaki. Akagi interviewed Ms. Arakaki, who was referred to as "Witness #1," but his summary of the interview was extremely brief. According to Akagi's CID closing report, Ms. Arakaki lived down the street from Gerard. Ms. Arakaki told Akagi "that during the evening of 06-21-13 she stayed home and ate leftover food." Further, "Arakaki related that she does not know the suspect and did not loan out her vehicle to anyone on 06-21-13." While it was great to know what Ms. Arakaki ate for dinner, no date was provided in Akagi's report as to when the "suspect vehicle" had been located by the police, nor why this particular vehicle was suspected to have been used in the theft, nor was any time or date given as to *when* Ms. Arakaki made these statements to Akagi. Normal police procedure is to list the exact date and time a witness is interviewed and makes a statement. It would also be normal to list who the suspect is whom the witness was questioned about and claimed she did not know. The fact that these critical facts were omitted was suspicious, particularly given that in other places in his CID closing report Akagi had been care-ful to note the exact date and time of other important events.

We knew from his closing report that Akagi did not name Gerard a suspect until June 29 at 5:00 p.m. But clearly when Akagi spoke to Ms. Arakaki, whenever that date and time was, he already had a suspect. Thus, if Akagi had spoken to Ms. Arakaki before 5:00 p.m. on June 29, something was awry. Perhaps that would explain why Akagi's closing report didn't list a date and time for his conversation with Ms. Arakaki, certainly a point we'd make to the jury in our quest to prove HPD's inves-tigation was being conducted with the intention of framing Gerard.

Under the heading "Polygraph Administered," Akagi detailed that Ms. Arakaki had participated in a polygraph examination that had been administered by CID detective Allan Kuaana. Again, no specific time or date was provided by Akagi as to when this examination was conducted. We were surprised to learn that Ms. Arakaki had been subjected to a polygraph examination. She had told Akagi that she did not know Gerard and did not lend him her car. That should have been enough, but it wasn't. It's not normal police procedure to subject this type of witness, a witness with absolutely no ties to the subject, to a polygraph, particularly in a simple theft of a mailbox case. The results? No deception was shown in her answers.

Luckily, Detective Kuaana's polygraph report had been turned over to us. Kuaana wrote that the polygraph examination of Ms. Arakaki began on "6-29-13 at about 1915 hours." This was two hours and fifteen minutes after Katherine had, for the first time, identified Gerard as the suspect. Kuaana initiated the polygraph testing by first having Ms. Arakaki sign a polygraph waiver/information form that informed her about the testing procedure and showed that she consented to taking the examination. Ms. Arakaki was then given her constitutional warnings, informing her that she had a right to remain silent and/or to seek advice of counsel. Ms. Arakaki signed the waiver indicating she freely gave up her constitutional rights and agreed to take the lie detector examination. This meant that anything she said during the examination could be used against her at a later time should questions arise about her sincerity.

A polygraph examination is made up of three distinct sections: the pretest phase, the in-test phase, and the posttest phase. The pretest phase is where a casual conversation takes place between the examiner and the subject, either a suspect or a witness, to review personal information about the subject or to go over some piece of the evidence that is going to be the focal point of the questions. It's meant to put the subject at ease and to formulate questions based upon the subject's answers. During this initial discussion the subject is not yet wired to the polygraph machine. It presents an opportunity for the examiner to bond with the subject over shared past experiences as the examiner attempts to obtain information for the second phase of the test. But this exercise has another purpose. It sets up the examiner's ability to more effectively question a subject during the final phase of the examination should there be a need to confront the subject if deception or inconclusive answers are indicated.

The in-test phase is the part of the polygraph examination that is commonly portrayed in television shows and movies. In this phase, the subject is wired to the polygraph machine and answers the yes or no questions put to them. The physical reactions of the subject are recorded and analyzed to determine if the subject is being dishonest. To a professional polygrapher, the criterion is whether the subject did or did not show deception from the established baseline, not whether the subject is telling the truth. There are three possible outcomes to a polygraph examination: no deception, deception or inconclusive. A finding of "truthfulness" is not an option. While many questions may be asked to establish a baseline to determine a subject's truthfulness, it is the customary practice that only up to three or four specific questions are asked that directly go to the subject matter at issue.

The posttest phase is often the most important part of the examination. It's during this phase that a subject is told the results of the examination and asked if they have any questions. But it doesn't end there. The examiner may question or confront a subject who has failed the examination by showing deception or whose results were inconclusive. And this is no accident. Law enforcement polygraphers are trained in techniques on how to question and confront a subject with the results of the examination in order to get a confession or lead the subject to make additional statements that can be used against them later if they are false or misleading. A subject whose answers have been found to be deceptive or inconclusive is not normally allowed to simply walk out the door without some attempt to engage him or her in a further discussion. This is why in the initial phase the subject is advised of his/her constitutional rights and asked to waive those rights.

But most importantly, not one part of this entire process is recorded, either by visual or audio devices. This is also not by accident. Not recording the interview allows the interrogator to do and say anything they want and deny it later if necessary. If a subject claims the interrogator did something improper, it simply becomes a swearing contest between the officer and the subject, who may by then be a defendant—a swearing contest a police officer will almost always certainly win.

Here, Detective Kuaana asked Ms. Arakaki only two relevant questions during the second phase of the polygraph examination, not the customary three or four.

Q: Did you let anyone use your Acura last week Friday night?
Q. Did you allow anyone [sic] use your Acura last week Friday night?

Ms. Arakaki answered "No" to both questions.

Kuaana found "no deception indicated" in her responses. In other words, she passed the lie detector test insofar as it related to these two specific, narrow questions. We wondered, however, why only two questions were asked and why these two very narrowly crafted and specific questions? Both questions addressed only whether she had "let" or "allowed" anyone to use her car. Kuaana did not ask if her car had been stolen. She could also have been asked if she knew Gerard. It was, after all, Kuaana who formulated the questions he wanted to ask. We questioned why the polygraph questions had been formulated in such a manner until we read Kuaana's pretest phase summary in his report.

Detective Kuaana wrote in his report:

> Part of the [pretest phase] examination was dedicated to reviewing information with the subject gathered during the investigation. I informed the subject that reviewing the case with her would allow me to formulate questions for [my] examination.

This indicated that, as he was trained, under the guise of preparing the questions he would ask during the second phase of the examination, Kuaana took the opportunity to reinterview Ms. Arakaki regarding her earlier statement to Detective Akagi. Based upon his own interview, Kuaana wrote:

> The subject related she is the owner of a white 2003 Acura TL. The subject [ ] did not allow anyone to use her Acura at any time last Friday night (6-21-13).

Kuaana noted that Ms. Arakaki stated she had the only set of keys to her vehicle in her purse, which had been in her bedroom that evening. Furthermore, Ms. Arakaki related that she is a short person and her "driver's seat is pulled forward, allowing her to reach the gas and brake pedals." She had placed a plastic magazine-type rack on the floor directly behind the driver's seat and said that "anyone driving her car would have had to move her seat back, which would have damaged the plastic magazine rack." For us, this was proof that Ms. Arakaki's vehicle was not used in the theft. Not, apparently, to Detective Kuaana, who wrote:

> The subject related *there were visible signs* [emphasis added] that her vehicle was stolen and that she found her car parked in the

same place as when she last saw it on early Friday evening.

Say what? At first glance, we gave Kuaana the benefit of the doubt, thinking that he'd simply forgotten to write "no" before the words "visible signs." Thus, the sentence could have, and perhaps should have read, "there were no visible signs" her car had been stolen. That would be consistent given everything else she had said. But a closer examination of what he wrote and the questions he had chosen to ask Ms. Arakaki led us to believe the missing "no" was more likely intentional, yet done in such a manner to allow Kuaana an easy out were he to be cross-examined about it.

First, it was strange that the two relevant questions Kuaana asked Ms. Arakaki were whether she had "let" or "allowed" anyone use her vehicle, but not whether the car had been stolen. Why not straight-out ask her if her car had been stolen when she was wired to a polygraph machine? Particularly odd when Kuaana had, within protocol, an unused third question he could have asked. Secondly, despite Ms. Arakaki explaining that had someone stolen her vehicle, they would most likely have had to push the driver's seat back, which would have crushed her magazine rack, Kuaana did not ask her if she had found her magazine rack intact or damaged. Kuaana was a trained police officer with years of experience, so there was no reason not to have asked this question when obtaining information about the condition of her vehicle. Perhaps Kuaana didn't *want* to know the answer to this question because it would make his claim that the car had visible signs of being stolen untenable. We therefore concluded that the lack of the word "no" before "visible signs" was not a simple typo. More importantly, we didn't have to prove to a jury that Kuaana had intentionally omitted the word "no." All we had to do was convince a jury that it *might* not have been a typo and, therefore, *might* have been intentional. Reasonable doubt was all we needed, and we reckoned Kuaana's report, coupled with Akagi's omissions, certainly helped us with that.

A month after Ms. Arakaki took the polygraph examination, on August 5, 2013, Brian contacted Ms. Arakaki and asked her if she would agree to speak with us. She told Brian that she did not know Gerard and, furthermore, did not want to talk to us. But Brian did not give up. He explained that all he wanted to talk with her about was her polygraph examination. Ms. Arakaki told Brian that she had been "told that she was done and that no one else would have to talk to her about her car."

While no witness can legally be told who they can and cannot speak to, such tactics are commonly employed by law enforcement officers to influence whom a person believes they can or cannot speak with, say, a defense investigator. To merely "suggest" that a witness shouldn't or doesn't have to talk with the defense is not improper, but to outright tell someone they cannot speak to anyone else, at all, crosses the line. Police officers will oftentimes come right up to the edge of what is legally permissible and, if caught going too far, simply deny they ever made such a statement in the first place. The witness simply "misunderstood." Then it becomes the officer's word against that of the witness, a civilian, and, again, we all know who wins that credibility battle in court.

Here, Ms. Arakaki had been told "no one else would talk to her about the car," implying that she didn't have to talk to anyone else because she was done. The officer never actually said she couldn't. Brian persisted. He told her that he had read the police report regarding her polygraph examination, which he determined she had never seen, and wanted to ask her about the statement that there were "visible signs that her car had been stolen." Ms. Arakaki immediately reacted with alarm, responding, "That's not true." Ms. Arakaki said that she did "not know what [was] going on and that she wanted to make a couple of calls and she would call [Brian] back tomorrow." We took this comment to mean that she was going to reach out to the detectives or perhaps to a lawyer friend to help her decide whether to call us back. We could only hope that she would, given the words she had spoken: "that's not true." But we knew, just like in the retail business, once a potential buyer walks out of your store saying they'll be back, they rarely do return.

To our surprise, Ms. Arakaki called us two days later, on August 7, and agreed to speak with Brian right then and there over the phone. According to Ms. Arakaki, she had been out of town and returned home on the evening of June 28. About twenty minutes later, two HPD detectives knocked on her door. Both were male; she couldn't recall their names but remembered that one detective went by the first name of "Dru." The detectives asked her some questions about her vehicle and asked if she'd be willing to come down to the main police station on Beretania Street in downtown Honolulu to answer further questions. Ms. Arakaki readily accepted their invitation and went to the police station where she spoke with the detectives for more than an hour. She returned the following day to take the polygraph examination. There was no mention in Detective Akagi's closing report that Ms. Arakaki had been questioned both at her home and again at the HPD station house nor any reference to what she might have said other than the few lines contained in his report. But since she had spoken to them on two separate occasions for more than an hour, there had to have been more said besides what she'd eaten for dinner.

Ms. Arakaki confirmed to Brian that her vehicle did not have any signs of having been stolen, which was what she told the detectives. By the tone of her voice, Brian could tell that Ms. Arakaki was quite upset that the report suggested otherwise. Brian asked for specifics about her vehicle, something the detectives should have done or had done and then omitted from their report. Mr. Arakaki said there were no signs the ignition had been punched out, no scratches, no broken windows, and that her seat was in the same position she uses to drive—very close to the steering wheel due to her height. She also confirmed that there was no damage to her magazine rack. Everything she told us refuted any inference that her car had any indication it had been stolen.

Of critical import was that Ms. Arakaki told us she was questioned about her vehicle by the detectives and had gone to the police station on June 28, the day *before* Akagi claimed in his report that Gerard was first identified as a suspect. Why, we asked ourselves, would Akagi even be in Gerard's neighborhood on the 28th, much less trying to connect a vehicle that might have been used in the theft to Gerard, who wasn't even a suspect yet?

Then came another surprise, again not mentioned in Akagi's closing report. Ms. Arakaki told Brian that right after she had completed the polygraph examination, she had been shown a videotape by Detective Kuaana of a car driving up to a residence and a person taking a mailbox. After watching the videotape, in silence, nothing more was said between them and she left. Kuaana never asked if the person in the video was Gerard, nor if the car was hers. He didn't say anything to her; he just showed her the video.

Ms. Arakaki told Brian the person in the video didn't look like anyone she knew, and that she would have told Kuaana that if he had asked her. She thought that she might have seen Gerard once or twice in his garage area, but she had never spoken to him or met him. But most importantly, now that she was being given the opportunity to say something about what she had seen on the videotape, Ms. Arakaki said that her car had several distinguishing features that made it clear to her that it could not have been her car. She did not elaborate further during the phone call but agreed to let Brian come to her residence and take photographs of her car. And, as she would later tell us when we came to take photographs of her vehicle, the detectives had also taken photographs of her car the very night they came to her residence on June 28. No mention of this was made in Akagi's report, and no photographs of her vehicle had ever been turned over to us as potential evidence. Only by having talked directly to Ms. Arakaki, and only because she had made the decision to speak with us, were we able to learn this fact. More circumstantial evidence that Gerard was being set up.

But it would get even better. Immediately prior to trial, we had Ms. Arakaki come to our office for witness preparation. Often this is the first time I actually meet some of our witnesses in person, as up to then either my investigators have dealt with them or I've only spoken to them over the phone. Prepping a witness to testify is critical, and I often learn new information during these sessions that may change their testimony or our view of the case. It can be an exhilarating process when the witness reconfirms or adds new helpful information to what they had previously told my investigators. It can also become an extremely depressing situation when a witness changes their story or claims they no longer remember key aspects of what they had earlier told my investigator on the eve of trial.

This was the first time I actually met Ms. Arakaki. Ms. Arakaki turned out to be a delightful and straightforward person whom a jury would easily find believable. I showed her Detective Kuaana's report and let her read for herself what he had written. She hadn't read it before, and I intentionally didn't read it to her. It was better she see his words in black and white for herself. She became very upset. She tensed up, and you could see anger in her face.

I asked her how it came to be that she took a polygraph test in the first place, given that she had told the detectives on June 28 that she did not believe her car had been stolen or used in committing the theft. She replied that the very next day, on the 29th, Akagi insisted that she undergo a polygraph examination due to his "boss's" alleged concern as to the veracity of her statements. His exact words. Akagi did not identify who he was referring to as his "boss." It could have been his immediate supervisor or, as we suspected, Chief Kealoha himself. She told us she was happy to comply. She thought she was just doing her "civic duty" to help catch a thief. But Akagi certainly knew the tactics that would be employed if she agreed to take the examination. Akagi was playing on Ms. Arakaki's desire to be a good citizen in order to get her to agree to take the polygraph examination and thereby, unwittingly, subject herself to further questioning. He had played her, plain and simple. But I kept these thoughts to myself.

After reviewing what she had told Brian about the polygraph exam-ination, I asked her why she thought Detective Kuaana had shown her the videotape at the end of the polygraph examination but had said nothing to her about it. Ms. Arakaki thought about it for a moment and then opined that he did it to see if she would react to seeing the car. Smart lady. She told me she did not react in any way. I asked her why? How could she be so sure it wasn't her car? Her answers were damning.

Ms. Arakaki requested to see the videotape surveillance footage again. We let her look at the image of the vehicle in the videotape as many times as she liked. Each time, Ms. Arakaki kept repeating that the car in the video surveillance was not hers. She was sure of it. One hundred percent.

I again asked why. Ms. Arakaki said that her car had several distinc-tive features that made it clear to her beyond a shadow of a doubt that her car could not be the car in the video surveillance footage. Ms. Arakaki pointed out to us that the grille of the car was different, but admitted it was a bit blurry. Ms. Arakaki's car also had a black strip running across the front portion of her car's sunroof. The photographs we had taken of her car clearly showed the presence of the black strip. It couldn't be missed and stood out because it was black against a white roof top. The car in the video, on the other hand, did not have any such strip. But the most significant difference, one that was readily apparent, was that the car used to commit the theft did not have a spoiler on the back. Hers did. This fact could not be missed or disputed despite the blurriness of the video. The car in the video clearly did not have a spoiler as it drove away. Without question the car in the videotape seen driving up to the Kealoha residence could not have been Ms. Arakaki's vehicle.

So how could it be that two highly trained detectives, who investi-gated murders, had ever thought it was her car that was involved in the theft? Given Ms. Arakaki's statement to Detective "Dru" Akagi on the 28th, denying knowing Gerard, denying he or anyone else had used her vehicle on the night of June 21, and having seen her car firsthand them-selves, how did these trained detectives miss these obvious differences between the two vehicles? And, even more importantly, given all this, why had Ms. Arakaki still been made to take a polygraph examination on the 29th? Ms. Arakaki's new information validated our belief that the missing "no" in Detective Kuaana's report, resulting in his statement that "there were visible signs that her vehicle was stolen," was not a simple typo. No, that was not a typo. ❖

CHAPTER 7

Meet the Press

Afternoon investigating the case for more than a year, I decided to try and get the press involved with the hope that they might help us get to the truth of what had happened. It was clear from the start that we needed to show the jury that Louis and Katherine were not the trustworthy and law-abiding people their esteemed positions in law enforcement made them out to be. In a trial, one of the best ways to demonstrate this to a jury is to use a witness's own words against them to show they said one thing at one time and something completely different at another time. This is called "impeachment" evidence, which simply means evidence attacking a witness's credibility by showing that they made inconsistent statements at different times. The bigger the inconsistencies, the more likely a jury will find a witness less believable. We desperately needed the jury not to believe either Katherine or Louis in order for Gerard to be found not guilty.

We knew that neither Louis nor Katherine would ever voluntarily speak to us. We felt we were well on our way to gathering strong evidence that Katherine had repeatedly lied. We had her own words, under oath, to prove it. Katherine had made several sworn statements to police and put her intentions in black and white in her letters to Florence. Louis, to our knowledge, had not made any sworn statements about the mailbox theft. We needed to get him talking and hope he said something we could use. And that is why we turned to the press. We knew Louis was required to talk to the press as part of his job. Perhaps we could get the press to ask our questions for us. We knew it could backfire if we couldn't first convince the press Gerard was innocent, and that would mean showing them some of our closely held evidence. But it was worth a shot.

When Louis, as chief of police, appeared in public and spoke to members of the press, he always dressed up in his smartest uniform, ribbons and medals shining. He was usually flanked by two or three captains or majors, also dressed in their finest HPD uniforms. Louis often read a prepared statement in a commanding, serious voice, as law enforcement people usually do when talking about crime. Crime is serious business, and Louis made sure he played the part. He seemed to enjoy the limelight when he was in control of the conversation, but not so much when he was forced to veer off his prepared remarks by questions. When pressed, he often reverted to bullying tactics, raising his voice, glaring at the questioner, acting authoritative and cutting short his remarks in response to questions he did not like. He made it clear that if you questioned him, you were the one in the wrong. Fortunately, during our preparation of Gerard's defense, several high-publicity cases were already making news, and one such case gave us an opening.

In early September 2014, a police officer had been caught on a store video seemingly beating the living daylights out of his girlfriend. The incident and the videotape appeared on all the local television newscasts. The length of the video was about the same as the video in Gerard's case. But this video was perfectly clear. There was no doubt who the people were in the video and that violent punches were being thrown by the officer. The woman was literally chased and beaten across the length of the store. Yet the officer was not charged with having committed any criminal offense. Members of the public, politicians and prominent women's groups spoke out, forcing Louis to respond.

At a press conference Louis lashed out at those who were calling for an arrest based upon what they had seen on the video. Louis aggressively responded, declaring, "If you want me to crumble under public and political pressure, if you want me to move away and compromise the integrity of the department and deviate from our policies, then I am not your chief." He claimed that the video was simply not enough and that a full investigation was needed before any charging decision could be made. Louis pointed out that by taking a more deliberative approach, he was standing up against the whims of politicians and the public who wanted quick action and was in effect "protecting [our] rights" through due process of law. "Someone has to stand up" against the rash calls for an arrest, Louis proclaimed, and he was that person. He told the press that there was more to what had occurred than could be seen in such a short videotape clip and that everyone should withhold judgement until they knew what had occurred prior to what was seen on the tape. However, Louis failed to mention that part of what had occurred prior to this incident was that the same officer had been involved in other incidents of domestic abuse, including one in which Katherine had represented the officer in defense of his actions.

As for the video that clearly showed the officer physically assaulting his girlfriend, Louis said that he didn't want to set up the expectation that anyone could send an "edited copy" of a video "and expect us to go arrest people. That [was] unacceptable because that can be any one of you." In concluding his remarks, Louis spoke about the courage, values and moral character of the men and women of HPD, values he was standing up for in refusing to bow to public pressure to charge the officer. As he put it, "Who wants to live in a city or in a society where you can be threatened with arrest and charged for an offense where there is only a sliver of evidence?"

Any other time I'd be standing and applauding any police officer who openly held these values. But not now. Not when a hypocrite was speaking these words. Louis's remarks incensed me. On the one hand, a videotape that clearly showed an officer beating a woman, in broad daylight no less, was not enough for HPD to charge the abuser, but on the other hand Louis had no problem arresting and having Gerard charged when it was almost impossible to make out the thief from a blurry videotape clip. No mailbox had been found in Gerard's possession, no pieces of mail, which according to Katherine had been in the mailbox. There was no physical evidence whatsoever to link Gerard to the crime. Yet, in his case, HPD had no hesitation in arresting and charging him with a felony offense based solely on "edited" and hazy videotape footage, when that same evidence was not enough to charge a police officer. In the officer's case, Louis was incensed that anyone would think the thirty-second video was enough. In this case, I was angry, too. No one could seriously question Louis about his position because no one knew anything about Gerard's case, so to some Louis appeared to be the voice of reason when he was anything but. I knew now that we had a hook that might interest the press and get reporters to start asking Louis questions about Gerard's case.

There was another important reason to try to get the press involved. No one outside of my office understood how explosive our case was, given the mounting evidence we were collecting that Louis and Katherine had used their law enforcement positions to frame Gerard. No one but the prosecution and us had seen the videotape surveillance footage. No one but us knew about the two different mailboxes. No one but us, apparently not even the prosecution, knew about all the contradictions and omissions in the police reports. We knew that the case was complicated and would only make sense to anyone in the press or public if the evidence was understood in its entirety. A trial can be confusing if you don't know what's going on. Lawyers may know what evidence is expected to come from witnesses, but those watching don't. Evidence doesn't necessarily get introduced in sequence nor with an explanation as to its significance. I wanted to ensure that as the evidence unfolded at trial, at least some members of the press would understand the importance and significance of each piece and would therefore be more likely to accurately report what was happening. Our goal was now to exonerate Gerard, not simply for him to be found not guilty. Accurate reporting would help make this point.

But the press is no one's ally. It's impossible to dictate to a reporter how to tell a story. What quotes to use. What photographs to choose that may make you look slimmer, handsomer or more trustworthy. Or the opposite... I've learned that when you see unflattering photographs of someone in a newspaper or television story, that is not by accident. Sometimes, too, no matter how thoughtful you think you've been in giving a carefully worded response to a question, it gets cut and used out of context, and there's little you can do about it.

It helps to remember and appreciate that reporters have a job to do and their own perspective on how to do it. First and foremost, they are people who, like everyone else, bring their own learned skill set to their job, which necessarily includes their own biases and opinions. Just like plumbers, mechanics or lawyers, there are those who take their craft seriously and others who are simply collecting a paycheck. Being a reporter is a difficult and complex job. In order to write a good story, an accurate story, the reporter has to understand the subject matter they are covering. While many of us do one job and learn the intricacies of that one subject, a reporter is called upon to cover stories on a multitude of different topics. Often, they have less than a day to learn as much as they can about an issue, interview people and put together a story by the evening news or the next day's paper. A story that may be only twenty to thirty seconds or a few columns long and must also satisfy their editors. The next day they may be sent out to cover a completely different type of story—a building fire, a labor strike or an interview of some government official about tax regulations. Reporters are not doctors, lawyers, accountants or mechanics. Yet they are called upon to report stories that may require intricate knowledge of each of these professions.

The good reporters, those who work hard at their craft, know this and enjoy the process. Many others, as in all professions, unfortunately do not. The Kealohas understood this and were very effective in using one reporter to get their opinions known to the public without their statements being seriously challenged. It was like watching "Kealoha News." I completely understood that talking to the press could be a perilous undertaking if we didn't establish a trusting relationship with the right reporters, but we needed to get Louis talking, so it was worth the risk.

I reached out to three reporters. One from the *Star-Advertiser*; one from Civil Beat, a local online news organization that specializes in public corruption investigations; and a television investigative reporter for Hawaii News Now. I met first with the *Star-Advertiser* reporter, just a meet and greet to see if he was interested in the story. Not so much. He resisted seeing the relevance and connection between the different ways Louis was handling the two videotapes in the officer's case versus Gerard's case. The reporter was also concerned about stirring up political trouble for his newspaper when he wasn't sure we could really prove Gerard had been framed. He wanted the story handed to him signed, sealed and delivered so he'd be safe in reporting on it. I told him that this was a story that was going to develop over time and would play out right up to and through the trial, which was still months away. He never got back to me. His reaction was not encouraging, but I moved on.

I next invited Rick Daysog of Hawaii News Now and Nick Grube of Civil Beat to come to my office at separate times to look at some of the evidence we had uncovered. Both had said they were interested in seeing what we had. I had had little if any previous contact with either of them prior to these meetings but knew them both by their reputations as aggressive investigative reporters. Exactly what we were looking for. Nevertheless, since I didn't yet know if I could fully trust either of them, we were going to be very careful in what evidence we disclosed. We only wanted to show them enough to get them curious and wanting more. Curious enough to want to do their own digging and their own questioning.

This time the meetings went better. Both appeared interested in the story, but they weren't necessarily convinced. It was like a first date, a little flirting and getting to know one another, but no commitment to a second date. Neither thought the person in the videotape was Gerard. Daysog was adamant that it wasn't. Grube was more reserved. Both were excited about the story but not sure whether my client or I were reliable sources. They agreed not to disclose the information I provided to them, and in exchange, I promised I would keep them informed of new developments in the case and make myself available should they want a quote for a story. Neither left my office saying they believed our story. After all, we were asking them to believe that two of the most important people in law enforcement were working in concert with other HPD officers to frame Gerard over what appeared to be nothing more than a mailbox theft. But at least they left with open minds. All I could do was hope. Hope that they would not betray my trust in them. Hope that they would be interested enough in our story to use their resources and, most importantly, start asking Louis questions about our case.

Our hopes were rewarded. They did, and with a vengeance. Finally, direct questions were asked of Chief Kealoha about Gerard's case, and he had no choice but to reply. And his answers were pure gold for us.

It all began at a press conference on September 24, 2014, less than three months before our trial date, at a time when all we knew officially about Louis's role in the case was that he was simply going to identify Gerard as the alleged thief. We did not have any additional information from Akagi's closing report regarding Louis's involvement, but we believed he was more involved than we were being led to understand. If we could get Louis talking and catch him lying in response to a question, it would confirm our suspicions. And the more involved Louis was, the more it supported our theory that Gerard was being framed by a ginned-up HPD investigation.

Rick Daysog asked Louis to explain what role he had in the investigation of Gerard. Louis stated that "he woke up one night and noticed his mailbox was missing." Louis said he knew it would be improper for him to take any active role in the investigation and prosecution of the case, since he was the victim. Louis was correct that it would be against standard police department policy for any officer to be directly involved in the investigation of a case that affected them personally. Louis claimed after he noticed the mailbox missing, he called deputy chief Marie McCauley and assigned the case to her. She in turn, he said, referred the case to CIU. After notifying McCauley, Louis said "he didn't keep track [of] or drive the investigation." Louis claimed he saw the mailbox missing during the evening of June 21, something not mentioned in Akagi's report. If true, why did Katherine call 911 at 1:29 p.m. the next day if HPD, specifically CIU, had already been notified the night before? Louis's statement contradicted everything we knew about how HPD's investigation of the mailbox theft was initiated, and this was, for our purposes, a good thing. Someone wasn't telling the truth.

But there was more. When asked about the presence of HPD surveillance cameras at his residence, Louis claimed that his house had been vandalized six times prior to the mailbox being stolen, including someone shooting out his windows with a BB gun, a crime Louis claimed he himself had reported to HPD. That was why, according to Louis, HPD had installed the surveillance cameras. When pressed about why at least six officers were assigned to work on a "minor crime," Louis responded, "I know what it looks like but there's no preferential treatment," explaining that such resources were routinely used when a crime involved a high-profile public official, and he was such a person.

Under normal circumstances, how a case is initiated and assigned to a particular division within HPD or to a specific investigative officer is not relevant in a criminal trial. In most cases that's not material to whether a defendant committed the crime for which he is charged. But not in our case. We were putting the chief of police and the entire HPD on trial. Any and all irregularities in the manner HPD conducted its investigation were relevant. Louis's comments in this one press conference would end up providing us with explosive information to use against Louis in the trial. Thank you, Fourth Estate.

We met to go over what we'd learned from the press conference. There was a lot to unpack. It appeared that Louis was saying he first noticed the theft "at night." We'd previously been told that Louis claimed he first noticed the mailbox missing when he went out to surf in the early morning hours of June 22. If Louis had gone out at night and seen the mailbox missing, he should have been caught on the surveillance cameras. But we only had surveillance video footage from half an hour before and after the theft, and Louis was not seen in that limited footage. We had issued a subpoena to HPD seeking more video footage and repeatedly asked the government if there was more footage than the half hour on either side of the theft that we had been given. Each time we were informed that no such additional footage existed. Due to Louis's statements to the press, the surveillance video footage was becoming even more important to our case, and the lack of it more meaningful.

Louis claimed during the press conference that he'd turned the entire case over to deputy chief of police Marie McCauley and that it was McCauley who contacted CIU. This made no sense to us. From the HPD reports, the investigation had started when Katherine called 911 at 1:29

p.m. on June 22. McCauley's name did not appear, ever, in any police report that we had received. There was no indication whatsoever that she'd been involved. But now Louis had not only named her specifically; he claimed it was McCauley who had first notified HPD of the theft, not Katherine with her 911 call. Why then make the 911 call at all? And why was there no mention of any of this in Akagi's report? Whatever the truth was, this claim was important, as we now had McCauley, an independent person whose testimony could directly contradict and bring into question Katherine's 911 call. And during closing argument I would bring all these contradictions to the jury's attention. At the end of the day, it's all about what the jury thinks, and that includes what they think about evidence that was *not* presented to them by the prosecution. I didn't believe the government would be calling McCauley as one of their witnesses, but we would. The jury would be wondering why, and I would point out that the prosecution was hiding evidence from them.

Nick Grube of Civil Beat wrote his first article on the case on September 25, 2014, entitled "Missing Mailbox Exposes Family Friction for HPD Chief, Prosecutor Wife." He would go on to write dozens of articles related to the case. This article detailed the claims made by Florence and Gerard in their civil case, the case that Gerard had mentioned at our first meeting was the reason he was being framed. I'll talk more about that in chapter 10. Nick linked this case to the mailbox charges against Gerard. It was the first article that began to let the public know our side of the story. Lynn Kawano of Hawaii News Now, who had taken over the story from Rick Daysog, would also air numerous stories on the case on television. She, like Nick and Rick, kept our evidence confidential. Nick and Lynn were relentless reporters, and through their own investigation came to believe Gerard's claim that he had been framed.

My hunch that if we got the press involved something useful might develop had paid off. Louis had been questioned. He had responded. And everything he said was something we could use to our advantage. Louis's statements to the press became Defense Exhibits KKK through OOO. I could only hope that Louis's temper would get the better of him on the witness stand and he would raise his voice, point his finger at me and give evasive answers when I confronted him on all of these issues. If he became aggressive and angry in front of the jury, his own behavior would help us undermine his credibility. We had indeed learned a lot from his statements to the press, just as we had hoped. ❖

CHAPTER 8

Gag Order

A witness's ability to perceive or to be able to properly recall and remember events to which they are testifying about is always subject to cross-examination to undermine their credibility. In other words, are they competent, either physically (eyesight) or mentally, for their testimony to be believed by a jury. If a witness is found to be legally incompetent, a judge will bar their testimony entirely. Otherwise, it is up to the jury to decide what weight to give that person's testimony. It is often necessary to obtain a witness's medical records to effectively mount a challenge to that witness's competency. But a witness's medical records are protected by the doctor–patient privilege, which is fully recognized and protected under federal law. Thus, it is often very difficult in a criminal case to obtain such medical records. A very compelling showing must be made to a judge that such personal information is relevant before the court will allow access to a witness's medical records. But Katherine, by her own hands, had put her competency in question and we were not about to miss this opportunity.

On June 19, 2013, Katherine had undergone the first day of her two-day scheduled deposition in the civil case filed against her by Florence and Gerard. A second day of depositions had been scheduled to follow shortly thereafter, but Katherine had been successful in delaying her continued deposition by claiming she was ill. As time went on, in a further attempt to justify the delay, and thereby also justifying a continuance of the trial in the state civil case, Katherine provided a doctor's note to Gerald Kurashima, Florence and Gerard's civil attorney. This note claimed that Katherine had a serious medical condition that rendered her mentally unable to work or perform daily activities. This included her ability to undergo further deposition testimony. The "effective date" of this alleged infirmity, according to the doctor who penned the note, was

June 26, 2013, even though the note was written on February 13, 2014. If Katherine's mental cognitive abilities were indeed impaired as of June 26, 2013, this raised significant legal questions regarding Katherine's competency to testify and her ability to correctly recall events. To our surprise, the government, fully aware of this issue, repeatedly asserted that Katherine was going to testify at Gerard's trial come hell or high water. Thus, Katherine's mental competency regarding her ability to accurately recall events would certainly become a factor that the jury would have to consider.

On June 29, 2013, just three days after her doctor claimed Katherine had become mentally unfit to answer questions in a deposition, Katherine made a written statement to HPD identifying Gerard as the individual in the videotape. Her statement contained new information she hadn't included in her original statement when she initially called 911. She now recalled going out to the mailbox the evening of June 21, thumbing through "a lot of mail" but only taking a few pieces of mail and leaving the rest inside the mailbox. We believed Katherine added that there was mail in the mailbox when it was stolen because she was under the mistaken understanding that there had to be US mail inside the mailbox to make it a federal crime. She made a second detailed statement to US postal inspector Brian Shaughnessy on July 3, 2013, reaffirming this new version and her identification of Gerard as the thief. Both of these statements, including her initial identification of Gerard as the person in the videotape on June 29, were made *after* Katherine's doctor claimed she was mentally unable to work or perform her daily activities.

By filing this doctor's note in her civil case, Katherine had inadvertently placed her competency at issue in our criminal case. It opened the door for us to seek subpoenas to obtain Katherine's medical records to determine her current fitness as a witness and to challenge the reliability of her testimony. If, on the other hand, she was lying about her medical conditions simply to delay her deposition in the civil case, then that also would be extremely relevant for the jury to consider in judging her credibility. We saw it as a win-win situation for us.

Normally a defense request for a subpoena is secret, in that the government doesn't know who we are subpoenaing or why, but because this involved Katherine's medical condition the law required us to notify her. This allowed her the opportunity to object, if she had a legal basis, to protect her privacy rights. As a result, all the subpoena paperwork and all the documents returned in response regarding Katherine's medical condition were sealed from the public, including all hearings held relating to the possible use of this information at trial and challenges to our subpoenas. A battle ensued, all behind closed courtroom doors. Katherine fought like hell to prevent us from obtaining her medical records and related documents. The government was aware of what we were doing because Katherine was not prohibited from telling them about our subpoena request once she was notified. They joined and filed their own objections on Katherine's side.

When the dust had settled, and all the objections and arguments had been heard by the court, we believed that, although we still needed the court's final approval during the trial, when the moment came we were going to get the green light to cross-examine Katherine on her mental capacity in front of the jury. And the Kealohas knew this as well.

The court, however, issued a gag order that prohibited me from disclosing what we'd learned from out subpoenas until the court made the final decision at trial. A gag order simply means that one is prohibited by a court from disclosing certain information. That order continues to this day regarding various facts related to Katherine's physical and mental health that we discovered through subpoenas. However, I'm not under any such order regarding information I learned through other means or which otherwise has become public. In 2019, long after Gerard's case was over, Robert Black, the attorney for the Civil Beat Law Center for the Public Interest, filed a motion under the First Amendment requesting that the court unseal all the documents in Gerard's case. This motion included our subpoena requests. The court agreed to unseal almost all the documents Mr. Black requested, excluding the subpoenas related to Katherine's medical records. But one of her medical record documents was unsealed by the court, a document we'd also obtained from sources independent of our subpoena requests. This was the note from the doctor testifying as to Katherine's mental unfitness. The press seized upon it and reported its contents.

According to the Civil Beat Law Center's website, where this document still remains posted, Katherine's doctor specifically stated that Katherine was under medication that affected her cognitive ability, such that Katherine was "unable to perform any sustained activity which requires mental focus or concentration, such as going to court or answering questions in a deposition." The note was addressed "To Whom it May Concern," and dated February 13, 2014, though as I mentioned, it claimed Katherine's condition began back on June 26, 2013.

On October 22, 2018, Lynn Kawano of Hawaii News Now reported that "Katherine had been diagnosed with transient global amnesia." From information gathered from her own sources, Kawano reported Katherine "took more than 200 hours of taxpayer-funded sick time in 2013 and 2014, before eventually going on sick leave without pay." As Kawano reported, "the Mayo Clinic describes TGA as a sudden, temporary episode of memory loss where the patient sometimes will draw a blank when asked [during the episode itself] to remember things that happened a day, a month or even a year ago." However, a TGA episode is rare, lasting no more than twenty-four hours, and can only occur once or twice in a person's lifetime to qualify for this diagnosis. There are no lingering effects. If episodes are repetitive, then there can be no TGA diagnosis. Moreover, when the episode is over, there is no general memory loss, although you may not remember what you did during the TGA episode itself. If this medical condition had been in fact the basis of Katherine's doctor's note in 2013, then it should not have justified a delay of her deposition testimony, as it was not an ongoing mental health condition that rendered Katherine incapable of doing legal work, much less ordinary daily tasks. It also would not have justified extended sick leave with pay.

We were fully prepared to use our information against her during cross-examination in Gerard's trial. But more importantly, Katherine and Louis Kealoha were fully aware of the medical and employment records that we had obtained through our subpoenas, as well as the court's sealed rulings regarding whether we could use that information at trial. They knew exactly what we were prepared to do on cross-examination should Katherine testify. If we had been able to use it, we believed this information would be devastating to Katherine's career and to the public image she had so carefully crafted over the years. It was that explosive. Trust me, there is so much more to tell than I have mentioned; I simply cannot legally discuss it at this time. I was therefore surprised that the government continued to insist that Katherine was ready and eager to testify. I had thought that the government, and Katherine, would make the difficult but necessary decision to keep her off the stand even though it would severely cripple their case. But again, maybe we knew more than the government did, or at least understood more than the government did. Regardless, when Katherine took the stand against Gerard it would be dramatic, and I was most curious to see how it would play out. ❖

CHAPTER 9

Subpoena Wars

I love subpoenas. Specifically subpoenas that request documents. These types of subpoenas are called *subpoena duces tecum,* which means "under penalty you shall bring with you" the requested documents. But HPD? Not so much.

The process of obtaining a subpoena in federal court is not as easy and straightforward as it might appear. As an attorney for an "indigent" defendant, Gerard, I could not simply write up a subpoena, serve it and obtain any document I wanted on my own accord. Under the Federal Rules of Criminal Procedure, while an indigent defendant has the right to seek evidence, records and documents from third parties through the subpoena process, as a federal defender I was required to apply to a federal judge to obtain a subpoena. In doing so I had to demonstrate three things to the judge: first, that the documents existed and were in the possession of the person or entity I was subpoenaing. Second, that the documents would not be voluntarily turned over to me without a subpoena. Third, and most importantly, that the documents were relevant to my defense. The government and defendants represented by their own attorneys do not have to follow this procedure and can issue subpoenas without justifying them first to a judge. But on behalf of an indigent defendant, subpoenas were actually issued *by and on the authority of a federal judge.* All of this is done under seal; otherwise, the prosecutor would unfairly learn of our defense strategy. This entire process is irksome to prosecutors; while they can see that I am asking the court for a subpoena, they don't know why or what specific documents I am seeking. They suspect I'm looking for something important to my defense and something perhaps they've overlooked, and they're usually right.

In Gerard's case, we served a number of subpoenas on Honolulu City and County agencies seeking information on the license plate numbers

Gerard had given us of the vehicles he believed had been following him in the days before his arrest. We were hoping they would reveal that the vehicles belonged to HPD officers. They did. This subpoena endeavor was met with little resistance or pushback from City and County agencies.

After we served our eleventh subpoena on the custodian of records for HPD, however, HPD had had enough. On October 24, 2014, the City and County Corporation Counsel, on behalf of HPD, filed a motion to quash all eleven subpoenas we had served on HPD between September 5 through October 2, 2014. We didn't believe for a moment that such a motion would have been filed without Louis's knowledge and consent, as he was chief of police. Corporation Counsel argued that we were serving too many subpoenas on HPD and that HPD was being "harassed and burdened by [our] fishing expedition." He further argued that our subpoenas sought "irrelevant and inadmissible" information and therefore were "unreasonable and oppressive." Corporation Counsel concluded by stating that the "broad sweep of the documents, records, and information" we were seeking could "hardly be characterized as satisfying the 'specificity' requirement" we needed to show in order to justify our subpoenas, and that without this showing "HPD and the City will not agree to participate."

While I wasn't surprised that HPD was fighting back and didn't want to produce the documents and records we were seeking, I was taken aback by Corporation Counsel's statement that HPD and the City would "not agree to participate" unless *they* were satisfied that our subpoenas were legally sound. By its very nature, a subpoena is coercive. It is not voluntary. One does not have the right to decide whether one will or will not "participate." More importantly, the City's position seemed to suggest that it had no understanding in whose name and under whose authority the subpoenas had been issued in the first instance—a federal judge's. We reckoned that when we appeared in court to argue the motion before the very same judge who had issued the subpoenas, this misunderstanding of the law would work in our favor. It was clear to us that HPD, and by extension the Kealohas, were trying to force us to expose our theory of defense by objecting to our subpoenas. That was not going to happen.

In fact, I had written detailed motions to the court explaining why each and every document I was seeking was relevant and material to our defense. But the actual subpoenas we served simply told HPD what documents I wanted and the date HPD was required to provide those documents to the court. HPD had the right to challenge the subpoena by filing a motion to quash if it believed the subpoenas were improper. But HPD did not have the right to know the underlying reason I wanted the documents. And refusing to "participate," like little children refusing to play a game, was simply not an option.

I was also troubled by the timing of the motion to quash, because up to this point we had been attempting, through emails and phone calls, to amicably resolve issues that had arisen. Corporation Counsel had simply asked me for more time to gather documents, and I had agreed. I had not agreed to give them more time to file a motion to quash.

Initially, HPD had complied with several of our subpoenas. The problem was that they had redacted parts of the documents, like dates of birth, addresses and names of witnesses, or even locations of events. We were told this was being done pursuant to HPD's own internal policies to keep certain information private. But often this was the very information we were seeking to uncover. If HPD wanted to black out information, they should have gone to the court, presented their case and clarified what was required of them. They didn't. Rather, without permission, HPD simply blacked out information and then claimed they had complied with our subpoena. We had repeatedly informed Corporation Counsel that HPD was not in compliance with the subpoenas if any information was blacked out, but we were told in response that unless the subpoena specifically instructed HPD *not* to redact information, they were going to continue to abide by their own internal policy.

A second issue that came up was whom at HPD we were supposed to serve our subpoenas upon. We'd originally been instructed to serve them on HPD officer Sonny Roden, the custodian of records for HPD. He was the same individual we had served subpoenas on for HPD in all of our other cases in the past. But as we filed more subpoenas in Gerard's case, Officer Roden began responding that he could not find any responsive documents *in his one department*. He claimed there were at least three other custodians of records for other departments within HPD and we would have to serve each of them independently every time we gave HPD a subpoena. We had never encountered this supposed "procedure" in the past. Such a requirement would be very cumbersome and time-consuming for us and could lead to HPD being able to claim, later, that documents did exist but we had just failed to serve the right custodian of records. We needed to know with certainty whether a document existed or not. And if it did, it had to be turned over. This new requirement seemed more like a shell game than anything legitimate.

Because we believed that HPD might deliberately hide documents from us, the subpoenas we issued also required that Officer Roden file an affidavit to the court if no documents were found in HPD's possession. If HPD did hide documents, and we later discovered this fact, the affidavit would serve to severely undermine HPD's credibility before the court and perhaps could lead to sanctions being imposed. But I also hoped that making Officer Roden file an affidavit would make HPD think twice before hiding documents. Initially, Officer Roden complied with this requirement. But as we served more subpoenas, he changed the wording of his affidavits and said he was *only* certifying that there were no documents *in his one specific department*. This was not acceptable. The filing of the motion to quash the subpoenas told me the gloves had finally come off. For both of us. Trial was fast approaching. HPD was stalling, and we were running out of time.

On November 12, 2014, after several not-so-friendly hearings, Judge Leslie Kobayashi, the judge who had been handling our subpoena requests and who would be our trial judge, ruled that our subpoenas were neither unreasonable nor oppressive and ordered HPD to provide unredacted documents. The court also ordered that our subpoenas did not have to be served on different custodians of records and that Officer Roden would be required to accept service and respond for the entire department. While this was a satisfying victory, the clock was ticking. We were now less than a month away from trial and we needed to see what was in those documents.

On Monday, December 1, one day before trial began, we finally obtained all the unredacted documents HPD claimed they had. In response to several of our subpoena requests, however, HPD claimed they could find no documents. But HPD was not done. On December 2, the first day of the trial, Corporation Counsel sent a letter to Judge Kobayashi stating that HPD had fully responded to our subpoenas and that because Officer Roden had filed an affidavit so stating, Officer Roden should not be required to appear as a witness. Apparently, Officer Roden had vacation plans, plans he had made even though he was aware he was going to be called as a defense witness. I objected. We'd subpoenaed Officer Roden specifically so we could put him on the witness stand to say that he had found no documents in response to several of our subpoenas. We intended to use his testimony to argue to the jury that documents HPD claimed did not exist were in fact required to have been generated by standard HPD policies and procedures. We'd previously obtained several of HPD's operating procedures manuals regarding the preparation of police reports, and these specified who was required to prepare a report, when and how. We also knew, according to these manuals, that police reports or documents authorizing the allocation of City and County property, such as in the placement of cameras at the Kealoha residence, should exist. The fact that HPD was saying they didn't exist simply didn't jive with their own policies and procedures, and we had already learned that HPD were sticklers for following their own internal rules and procedures.

Specifically, we had asked for these pieces of evidence:

Any reports that Louis had reported shots being fired at his house.

Reports relating to deputy chief McCauley or Louis reporting the theft of the mailbox and referring it to CIU.

All documents stating when the surveillance cameras had been installed at the Kealoha residence and under whose authority and for what purpose.

The hard drive of the video surveillance footage or a longer version of the footage given to us.

And lastly, any and all CIU reports regarding any CIU involvement in the mailbox theft investigation.

According to HPD, none of these reports or pieces of physical evidence existed. Sometimes the failure to file a report can be as damning as having filed a false or incomplete report. The fact that HPD's custodian of records had sworn in an affidavit and we presumed would swear again under oath on the witness stand that subpoenaed documents that should exist did not, only further supported our theory that Gerard was being framed. But in order to present this evidence to the jury, we needed Officer Roden as a witness. Judge Kobayashi agreed and denied the City's request, ordering that Officer Roden be present to testify.

In the end, despite resistance, our subpoena efforts paid off. Through these protracted battles we had uncovered CIU officer Niall Silva's altered chain of custody report—tangible proof that at least one HPD officer had improperly altered a report. While we had found police reports that we could argue omitted critical evidence, and police reports that seemed to falsify evidence, shockingly we now had a report that *had* actually been altered, and we could prove it. And, even more importantly, HPD had hidden this document from federal prosecutors.

But HPD was not the only subpoena fight we had. Katherine was fighting us tooth and nail over the subpoenas we had issued for her medical and employment records. That fight was bitter, and when the district court finally ruled against her and in our favor, Katherine appealed to the Ninth Circuit Court of Appeals to prevent us from getting her records. We won that battle as well. But all of this took time, and the clock was ticking.

Katherine's boss, Keith Kaneshiro, had also decided to enter the fray. Katherine's employment records were located at the Honolulu Office of the Prosecuting Attorney. Brian, my investigator, went to serve our subpoena seeking her employment records early in the morning of June 3, 2014. He was met at the door by Vernon Branco, who was working as one of Keith Kaneshiro's right-hand men. Branco not only refused to allow Brian to enter the office; he refused to accept the subpoena. This was a federal subpoena issued by a federal judge being served on a law enforcement office, and they were refusing to accept service. And it just wasn't any office, it was the office of the prosecuting attorney, whose very job it was to uphold the rule of law and who themselves routinely issued subpoenas. And Branco, of all people, knew we had obtained the subpoena from a federal judge because he used to work in my office and had served subpoenas for us on numerous occasions. Kaneshiro's refusal to accept service of a federal subpoena was unprecedented and, quite frankly, mindboggling.

I immediately called the US Marshals, explained the situation and asked that they serve the subpoena for us. A deputy marshal went to serve the subpoena. She had told me she did not expect any of the difficulties we'd run into. After all, she said, she was a US marshal serving a subpoena on a prosecuting attorney, people the US Marshals worked with on a daily basis. Surprise. At around 1:30 p.m. she called me and told me that she too had been refused entry into the office and that they had refused to accept service even from her. I could hear the shock and amazement in her voice. But I also heard anger. She informed me she was going to get two large male deputy marshals and they were going back and would serve the subpoena one way or another. While I enjoyed the image of US marshals breaking down the door to the City and County Prosecutor's Office, I asked her to let me make some phone calls to see if I could work things out.

I called the office of the Corporation Counsel, who represented the prosecutor's office in such matters, and explained the situation. I told them that they had until 3:00 p.m., about an hour from my phone call, to convince Kaneshiro to accept service of the subpoena or I was going to hold a press conference and disclose to the public that Kaneshiro, the City and County prosecutor, was refusing to accept lawful service of a subpoena issued by a federal judge by US marshals. Finally, fifteen minutes later, we were told that the US marshals could go ahead and now serve the subpoena.

In total, we'd obtained and served twenty-four subpoenas seeking documents in this case. Never before had so many subpoenas been issued in any one case by my office. Maybe we'd sought three or four subpoenas in a case before, but never twenty-four. We'd been persistent and won almost every battle that came our way. And we had struck gold. We found damning evidence that we could use to undermine Katherine's credibility. We found a police report that was concrete evidence that at least one document had been improperly altered. We found that no reports existed when they should have. And we had tied vehicles Gerard claimed were following him to undercover police officers. It had all been worth the effort, time, energy and fight. And maybe, just maybe, in the future some doors would be opened just a little quicker when we came calling with a subpoena. If not, I knew a couple of US marshals who were eager to kick them open for us. ❖

CHAPTER 10

Florence

G erard believed he was being framed because of a civil lawsuit he and his mother, Florence Puana, had filed against Katherine in March of 2013. This was just three months before Katherine claimed Gerard stole her mailbox. I needed to determine if this was plausible. Brian Wise, my investigator, spoke to Florence in early November of 2013. I met Florence a few weeks later to get more precise details and to judge her credibility for myself. If we were going to use the civil lawsuit as a motive for why a person of stellar reputation and status in the community like Katherine Kealoha would go to all the trouble of framing her uncle over, I needed to fully understand and hopefully be able to verify every detail. There could be no holes, no half-truths, or our motive would fall apart under cross-examination at trial. If that happened, our credibility with the jury would instantly vanish and it wouldn't matter what other evidence we presented; we'd lose.

I met Florence at her daughter Charlotte's apartment in Kailua when she was ninety-three years old. Florence had been living there since getting out of the hospital in April of 2013. Needing twenty-four-hour care, she was not well enough to live in her own home, which was located on a hill and had stairs to the second floor. Charlotte's place was a two-bedroom apartment, small for three adults to live in, but they made it work.

I brought Brian with me. Brian had told me how warm and friendly Florence had been to him, so I thought he'd be a familiar, friendly face for her to see. Many times, people close up when talking to an attorney. I wanted Florence to feel at ease, to talk freely. I also needed Brian to listen and record our conversation so he could be a witness to what Florence said if that became necessary in the future. Sometimes witnesses change their stories or a prosecutor might allege at trial that they were making things up during their testimony. If that happened, I could put Brian on the stand to testify to what Florence had told us during this meeting, months before the trial, when her memory was fresher.

When I walked in, Florence was seated at the kitchen table, her walker by her side. I immediately noticed she was wearing white compression socks like my father-in-law had worn. While she didn't get up to greet me, she reached out both her hands and cupped my hand in hers and welcomed me. She held my hand in hers for a long time. She immediately made me feel like I was family. She smiled, and I could see the spark of life in her eyes. Instant acceptance. I now understood why Brian felt like he had connected to Florence so easily. While her speech was a bit slurred, she was clear, concise, logical and coherent. She spoke in a manner well beyond what her eighth-grade formal education would suggest, demonstrating that her efforts at self-education had served her well. She proudly told me that she continued to exercise by using a small bicycle machine for her arms and kept her mind sharp by doing crossword puzzles. I told her about my father-in-law and how he used to walk around our house in his compression socks, white T-shirt and shorts. The image in our minds brought a smile to both of our faces—a good icebreaker if one was needed.

We sat down at the family dinner table, and I asked Florence to tell me first about her life, a safe subject that she didn't have to think hard about to remember. This would make it easier to later transition into a subject she might not want to talk about as much. She told me she was born on August 24, 1919, and grew up on the island of Maui where she went to school through the eighth grade. As a teenager she worked in the fields and at the pineapple cannery. I interjected to tell Florence that as a teenager my wife had also worked at the Dole pineapple factory on Oʻahu. The sweet smell of pineapple became overwhelming after working eight-hour shifts. Florence smiled knowingly.

Florence told me she moved to Oʻahu in June 1941 when she was twenty-two, with her husband, John Kenalio Puana. Six months before the attack on Pearl Harbor. On Oʻahu, Florence worked at Star of the Sea Church for thirty-two years, where she cleaned and did ironing. The Puanas were married for sixty-four years before John's death. Florence and her husband had built their family home in the Wilhelmina Rise section of Honolulu, where they raised their nine children. On his deathbed, Florence promised her husband that the house would go to their children. It was to be their inheritance. It was all they had to give them.

Gerard was her youngest son. Katherine was the child of Florence's second-oldest son, Rudolph or "Rudy." By now, Florence said with a big grin, she had too many grandchildren to count. The Puana family was large, and Florence was its matriarch. Family was, as Florence proudly and sternly said to me as she looked directly into my eyes, "everything." Florence told me she was particularly proud of Katherine and had always trusted her because she was the only one of her extended family who became a lawyer. Katherine, Florence said, was the "smart one."

Now that Florence herself had brought Katherine's name up, the transition to the topic of the reverse mortgage and the lawsuit was smooth. I asked Florence to tell me why, given how well she thought of Katherine, she had filed a civil lawsuit against her own granddaughter. Florence paused, put her hands together on her lap and looked down for a for few seconds before answering. It was clear that discussing what had happened between her and Katherine troubled her. Katherine, Florence wanted me to know, was still family, no matter what she had done. Florence just wanted to know why she'd done it.

Florence took a deep breath, looked up and began telling me the story. In 2009, Florence and Katherine were on good terms. Florence, as she would tell people time and time again, was very proud of Katherine for her accomplishments and trusted her completely. Gerard, Florence said, also had a good relationship with Katherine in 2009. Katherine called Gerard her "favorite uncle" and lovingly referred to him as "Uncle Gerrsters." When Katherine and Louis renovated their Kāhala home, Gerard pitched in and worked for many weeks alongside his older brother Rudy on various projects around the house. The relationship between Katherine and Gerard was so solid and trusting that, over the course of several years, Gerard gave Katherine thousands of dollars to invest for him. This was money he'd been able to save up while living with Florence. Gerard promised his father on his deathbed that he'd take care of her, and he had. For years after John's death, Gerard lived at the family home with Florence, taking care of her. Now Florence wanted to buy a place of his own for Gerard.

But like many families in Hawai'i, Florence was house-rich but cash-poor. Many people in Hawai'i own the homes they grew up in, homes that have greatly increased in value. Salaries and income, on the other hand, have not kept up with the cost of living. As a result, generations of family members often live together in one residence because they cannot afford to rent or buy their own homes. The Puana family was no different. Neither Florence nor Gerard could themselves qualify for a bank loan, as neither had a steady source of income. Gerard was living mostly on disability insurance and Florence on social security. Years earlier, Gerard had lived in a condo unit in the Greenwood Condominium apartment building in the Salt Lake area of Honolulu with his now ex-wife. Katherine told Florence and Gerard that same exact unit had just come on the market. Florence and Gerard thought it would be a good investment, but neither had the money nor financial credit to get a loan. Thus, it was no surprise they turned to Katherine for financial advice.

Katherine suggested that Florence obtain a reverse mortgage. And Katherine had a plan. As she explained, if Florence got a reverse mortgage, Florence could use that money to buy Gerard the Greenwood condo. And to help Katherine, who was experiencing her own unexplained financial difficulties, Florence would allow Katherine to use a little of the monies left over from the reverse mortgage to pay off debt of her own. With Katherine's credit restored, Katherine promised to obtain her own personal bank loan and pay off the reverse mortgage. That way, Gerard would have his condominium, the reverse mortgage would be paid off, and Florence would keep her home without having to make any payments. Gerard would then make monthly payments directly to Katherine to reimburse her for the personal bank loan she had obtained to pay off the reverse mortgage. This solved, as Katherine explained, any problems with the fact that neither Florence nor Gerard could get a loan based upon their own credit. It seemed like a win-win solution for everyone, and even though Gerard was hesitant, the plan was set in motion.

Katherine explained she would handle all the paperwork and the financial transactions, and she opened a joint bank account with Florence so everything would run smoothly. All the monies from the reverse mortgage were deposited into this account, and all payments made out of it. Katherine also opened up a joint post office box with Florence so all the bank paperwork and bills would be sent to this one mailing address. While Florence had legal access to the postal box, only Katherine had the keys and collected the mail. Katherine said this would make it easier for her to manage all the transactions and the paperwork that needed to be filed. Florence gave Katherine power of attorney so Katherine could handle all the financial documents.

Florence was pleased. All seemed to go well, at first. By the end of 2009 Florence had obtained a loan in the amount of $513,474 from the reverse mortgage and bought Gerard the Greenwood condo in Salt Lake for $360,000. The remainder, approximately $137,235 was deposited into the joint account. In emails, Katherine instructed Gerard, or, as she wrote, "My Favorite Uncle Gerrsters!!!" exactly how much he had to pay her each month for the personal bank loan she claimed she had obtained to pay off the reverse mortgage.

Then, in late 2009, Florence received a mortgage statement that had been sent to her home address instead of the post office box. It showed that there was still an outstanding balance on the reverse mortgage. Florence immediately contacted Katherine and questioned her as to why there was still a balance on the loan, a loan that Florence thought had already been paid off. Katherine explained that the loan had, in fact, been paid off in full and the bank's paperwork just had to "catch up." Florence did not receive any more bank statements, and life went on. Gerard continued to faithfully pay his monthly debt to Katherine, month after month.

Three years later, in February 2012, Florence received a second bank loan statement. The originating mortgage company had sold the loan to another bank and had used Florence's home address rather than the post office box. The notice contained the amount of the outstanding balance due, which was now well over what she had originally borrowed since no payments had ever been made against the loan. Not a penny. The mortgage statement stated Florence now owed $651,783. Florence didn't know what to make of this, as she assumed that the reverse mortgage had been paid off in full by Katherine years earlier. Gerard's monthly payments to Katherine were proof of that, Florence thought. Surely this bank statement was a mistake, and that was why, Florence surmised, she had not received any other mortgage loan statements for years.

Florence reached out to Katherine to find out what was happening. Surely Katherine would make some calls and straighten this whole matter out. But no matter how many times Florence tried to reach her, Katherine never answered her phone and never returned messages. Just a voice machine with 'ukulele music strumming in the background. Gerard also reached out. No response. Two of Florence's daughters called Katherine. Nothing. Radio silence. Unable to contact Katherine, and fearful that she was going to lose her home, Florence spoke to an attorney for advice. He instructed her to write Katherine a letter asking her to explain what had happened and notifying her that Florence was revoking Katherine's power of attorney. In September Florence sent a one-page typed letter to her. It was polite but sad. It sought answers from Katherine as to why the reverse mortgage had not been paid off and said that while Florence was still open to working it all out, if she didn't hear back from Katherine, she'd be forced to take legal action to "correct this mess."

Florence went on to tell me that Katherine had finally responded, in writing. Katherine wrote two letters, one addressed to Florence and Gerard and the other to the entire Puana family. In these letters Katherine not only denied she'd done anything wrong; she claimed she'd done everything she could to help Florence and Gerard buy his condominium, even having to put money up front and buying furniture out of her own money to make the transaction work.

At this point Florence stopped and looked at me, her hands reaching out to hold mine, and said, "Everything she said in the letters was a lie. Everything. Why would she do that?" Florence withdrew her hands and put them back in her lap and, looking down, said that Katherine had said many other things in the letter that she simply would not repeat to me. While I knew Florence was trying to contain herself, I could see fire in her eyes. Anger. I wanted to see the letters, but I didn't want to interrupt her, so I let her continue.

After receiving the letters and with no further communications from Katherine, Florence was told to find out how much money was in the joint bank account that Katherine had opened at the Kāhala branch of the Bank of Hawaii. It was Katherine's bank, and they knew Katherine. They did not know Florence or the rest of her family. After several failed attempts by Rick Hartsell, her son-in-law, and Gerard to gain access to the bank account on Florence's behalf, in early February of 2013 they finally found out that there was no money in the account. It was all gone. All $137,235. Florence stopped talking and just stared at her hands. "I don't know where it has all gone. What happened?" That's why, Florence told me, she felt she had no choice but to file a lawsuit against her own granddaughter.

I showed Florence a copy of the lawsuit she and Gerard had filed on March 7, 2013. The lawsuit alleged fourteen separate claims related to Katherine's alleged misconduct regarding the reverse mortgage transaction and other monies, over $70,000, which Gerard had given Katherine to invest in "huis," which he claimed she also stole. (A *hui* refers to a group of people who join together for some purpose; in this case, financial investments.) The claims filed against Katherine included allegations of breach of fiduciary duty, fraud, intentional misrepresentation and fraud against the elderly. The civil complaint, if true, was damning. It outlined allegations of serious misconduct and possible criminal fraud violations committed, intentionally, by a high-ranking prosecuting attorney against her now ninety-three-year-old grandmother and her uncle, Gerard. The civil suit sought punitive damages in addition to the actual monetary losses suffered, which could run into the hundreds of thousands of dollars.

Katherine filed a response to the lawsuit denying any wrongdoing. She referred to Gerard as a "ne'er-do-well" and a "deadbeat." But Katherine didn't stop there. She filed a counterclaim alleging that the allegations were false, and because they impugned her character and reputation in the community, she sought monetary penalties against Florence and Gerard. As Katherine stated in her response, "I deny all of the so-called factual assertions claiming that I breached any duties to either of the plaintiffs." She added, "The claims contained in that document are so detached from reality that it amounts to a work of fiction."

I asked Florence if there was anything in writing, anything tangible to back up her story about the reverse mortgage agreement between her and Katherine. Other than a few email exchanges mentioning the reverse mortgage and Gerard's payment schedule, there was nothing else. Nothing to show Katherine had agreed to pay off the mortgage as part of the plan. Gerard had been making payments to Katherine every month, but even these payments did not indicate what they were for. Without real proof, Katherine could simply come up with some story that Gerard was paying her back for some other debt or for some financial investment gone bad. Only Katherine, Florence and Gerard had known about the agreement. No one else in the family knew.

I had heard from Brian that something unusual had happened to Florence during the deposition of Katherine in the civil case, so I now asked Florence to explain. The first day of Katherine's scheduled two-day deposition in the civil case was on June 19, 2013, just two days before the mailbox theft occurred. Florence said that after a few hours into the deposition she could no longer listen to the lies that Katherine was saying under oath, and her back hurt, so she had asked to leave. Gerard took her downstairs to sit on a bench in the lobby of the office building while he went off to get the car.

Bobby Nguyen, a CIU police officer who was married to Katherine's niece and thus was family to Florence, sat down next to her on the bench. Florence's memory was clear as a bell as she repeated to me the conversation she had with Bobby while she waited for Gerard to bring around the car and drive her home. Initially, Bobby just sat next to her texting on his phone. He didn't even say hello. Then he turned to Florence and asked her what car Gerard owned. Florence mistakenly told Bobby that Gerard owned a white car, rather than the silver car he actually owned. She didn't mention the type of car. She was a bit embarrassed that she had told Bobby that Gerard's car was white, not silver. She looked up at me smiling shyly. Florence didn't like the fact that her memory had betrayed her in that moment. I purposefully went over this conversation with her several times to make sure she had told me everything about it, leaving nothing out. Every time her version of the events was consistent. Florence remembered it clearly because Bobby didn't ask her anything else and he was not very friendly to her, given that he was family through marriage. Rather, he simply sat next to her for most of the time using his cell phone. He didn't help her get up. He didn't walk her to the car. She was, to say the least, less than pleased with his behavior.

I looked over at Brian to make sure he'd caught this detail. A white car. Had this little mistake by Florence sent HPD on a wild goose chase looking for a white car? Could it have really been that simple? As crazy as it seemed, all the evidence seemed to point in this direction. But why was Bobby even at the deposition? It was a deposition in a private civil case. Not connected in any way to any official HPD business. What was Bobby even doing there? Why did he sit next to Florence if he wasn't going to talk to her as any family relative would do? Why ask this one and only question? There was one reasonable explanation for Bobby to have taken the opportunity presented to him to ask Florence that one question. We knew that Katherine did not necessarily know what kind of car Gerard drove because they hadn't seen or spoken to one another for some time. We also knew that if an officer ran a check on someone's vehicle in the police computer system, there would be a notation of who the officer was and the time and date. In other words, it could be traced. Talking to Florence, on the other hand, was untraceable, and Bobby probably figured she'd never even remember the conversation.

Bobby had underestimated Florence. She had remembered. To us, the fact that Bobby had asked Florence this question just two days before the mailbox theft explained why Detective Akagi went looking for a white car. If the theft was staged, Katherine needed to know what color car Gerard drove, to make sure the car make and model could not be made out in the videotape surveillance footage. And what color car showed up in the video surveillance footage? A white car. And, because of the blur of the streetlights and where the vehicle had pulled up on the street in relation to the surveillance cameras, the make and model of the car couldn't be determined. We could now offer an explanation to the jury as to why there was a white car in the video and why Detective Akagi was trying to tie a white car to Gerard.

Florence told me that Katherine was scheduled to return for a second day of depositions. It was going to be during this second day that Florence's attorney was going to confront Katherine with the bank account information and receipts for expenditures that were not authorized by Florence. But Katherine kept stalling, giving medical excuses to delay taking her deposition. And then, after Gerard was arrested for allegedly stealing the mailbox and his criminal case was moving forward, the civil case was delayed by court order for the criminal case to proceed first. It's normal procedure for a criminal case to take precedence over a civil case when one of the parties in the case is facing criminal charges. This protects that person's Fifth Amendment rights not to incriminate themselves by saying something in a civil proceeding that could be used against them in their criminal case. As a prosecutor, Katherine certainly would have known this delay would occur. A delay meant no verdict against her in the civil case. And if Gerard was convicted in his criminal case, his credibility as a witness would be severely damaged if he later testified in the civil case. And that would greatly increase Katherine's chances of success in the civil case. Framing Gerard for stealing the mailbox would be a win-win situation for Katherine.

Sadly, Florence realized that the bank would eventually own her home if the reverse mortgage was not paid off, and Florence would get nothing. With the $137,000 that had been in her joint account gone, Florence made the difficult decision to sell her family home so she could pay off the mortgage. It was to have been her family's inheritance, a promise she had made to her husband on his deathbed. It was not to be.

As we parted, Florence handed me the three letters written between herself and Katherine. I would read them later. But even at a glance I could tell the letters written by Katherine appeared strange. The letters were typed, with many words capitalized and in bold print. In fact, entire sentences and sometimes entire paragraphs were capitalized. It was as if Katherine was shouting at the reader. The letters did not at all appear like they had been written by a lifelong seasoned attorney. The one word that came to my mind as I glanced over the letters was "unhinged."

On November 25, 2013, I took Florence's videotaped deposition for possible use at Gerard's criminal trial. If Florence was unable to testify in person, we'd show the videotaped deposition to the jury as her testimony in the case. Unlike civil cases, where depositions are routinely taken, depositions in criminal cases are rare and only allowed to preserve the testimony of a witness who may be unavailable at the time of the trial. Florence's doctor had written me a letter that I had presented to the court saying it was his opinion that she was too ill to testify in person at a trial. The government offered no objection to taking her deposition, on the condition that, should Florence's health have improved by the time of trial, she would have to testify in person. The downside to taking Florence's deposition before the trial even began was that I was exposing an important piece of our defense to the government before they put on their evidence. Florence was a defense witness, and under normal circumstances she would testify *after* the government had presented all its evidence and witnesses at the trial. By taking her deposition before the trial began, we were putting one of our most important witnesses up first. The government would now have the opportunity to learn something about our defense and counter it in their own case. We felt we had little choice. Florence's testimony was simply too critical to risk should her health fail and she lose the chance to testify altogether.

At the deposition, because Florence was a defense witness, I asked her questions first. I began by asking her a series of questions to establish she was fully competent to testify. General questions about her life, significant events and names of her children. These questions not only demonstrated that her memory was intact; they also allowed the jury to get to know her a little. Florence then described the reverse mortgage agreement, the monies Katherine had stolen, her encounter with Bobby at the deposition and the civil lawsuit she had filed against Katherine as a result. I moved my questioning along as fast as I could because I didn't want to tire Florence before she underwent cross-examination. Florence concluded by stating she had seen the videotape surveillance footage of the theft of the mailbox several times, and the person in the video was definitely not her son Gerard. No chinks in her testimony. So far, so good.

During my examination of Florence, I never brought up the two mailboxes, nor any suggestion that the lawsuit was a means to frame Gerard, nor that there was anything wrong with HPD's investigation. The less I exposed about our defense the better, particularly at this stage of the proceedings. Florence's testimony would simply set the stage for what would come later at trial. Most importantly, Florence verified the letter she wrote to Katherine in September of 2012 and the two letters she received in response from Katherine. I introduced them into evidence. I did not ask Florence any further questions about them. They spoke for themselves, and I didn't want to draw too much attention to them. I didn't believe the government had ever seen or read them before, or, if they had, they hadn't paid much attention to them, so I kept my questioning low-keyed. Maybe, I hoped, the government would fail to understand their significance.

The government's cross-examination focused mainly on small details, like who helped her write the letter to Katherine and details about the reverse mortgage. No direct challenge to Florence's credibility. No questions at all about Florence's conversation with Bobby. As the cross-examination went on, Florence began to tire and became confused in some of her answers. I chalked it up to the lack of clarity of the questions being asked of her by the government more than her mental state. The prosecutor was also being somewhat aggressive in his questioning of Florence, using an unpleasant tone of voice and talking over her when she did not directly answer his question fast enough. I was convinced that this would upset a jury and make them even more sympathetic to her, as it seemed that the government was purposefully trying to confuse a ninety-three-year-old lady. Bad form, but good for us.

When it was all over, I was very satisfied with Florence's testimony. I did not think they understood how we were going to use her testimony and how significant it was to our defense. Florence, for her part, was tired but glad it was over and grateful that she had had her say. She turned to me as she left and said it was now up to me to "get it done."

I knew Katherine would be given a copy of Florence's testimony, which would give her the opportunity to craft her trial testimony accordingly. Katherine did more than that. She certainly understood the significance of Florence's testimony, even if the government did not. One day before the start of Gerard's criminal trial, on December 1, 2014, Katherine filed a motion to a state probate judge asking the court to appoint a conservator for Florence, claiming that Florence was mentally incompetent and under the undue influence of Gerard. Katherine wanted Florence's finances under the control of someone else, like herself. Katherine did not attach a single medical document supporting her claim that Florence was mentally unfit. She simply averred Florence was incompetent, pointing to Florence's confusion in some of her responses to the government's questioning during her deposition testimony in Gerard's case. If Florence was found mentally unfit, Katherine could try to prevent Florence's testimony at the civil trial on the basis that she was not a competent witness. Many months later the state court would find Florence competent and the motion filed by Katherine to have been frivolous.

But Katherine never did anything without a purpose. We surmised Katherine was setting the stage for the government to challenge Florence's competency as a witness in Gerard's criminal trial, which was scheduled to begin the very next day in federal court. Even though we had already taken Florence's deposition, there was still time for the government to challenge her competency as a witness and perhaps keep the jury from hearing her testimony at all. Something unexpected always happens right before a trial starts. It never fails. And this was one more last-minute crisis to deal with as we prepared to walk into court on December 2, 2014, to begin the first day of trial. ❖

CHAPTER 11

Rue the Day

Motive. It's often the key to determining whether a defendant is guilty of the crime they are charged with. If you can explain to a jury why a person would *want* to commit the crime, then it's that much more likely they will follow along with you as you show them the evidence that they *did* commit the crime. Every crime drama has a plot that focuses on a defendant's motive. The more twisted the motive, the more interesting the story. Sometimes it's pragmatic: a person robbing a store for money to buy drugs or to pay bills. Sometimes it's emotional: a spurned lover or a domestic relationship gone bad. Sometimes it's just plain greed. And sometimes it's a combination of all of the above.

Many people are surprised to learn that while there are legal elements of every crime that the government must prove, motive is not one of them. The prosecution need only prove the defendant committed the charged crime beyond a reasonable doubt. Proving that the defendant had a reason, a motive, for committing the crime is not relevant to a finding of guilt. Nevertheless, prosecutors often seek to develop a defendant's motive because it's more convincing to a jury. A jury is more likely to convict if they understand not only the how, when and where, but also the why.

In Gerard's case the tables were turned. It was we, the defense, who needed to prove motive if we wanted to convince a jury that Gerard was framed. And we needed a damn good one if a jury was going to believe that the HPD chief of police himself, his high-level prosecutor wife and various members of the Honolulu Police Department had all conspired to frame Gerard, a family relative of the Kealohas, no less, for stealing a mailbox. This was no small task. I was used to picking apart motives suggested by a prosecutor to explain my client's criminal behavior, not putting one together.

Greed. Power. Prestige. We thought any one of these vices would suffice as a motive if it was strong enough. If we could check off more than one, we'd have found good reasons why Gerard would, or at least could, have been framed. The civil lawsuit clearly put Katherine at risk; that much was obvious. If she lost and it was proven that she had actually stolen hundreds of thousands of dollars from her uncle and grandmother, Katherine would most likely lose her law license and might even become the subject of a state criminal investigation herself; certainly her standing in the community would be destroyed. But we had to show that this wasn't just our opinion but something Katherine actually believed to be true. We needed something that proved beyond any doubt that she feared the civil lawsuit and what might happen to her if the truth came out. And we found it. In Katherine's own words, in the letters Katherine had written in September 2012 to Florence.

We'd learned during our investigation that Katherine Kealoha was the daughter of Florence's son, Rudy. She was Florence's granddaughter. She was the only attorney in the family, graduating from the University of Hawai'i Richardson School of Law in 1996. She began her legal career by serving as a judicial law clerk for three different state judges, then working on and off in small private law firms before steadily rising through the ranks of the City and County's prosecutor's office. Katherine was also an adjunct professor at Chaminade University's Department of Criminology and Criminal Justice Administration. In 2008, Governor Linda Lingle appointed her as director of the Office of Environmental Quality Control, where Katherine served for several years before returning to work at the prosecutor's office. There she became the supervisor of the Career Offender Unit. Katherine's résumé was, to say the least, impressive.

Louis had risen through the police ranks, going from captain to being selected as the chief of police after having been passed over for promotion to major several times. One local magazine dubbed them the "Dynamic Duo." They had several homes, including a house in Kāhala, one of the wealthiest suburbs of Honolulu. Katherine drove a Maserati. Clearly Katherine's standing in the community meant a lot to her. Together, the Kealohas lived a good life and were considered a Hawaiian power couple. Katherine understood that the mere accusation that she had stolen money from her grandmother and uncle could cause serious problems for both her and her husband, let alone the problems a verdict against her would create.

We'd learned that by February 2013, Florence had found out that not only was the reverse mortgage not paid off, but the $137,235 balance in the joint account Katherine had set up for them was gone. It was later discovered that Katherine had spent $37,405 of this money on hotel fees, including $23,976 for an inaugural breakfast celebration for Louis when he became chief, at the Sheraton Waikiki in 2010. Another $10,171 was spent on miscellaneous personal expenses of Katherine's, including Elton John tickets, insurance and cell phone payments. And over $9,000 went to car expenses, including payments on her Maserati and Mercedes-Benz, and another $10,000 on shopping and restaurant charges. All without Florence's knowledge or consent.

In June 2013, when Katherine alleged Gerard had stolen the mailbox, the civil lawsuit was slowly moving towards trial. We reckoned Katherine badly needed to win the civil case, and she wanted Gerard to be convicted of a felony offense. But our case was not the only effort Katherine made to saddle Gerard with a felony conviction. In 2011, Gerard had been arrested for going onto his neighbor's front porch in an argument over a parking space. The neighbor kept parking on the street right in front of the steps that led down from Florence's home. Gerard needed to park there to make it easier for Florence to get in and out of the car and up and down from the house. Gerard had asked his neighbor on several occasions to leave the space available, but to no avail. For going onto his neighbor's porch to argue, Gerard had been arrested for unlawful entry, a state felony offense. In March 2013, Gerard pled guilty, but in June, the same month Katherine alleged Gerard stole the mailbox, a state court judge granted Gerard's request for a deferred plea, commonly referred to as a DANC plea, for "deferred acceptance of no contest." This meant that there was no longer a conviction, and so long as Gerard complied with the terms of his probation, the charges against him would be expunged from his record. Thus Gerard was no longer legally convicted of any crime. But in September, just three months later, with the civil case still pending, Katherine tried to get the state judge to reverse his decision by ordering one of her deputy attorneys to file a motion challenging the legality of the DANC plea. The challenge was unsuccessful. Gerard remained felony free.

But if Gerard was convicted of a felony in our federal case before the civil case went to trial, this "bad" or "illegal" act could be used during the civil trial to undermine his credibility. This was possible because Katherine alleged that Gerard had stolen the mailbox for the specific purpose of obtaining important bank statements that he thought were inside the mailbox that night. This allegation made it more likely that the state court judge would allow his criminal conviction for stealing the mailbox into evidence because the theft was directly related to the civil lawsuit. While Katherine, we believed, might feel that she stood a good chance of discrediting Florence's testimony as nothing more than that of an old lady who couldn't and didn't remember what really happened, Gerard was younger, with no memory issues, and presented a real threat. He needed to be dealt with. As outlandish as it might at first seem, framing Gerard for stealing the mailbox was the solution to her problem.

Katherine apparently believed she'd be able to orchestrate the investigation and the prosecution of the case from start to finish. Her husband, the chief of police, would conduct and therefore control the investigation. Katherine's office, or the state's attorney general office, where she had many close associates, would prosecute the case. No one, we thought Katherine believed, would ever seriously question the investigation or their credibility. In state court, Gerard would be appointed a state public defender with a heavy caseload, who would most likely not have the resources or time to fully investigate the case. And if any issues arose with the prosecution, Katherine could call upon the prosecutor to offer Gerard, her poor uncle, a sweetheart deal to plead guilty to avoid jail time. Gerard might then have had no choice but to take the deal to get himself out of jail. If this happened, as a further benefit to Katherine, she would look good to her entire family for having prevailed upon the prosecutor to go easy on Gerard. And presto, a felony conviction would be in place, and Gerard's family would be indebted to Katherine. Brilliant. It simply had to go according to plan. But when it didn't, and the case ended up in federal court, she was already too committed. She just had to get Gerard convicted, now in federal court. He was still charged with a felony. Her plan could still work…if everyone stuck to the plan.

On September 10, 2012, Florence took her attorney's advice and sent the letter to Katherine revoking her power of attorney and questioning what had happened with the reverse mortgage. Florence wrote:

> I am brokenhearted and have been anxious and worried since I discovered that there is a balance owed on my home of over $637,000. As you know, I've tried again and again to talk to you by phone, offered to meet with you at any time or place. But you've refused my requests. You have not been truthful, have

turned your back on me and will not return any of my calls. I'm confused by your actions and am worried sick. I <u>don't</u> understand what you've done and why.

I trusted you when you came to me in October 2009 with the idea of a reversed *[sic]* mortgage on my house so I could buy a condo…and you could borrow around $300,000 which you said was to consolidate your debts. You promised you'd repay the money within 3 to 6 months at most….

I am still willing to work this out with you. But if I do not hear from you…by 9/18, you will leave me no choice but to take whatever steps necessary to legally correct this mess.

Florence signed the letter, "Your grandmother." Gerard's name was not affixed to the letter. In fact, his name did not appear in the letter at all.

We knew it would be challenging to find a way to explain all of this to the jury. But, luckily for us, we had Katherine's own words to do it for us. The two letters Katherine had herself penned five days later in response to Florence's one-page, desperate letter seeking answers exuded greed, power and prestige.

One letter, containing forty-one numbered paragraphs and consisting of ten pages, was addressed to "Puana Family Member, Party Participant, and Interested Party." We've never figured out why Katherine used these terms when addressing her own family other than to make her letter appear more "legalistic." The second letter was six pages long and addressed only to Florence and Gerard Puana. Both letters were typed and signed by Katherine. The number of capitalized and underlined words contained in these letters was both striking and odd. The style of writing made it appear as if Katherine was so angry that she could hardly contain herself, almost yelling at the reader through the words on the page. The letters certainly did not appear to be written by an attorney with over sixteen years' experience, let alone someone who once ran a state office and was now one of the highest-ranking City and County prosecuting attorneys on Oʻahu.

In the letter addressed to "The Puana Family," Katherine denied, point by point, that she had done anything wrong. She absolutely refused to accept any responsibility, focusing on the fact that she had not and never would have borrowed any money from Florence. As Katherine stated, "I can assure everyone that I did not borrow even a dime from these people." "These people" referred to Katherine's own grandmother,

Florence, and her now presumably no-longer-favorite uncle, "Gerrsters." Throughout the letter Katherine referred to Florence and Gerard as "the individuals" and "the likes of these people," noting that while she "may be related to Florence and Gerard by blood [she] DID NOT grow up close to them." Katherine repeatedly asserted that she had used her own funds to secure the reverse mortgage, which was why Florence's claim that Katherine borrowed money to repay her own debts "INFURIATES ME ABOUT THE LIES"; this "FALSE assertion is BEYOND ABSURD." Unrelenting, Katherine asserted that "these allegations are BOGUS and FALSE because I DON'T EVEN HAVE ANY SIGNIFICANT BILLS TO CONSOLIDATE...." Several times in the letter Katherine stated she would not be "THE SCAPEGOAT ANY FURTHER!"

Katherine's claim that she was not in debt and would never borrow money from "the likes of" Florence was simply false. We learned through extensive subpoena efforts that on August 2, 2009, at the very time the reverse mortgage loan was being negotiated, Katherine had filed a police report claiming that someone had stolen her identity, causing her financial problems. The police report corroborated Florence and Gerard's claim that Katherine had suggested the reverse mortgage in part so that she could use some of the money to clear up her own financial difficulties.

Katherine's letter went further, threatening Florence and Gerard with retribution should they continue making their false accusations:

> This time may have been wasted, but IT WILL NOT BE SOON FORGOTTEN! I will meet these FALSE ALLEGATIONS with necessary and justified LEGAL ACTION and I can assure all of you that I will not rest until I have the JUST RETRIBUTION sought for these deplorable, libelous and defamatory statements...everything I did has been JUSTIFIED and THEY SHOULD BE ASHAMED OF THEMSELVES FOR THOSE LIES ABOUT ME!

Katherine's letter ended with a discussion of various bad acts allegedly perpetrated by Gerard against her and her family and how she had tried to help Gerard work through his legal problems in the past. But, due to Florence's letter, Gerard should not "EXPECT ANY SYMPATHY, FORGIVENESS OR RECONCILE FOR ANYONE WHO PUTS MY FAMILY IN HARMS WAY!"

While this letter, which Katherine sent to the entire Puana family, contained many quotable phrases that we would present to the jury to demonstrate Katherine's extreme level of animus towards Gerard, it was the second letter addressed to Florence and Gerard that contained even more venomous words from Katherine. In this letter, Katherine once again defended her actions as nothing more than her own good-hearted attempt to assist Florence with obtaining funds to buy Gerard a condo. Katherine began her defense of her actions by denying that she received any calls or messages from Florence, stating she had "never once received a telephone call, a telephone message, a letter, an e-mail or any other form of communication on Florence's behalf wishing to speak or meet with me about this situation." Katherine again repeatedly refuted that she borrowed any money from Florence, stating,

> I HAVE NEVER, WILL NEVER OR WOULD NEVER BORROW, TAKE OR EVEN REQUEST to BORROW ANY MONEY FROM FLORENCE PUANA!…. I am ASHAMED and APPALLED at both Florence and Gerard for allowing SUCH A LIE to be STATED!…I WILL PROVE that this is a HORRIBLE LIE! ANY PERSON who perpetuates this LIE should be damned ASHAMED of THEMSELVES for stating such CRAP!… HOW DARE ANYONE make such MALICIOUS and FALSE STATEMENTS against me!…you are now a Tortfeasor under the Law! YOUR tortious conduct is Outrageous, Unacceptable and beyond reprieve!

Katherine further claimed that she had documentation to prove the truth of her statements and "WELCOME[D] ANY AND ALL 'legal action.'"

Then, in her own words, Katherine's desire to strike back at Gerard became readily apparent. What she wrote, with such rage, made her intent crystal clear and later would become the mantra of our case and the capstone of my opening statement to the jury. In its simplicity and brevity, it revealed why a top state prosecutor and her chief of police husband would go to great lengths to frame an innocent man, to see that he was arrested, imprisoned and charged with a felony for a crime he did not commit:

I WILL seek the highest form of legal retribution against ANYONE and EVERYONE who has written or verbally uttered these LIES about me!

They will rue the day that they decided to state these TWISTED LIES!

These were ugly words, ugly letters. We would use them to make things right for Gerard. ❖

CHAPTER 12

Organized Chaos

The days and weeks leading up to the start of Gerard's trial were hectic and nerve-racking, with long, long hours in the office for everyone. Even though we'd been working on the case for over a year, that time had been spent gathering evidence, finding witnesses and formulating a defense. Now it was time to put it all together.

Trials are a rarity. As I mentioned, 90 percent of cases brought in federal court end up in a guilty plea. While my office may begin to prepare a number of cases for trial, most end up settling long before the real trial prep work begins. In an entire year my office normally has only one or two cases that actually result in trials. Thus, when we do go to trial, it's all hands on deck.

My investigators, my administrative assistant Lynelle and several other staff members all pitched in and shared the collective pain. While I had many trials under my belt and knew what had to be done, I'm simply not that organized—an understatement, if you asked Adam and Lynelle. Nevertheless, there was purpose to my insanity, and everyone knew I would be prepared by the start of trial, no matter how disheveled my office appeared or how unkempt my hair. But some of the chaos was unavoidable, a result of receiving numerous documents from the government and from HPD in the days before trial began.

The week leading up to trial, Adam and I pored over the hundreds of documents we had gathered to determine which we would need to use during the trial. We ended up with seventy-eight documents. Many other documents were held in reserve to use to impeach witnesses, such as the two mailboxes and all the photographs showing the Solar Group mailbox standing before the Kealoha residence. We weren't required to include that evidence in our trial exhibit binders. Six sets of trial exhibit binders had to be prepared for the court and the prosecution. Grunt work to be sure, but absolutely critical. If we missed a document, the court might not allow us to use it during the trial, and that could be fatal.

At 5:00 p.m. on Friday, November 29, just three days before Tuesday's trial, we received a witness list and additional documents from the government. The rules permitted such late discovery, and the government always waited until 5:00 p.m. to turn over these documents. It left us with only the weekend to review them and conduct further investigation if necessary. Remember, it's trial by ambush. After we had reviewed the new documents, we were relieved we hadn't gotten anything from the government that we hadn't already anticipated. We still believed we knew far more about what was really going on than they did.

The weekend would also be spent reviewing the information about more than a hundred potential jurors that we'd received from the court. Each had filled out a short questionnaire with their age and occupation, the name and occupation of their significant other, and where they lived. Not a lot of information. Adam and Kate spent countless hours on the Internet obtaining more information about each prospective juror and preparing a flow chart of the information they found to assist us during the jury selection process. The government was doing the same thing, but their resources were far more extensive and intrusive, including the ability to get tax records for each juror.

Throughout trial preparation, my responsibilities to my thirty-five other cases and my administrative duties continued. Calls, meetings and court hearings created constant interruptions. As a result, in the weeks before trial I often came into the office before 6:00 a.m. and stayed past 10:00 p.m. Organized chaos and long hours—par for the course.

In preparing for Gerard's trial, the single most important task was to formulate the direct and cross-examinations of each witness. My trial notebooks for Gerard's case contained over twenty prepared examinations, with supporting documents under each witness's name. The two most difficult and most important were, of course, the cross-examinations of Katherine and Louis Kealoha. Each would merit their own separate trial notebooks.

Cross-examination is a learned skill that comes from doing trial after trial. It can be an art when done well and agonizingly painful when not. Sometimes, it just comes down to a gut feeling when you're questioning a witness and you sense that they're not being truthful. A gut feeling that you have to learn to trust and to act upon in the moment. It takes a certain mentality that not all attorneys, even defense attorneys, possess.

Trial work isn't for everyone, certainly not for the faint of heart. You have to have the instinct and the willingness to go for the jugular when a witness is reeling and their credibility is on the line. If you don't have that instinct or will, my advice is to find another occupation.

But before I even start formulating and writing down my cross-examinations, I have to be completely familiar with all the evidence in the case. What information each document contains, what each witness has previously said and in which document I can find that exact statement. I also have to know which rule of evidence permits me to introduce a particular piece of evidence or statement, in case the government objects. The process of preparing an effective cross-examination is never-ending and continuous, right up to the moment you stand up to do the cross-examination during the trial. I'm constantly reworking my examinations as new ideas pop into my head at any time of the day or night. I've often woken up in the middle of the night and jotted down ideas that came to me while I slept, sometimes unfortunately only to find the next morning that I'm unable to read what I wrote. By repeatedly fine-tuning my cross-examination in this way, I have memorized it. This is critical, because a trial is like an improvisational play, with the courtroom its stage and each witness a scene. One never knows what a witness will say that may contradict what they may have previously said. I have to listen closely and observe the mannerisms of a witness in order to pick up on inconsistencies or deception in their testimony—opportunities to formulate new questions that further my case. The body language of a witness can tell you a lot about whether they are being truthful. You have to be able to recognize the signs when you see them and figure out what it is they are lying about and then adjust your cross-examination notes accordingly. All in a matter of minutes.

Cross-examination is not just about asking questions. There has to be a plan, a structure and purpose to your questions. Every question should serve to bring out information that is helpful to your defense. For example, I never have a prosecution witness repeat what they have already said on direct examination. They'll just say the same thing, and that will make them appear more credible. The goal of most cross-examinations is to discredit the credibility of a witness, not necessarily to confront them directly on the facts…unless, as we could, you absolutely can.

One way to do this is to keep witnesses off balance. I never want a witness to be comfortable on the witness stand. I don't examine witnesses on a linear chronology of events, because they're prepared for that, and it feels natural and comfortable to them. By not going chronologically, I make sure the witness never knows what issue is going to come up next. It's unsettling to them, and that's exactly the dynamic I hope to create to foster opportunities to find inconsistencies in their testimony and thereby damage their credibility.

I've learned that there's no one right way to prepare a cross. You just have to find the method that works for you. Some attorneys type out every question they plan to ask and spend hours agonizing over the exact wording of the question. My style is more fluid. I don't type out anything. No specific questions. Instead, I write out concepts, areas I want to cross-examine a witness about. Key words that will remind me what points I want to make. Some words larger than others, some highlighted and circled so I don't miss them. Each area I intend to cross-examine a witness on contains references to specific documents or statements by that witness that are contradictory or inconsistent. I draw lines to connect ideas or facts that I want to highlight with a witness. As a result, my cross-examination notes look more like a Jackson Pollock painting than an organized, lawyerly cross-examination script.

In preparing my witnesses to testify, I instill into them three basic principles: Don't guess. Don't exaggerate. Don't lie. If my witnesses understand and follow these three principles, they can withstand any cross-examination the government throws at them and will be seen by the jury as credible. Conversely, I use these same three principles in formulating my cross-examinations. I design them to get government witnesses to take guesses, to exaggerate and thus to lie. The more times a witness guesses, exaggerates or outright lies, the less credibility they have with the jury.

Sometimes getting a witness to guess, exaggerate or lie is easy because we've already uncovered evidence, through prior inconsistent statements or in comparison to statements of other witnesses, that clearly shows a witness has exaggerated or lied. For example, when Louis told the press he first noticed the mailbox missing during the evening of June 21 and that he notified deputy chief of police McCauley, that statement was completely inconsistent with Katherine having called 911 the next day at 1:29 p.m. to report the theft. Or when Officer Silva stated he recovered the hard drive of the surveillance videotape footage at 8:59 a.m. on June 22, that conflicted with the fact that it was four hours before Katherine called 911 to first report the theft. While it was readily evident that these facts were mutually exclusive, it was my job to formulate a cross that brought this information to the jury's attention in such a way that it would diminish if not outright destroy Katherine's and Louis's credibility. And lastly, we had in our back pocket the bold-faced lie about the type, make and value of the mailbox. But it was essential to craft my cross-examination to ensure that this lie had the greatest explosive impact on the jury as possible. I would get only one shot; after that, the element of surprise would be lost.

In other circumstances, I have to anticipate a government witness who chooses to guess, exaggerate or outright lie in response to my questions. Oftentimes a witness will "gild the lily." A police officer will elaborate on an event to make it seem more incriminating for a defendant. These elaborations or exaggerations are often little details that are not in any report or statement that the witness previously made. But make no mistake, these "small" lies are nonetheless lies with a purpose, which is to convince a jury to convict my client. Therefore, they are not small lies but huge ones, and it's my job to make the jury understand that. I prepare my cross-examinations to foster and take advantage of such opportunities. Jurors don't like someone lying to them. When a witness lies, I bring a sledgehammer to the party. Even though calling a person a liar in front of other people is uncomfortable, in my experience jurors appreciate it and sometimes are even waiting in anticipation for that moment. Watching TV shows and movies has primed them to expect theatrics in the courtroom, some sort of Perry Mason moment. I want to give them that moment. Maybe, just maybe, it will be a moment that is important enough that it will carry the day in the deliberation room when they decide the credibility of a witness and thus my client's fate.

Fortunately, I learned these principles early on in my career. Right after law school I began working as a state public defender in Philadelphia. A Philadelphia police officer had been shot and killed by someone who looked Hispanic. A manhunt was underway, focused on the Hispanic neighborhoods throughout the city. The police had literally cordoned off entire neighborhoods and were conducting mostly illegal door-to-door searches without any suspicion of wrongdoing on the part of the homeowners. I was a young and inexperienced public defender assigned to the courtroom at the main police station, aptly called the Roundhouse because of its circular construction. It was a drab makeshift courtroom located in the heart of the police station, with a solitary steel door leading to a bank of cells where my clients were being held. The magistrate judge stood behind an unadorned podium with two long folding tables on each side. The prosecutor sat on one side and I on the other, along with handcuffed defendants in torn or bloody clothes, many with fresh cuts and bruises. They often had not slept, or they were still high or reeking of alcohol. Every new arrestee in the city of Philadelphia was brought here to have bail set. The Philadelphia Public Defenders Office manned the station twenty-four hours a day. Paralegals were hired to cover the day shifts, but newly hired public defenders were required to man the night shift, 10:00 p.m. to 6:00 a.m. It was not a good assignment. Thankfully, we only had to do these weeklong shifts two or three times a year.

One evening, a young Hispanic man was brought in on a relatively minor charge. He had been beaten up, and the room was awash with homicide detectives. I quickly learned that this young man was the suspect in the killing of the police officer, but he had not been charged with that crime yet. I read him his Miranda rights and had him sign a form invoking those rights, both as to the minor crime he was charged with as well as the homicide in which he was a suspect. I then gave a copy of the form to the prosecutor and the court, informing them and the police that my client was invoking his constitutional right to remain silent and would not answer questions without his attorney being present. This was supposed to prevent any further questioning of my client. It didn't. Later, the commonwealth prosecutor claimed my client had waived his rights outside the presence of counsel and made incriminating statements that the prosecutor wanted to use at his murder trial.

About a year after his arrest, I was called as a defense witness at a hearing held before a state judge. The issue was whether the prosecutor could use those statements against him at his homicide trial. Such hearings occur prior to trial and present legal issues for a judge to decide. The question before the court was not whether the statements were true, but only whether the statements had been illegally obtained by the police in violation of his constitutional rights. If they were properly obtained, the prosecutor could use them at trial; otherwise, they could not. The outcome of this type of hearing can sometimes determine the entire case.

It was during my own testimony that the principles "Don't guess," "Don't exaggerate" and "Don't lie" became evident to me. It wasn't an easy lesson. It's human nature to want to answer a question. People have an internal drive to answer a question even when they're not sure. No one wants to look dumb or forgetful. This tendency to want to answer a question even when you're only making an honest guess can get a witness into serious trouble in the hands of a skilled cross-examiner.

In that case the prosecutor asserted that at the time of the young man's arrest he was not a suspect in the homicide case and, therefore, the Miranda warnings I'd given him applied only to the minor charge he'd been arrested for on that day, not for the homicide. Thus, the presence or absence of homicide detectives in the bail courtroom was critical. I was cross-examined on my claim that I saw homicide detectives in the hearing room that day, with the insinuation that I was mistaken.

I calmly related my story. But then the prosecutor asked me a straightforward question: "Sir, can you describe to us the shape of the badges the homicide detectives were wearing?" Besides the fact that I wasn't used to being called "sir," I had no idea. It was a simple detail; I should have been able to describe the shape of a badge. After all, if there had been as many homicide detectives in the room as I had alleged, I should have at least noticed their badges. But I had no such memory. None. But I really, really wanted to answer the question. I should have known. My credibility was at stake. How could I not know? Every part of my brain was telling me to make an educated guess. I knew the shape and design of a regular cop's badge, so the badges for homicide detectives had to be a different shape. I could guess and maybe be right. And if I wasn't, what was the big deal anyway in the larger scheme of my overall testimony? I remember pausing and thinking about it before I answered.

I took a breath and said, "Sorry, I have no recollection as to the shape and size of the badges." And that was it. It was the truth. The prosecutor, who had asked the question calmly and without any indication that she really cared about the answer, had been ready to spring upon me like a panther had I dared to guess. Now she had no choice but to move on. By not guessing, I had avoided what would have been a major trap. By not letting my ego, my desire to be right, get in the way, by not "gilding the lily," I had avoided going down a path of witness destruction. Lesson learned. Don't guess. Don't exaggerate. Don't lie. There's nothing like your own personal gut-wrenching experience to make a lesson stick. I often tell this story to my witnesses to drive it home. It helps when they know I've experienced what they are about to go through.

By Monday evening all but one of our witnesses was ready to testify. Mr. Dryer flew in the weekend before trial, to be followed by Mr. Slaugh, who would arrive a few days after trial started. The sessions with these two representatives from the mailbox companies provided new critical information. For example, we learned from Mr. Dryer that he believed the placement of the nut on the pedestal rod indicated the mailbox was rigged to be removed. It was also at this point that we learned from Ms. Arakaki why her car could not possibly have been the vehicle used in the theft, because the car in the videotape was missing several of her car's features, like the spoiler on the trunk and the black strip on the sunroof. The information we'd gleaned from these prep sessions led me to modify my examinations, particularly my cross-examination of Detective Akagi. It's exactly because my cross-examinations are not written in stone that I can easily modify and adapt them to take this new information into account.

We were all set to go. Jury instructions were agreed upon and drafts submitted to the court, all six copies of our trial exhibits were filed, the jury pool list was organized and updated with all the latest information Kate and Adam had dug up, and my opening statement and cross-examinations were completed and in my trial notebook. We were as ready as we were going to be.

No matter how many trials I've done, I'm always nervous before they start, which includes each and every morning of the trial itself. But at the sound of the gavel signaling the commencement of a new day of trial, my nerves vanish. Being in court is energizing. Immediately after jury selection is concluded, each side may make opening statement. Then the government will call their first witness in their case. All this could happen on the very first day of trial. That night, I reviewed my Pollock-like notes one last time. I focused on the three government witnesses I believed would most likely be the first to testify: Officer Niall Silva, Katherine Kealoha and Louis Kealoha. While the government had given us a witness list, they were not required to tell us the order of their witnesses. We had to be prepared for everyone, but from years of experience we made an educated guess that these three would most likely be the first. All I could do was be prepared and hope we weren't suddenly caught off guard. But there are always surprises during a trial. Nothing goes as planned. Ever. You just have to be flexible, not get anxious, because something unexpected is bound to happen.

After a year and a half of investigation and trial preparation, it was finally here. Trial. ❖

CHAPTER 13

Trial, Day One: Jury Selection
Tuesday, December 2, 2014

Most if not all of the first day of trial is dedicated to selecting a jury. Through the process of voir dire, prospective jury members (the jury venire) are asked a series of questions providing us with information in order to select twelve fair and impartial people to sit as our jury. Why twelve jurors in a federal criminal trial? It's based upon the twelve apostles. Moreover, the number twelve is a recurring and significant number throughout history and throughout different cultures. Just ask pro football quarterbacks Aaron Rodgers and Tom Brady. In addition to the twelve jurors who make up the actual jury, two extra jurors are selected as alternates should it become necessary to replace any of the original twelve jurors during the trial.

In jury selection, any number of jurors can be struck "for cause," usually due to personal or financial hardship, physical or religious issues, or because they claim they cannot be impartial. The prosecution and the defense can also strike jurors for any reason whatsoever, so long as the strike is not based upon some constitutionally protected status, such as a person's race, ethnicity or gender. These strikes are called "peremptory strikes." In our case, the government had six peremptory strikes, while we had ten. These strikes would be used after we had heard all the prospective jurors' answers.

A few days before jury selection began, we received a list containing the names of approximately a hundred or more prospective jurors. Ninety of them had shown up for jury selection. Because so many potential jurors are likely to be excused from serving on the jury before it is whittled down to the lucky twelve, plus the two alternates, all ninety people were sworn in as prospective jurors in our case. We had been provided with limited information about each juror from a short jury questionnaire, and the weekend before trial began Adam and Kate had gathered as much additional information as they could about each from various online social media websites. As we walked into the courtroom, we already had a vague idea of which jurors we wanted and which we did not. We didn't employ any so-called "jury selection expert" to assist us in this process, as is portrayed in television shows like *Bull*. We simply used our common sense and years of experience. More often than not, picking a jury is really about eliminating jurors you don't want rather than selecting those you do. It often simply comes down to a gut feeling.

In this case, we wanted to eliminate anyone with an overly positive view of law enforcement, particularly anyone who thought that law enforcement officers or prosecuting attorneys always told the truth. This sometimes can be indicated by what county the juror comes from. In the District of Hawai'i, prospective jurors are pulled from all the islands, not just O'ahu, where the courthouse is located. Jurors who live on the Neighbor Islands are flown in and their travel expenses paid for by the court. It may be humbug, but it's their civic duty. Many people take advantage of the opportunity to stay with friends or relatives and shop at the larger, fancier malls on O'ahu. But there are some social and political differences between O'ahu residents and Neighbor Island residents that lawyers have to take into account when selecting a jury. O'ahu jurors are more urban and used to dealing with all the associated issues and problems that come from living in a more densely populated area, while those from the Neighbor Islands live in more rural areas and aren't exposed on a regular basis to the same concerns. Some attorneys fear that Neighbor Island jurors become awed by the power and importance of the law enforcement agents—FBI, DEA, ATF, Secret Service or Homeland Security—who will be paraded before them as prosecution witnesses and, as a result, will more readily side with the prosecutor. Defense attorneys also fear that Neighbor Island jurors, who have not been exposed to the nitty-gritty of urban living in their rural lifestyles, are generally more inclined to be pro "law and order."

We were particularly looking for people who were not "followers." We wanted people who had the character to think for themselves and be able to stand up against the will of the majority, who would have the conviction and inclination not to bow to those in power and authority. We also didn't want anyone who had any reason to reach a quick verdict and go home. We knew the trial was going to be more complicated than anyone thought, and we didn't want anyone on the jury rushing to judgement just because they had more pressing personal obligations.

We knew coming in that selecting a jury normally takes less than a day in our district court. If we did not use the full day to select the jury, the judge could decide to immediately proceed to opening statements and even have the government call a witness to testify if there was enough time left in the day. Thus, going in we had to be prepared not only to pick our jury, but to make an opening statement and possibly cross-examine a witness. This makes for the possibility of a very long, grueling first day.

We were ready. We intentionally came to the courtroom early, before the prosecution team had even arrived. We placed the two mailboxes, hidden in cardboard boxes, under our counsel table. We'd given the government the opportunity to view them prior to trial, but they had chosen not to see them. Their loss. Now we didn't want to lose the element of surprise. If someone from the prosecution team wanted to see them, we would, of course, have to show the mailboxes to them. Otherwise, they would remain hidden from view until we used them in trial.

Members of the jury venire were already in the courtroom as we entered. Everyone became quiet as we walked in, all eyes on my client, Gerard. When a jury venire first enters the courtroom for jury selection, they don't know anything about the case. They don't even know if the trial is civil or criminal. Only when the judge reads the indictment to them and starts asking questions do they know what type of case they may be asked to render a verdict upon. And because jury selection is the first time the jury meets a defendant, we knew that the jury would immediately be formulating impressions about Gerard and us. It's human nature to do so. Some of those opinions are about the case itself, but some impressions are very basic, as in whether they like the way the defendant looks or how the defense team are dressed. Impressions could be made simply from an inadvertent look from one of us that a juror did not like. Or perhaps a juror might think Gerard was smiling too much, giving the impression that he was not taking his case seriously or that he was trying to sell himself as a good guy.

We had discussed with Gerard beforehand how to act and what to wear in court. How Gerard or Adam and I interacted with the jury throughout the trial could be as important as any of the evidence the jury saw and heard. It's harder to acquit someone if you don't like them or fear them. A jury has twenty-four eyes, and while some might be looking at a witness while they testified, others might be looking at how Gerard or I were reacting to that testimony. One never knew what act or look would make a negative impression on a juror, so we had to be constantly aware of this. I had asked Gerard to wear his best aloha shirt. I wanted the jury to understand he was a local boy, someone they could easily relate to. That he was one of them. He looked good.

Adam, who was now also my courtroom assistant, and I took our seats at our counsel table. The prosecution's table was to our left, closest to where the jury sat. Although this is the usual custom in the District of Hawai'i, I had filed a motion with the court seeking to allow us to sit closest to the jury. I thought it would give the jury members a better opportunity to see Gerard during the trial and perhaps become more attached to him, just as the prosecution believes being closer to the jury gives them that same advantage. But I had lost that motion. Change does not come easily to a court.

I wore my best suit, looking like the serious lawyer they expected me to be. I too needed to create a positive relationship between myself and the jurors during the jury selection process. I don't look local, nor do I sound local. Even after living in Hawai'i for more than twenty-five years, my accent and rapid speech pattern has a New York City flair to it. But I am a *kama'āina*; my wife grew up in Hawai'i and went to high school here, and our two sons were raised in Hawai'i, one born here. Still, pronouncing Hawaiian words correctly is challenging to me. I also knew that I was going to call many law enforcement officers liars, including the Kealohas, so it was more important than ever for me to create a relationship with the jury such that they would not be offended when they heard me make these accusations during the trial. Calling a witness a liar, to their face in public, is off-putting to a jury—unless they believe it is justified. While a jury does not necessarily have to like me, they do need to understand and appreciate that it is my job to give my client the best defense possible, and that may include calling witnesses liars. If I do my job right, by the end of the trial I want the jury to be thinking to themselves that if they or a family member were ever charged with a crime, they'd want me defending them. If I can get a jury to think about me like that, then I know they will forgive my directness.

Judge Leslie E. Kobayashi, the presiding district court judge for the trial, was fully aware of the nature of the case as she entered the courtroom to conduct jury selection, due to all of the pretrial filings she had read and hearings she had conducted. Judge Kobayashi is a very personable judge, and she is good with juries, making them feel welcomed, important and relaxed. Smiling, she greeted the jury venire and thanked them for having shown up and for honoring their civic responsibility to serve on a jury. We all knew that, with rare exceptions, almost every single prospective juror wanted to be doing something, almost anything else with their day than being here with us. And most were crossing their fingers hoping they would not ultimately be chosen to be on the jury. Judge Kobayashi's opening remarks reminded them that jury service is the foundation upon which our criminal justice system stands, and they should feel proud to play an important part in this process. She explained that it is the jury, members of the community, who have the awesome power to decide the guilt of their fellow citizen, not some impersonal governmental entity or policing authority. Just ordinary people, like them, she said, "and it is by this very act that our democracy lives and breathes."

The government's prosecution team then introduced themselves, and we followed suit. After describing how the jury selection process was going to work, Judge Kobayashi explained a little about the nature of the case before them by summarizing the allegations specified in the indictment. Then she proceeded to ask the prospective jurors questions. Most if not all required that they simply respond "yes" or "no" by raising their hand. These initial questions were designed to solicit information as to whether a juror had any medical, religious or personal reasons that would make serving on the jury difficult. Several jurors were dismissed in response to these questions.

Judge Kobayashi next asked questions regarding the jury panel's knowledge of the case and any exposure they might have had to any pretrial publicity. Despite the fact that the case had been in the news on a semi-regular basis for some time, only a handful of jurors indicated they knew anything about it, and none thought it would have an impact on their impartiality. I wasn't surprised. In my other cases that had received a lot of pretrial publicity, the jurors rarely indicated that they knew anything about the case or felt that what they had heard would influence their decision. People don't pay as much attention to the news as we think.

Judge Kobayashi next asked more meaningful questions designed to elicit bias. She asked if any juror or juror's family member was currently or had been a law enforcement officer or worked for such an agency. It's here, in my opinion, during this question and answer session, that the difference between federal and state court jury practice in Hawai'i is the most significant and has the biggest impact upon the fairness of the jury selection process. In state court, after a brief questioning by the court, it is the attorneys who ask the majority of the questions, and it is the attorneys who get to individually question each prospective juror. The attorneys thus control how to phrase a question and how to follow up with a particular juror if they want to know more about an answer. This type of discussion solicits much more information from a juror than simply a yes or no response. It also allows an attorney, through a discussion with one particular juror regarding their ability to be fair and impartial, to "educate" the rest of the prospective jurors as they listen. In federal court, however, it's the judge who asks the majority of the questions, normally in a yes or no format.

For example, the court may ask, as Judge Kobayashi did, "Does anyone know anyone who is a law enforcement officer or agent?" This will usually draw a number of raised hands. Judge Kobayashi asks each juror what their relationship is to that person. The court then asks, "Can you put this relationship aside and be fair to the defendant and to the government?" Almost always the juror's response is "Yes," and the court moves on. Only if a juror says they can't be fair or is indecisive does the court make a more detailed inquiry. You can imagine how much more information I would want to flesh out about the juror's relationship to this law enforcement person if I were doing the questioning, particularly in Gerard's case. But more often than not we simply have to accept that a particular juror, who has a relationship with law enforcement but honestly believes it will have no impact on their decision-making process, will be fair. "Yes" does not tell us a whole lot.

After several hours, Judge Kobayashi finished asking her questions. The government and I then had the customary twenty minutes each to ask questions of the jury pool ourselves. We could not question each prospective juror; there simply wouldn't be enough time. We had decided to use the time to accomplish two very different but important objectives. First, I needed to use this opportunity to have the jury warm up to me, to get them to know a little about my style. Second, I needed to address a critical issue, whether a juror was more likely to believe a police officer or prosecuting attorney than a civilian witness. This was particularly important in this case, since almost every witness in the prosecution's case would be a law enforcement officer, while almost all of our witnesses were civilians.

Assistant US attorney Leslie Osborne, the prosecutor, went first. Osborne was all business. Serious, direct, no nonsense. Pressed suit and tie. American flag on his lapel, very commanding in both tone and style. His questions and mannerisms conveyed that he was a prosecutor for the United States of America and this was a serious case, even if it was only about a mailbox theft. Not much warmth and certainly no humor in his approach. But it made the prospective jury members sit up and pay attention. His presentation played nicely into what I had planned, which was to be friendlier and more personable, yet still be taken seriously. I had worn a suit too, but my suit was not pressed and certainly was not as expensive-looking as his. We presented very contrasting styles.

I bear a striking resemblance to one of Hawai'i's recent former governors, Neil Abercrombie. I've often been mistaken for him all over town, but particularly in the federal courtyard, by scores of newly sworn-in United States citizens who see me from a distance and wave or bow as I walk across the courtyard to go into the courthouse. I've long ago given up acting like I'm not the former governor when people wave at me. Instead, I just return their waves or bows with a royal hand wave as I pass by. If people want to believe they saw Governor Abercrombie, who am I to rain on their parade? At the close of Osborne's presentation I stood up and asked my first question: "How many of you, upon entering the courtroom, looked at me and said, 'I wonder why Governor Abercrombie is here?'" Some people laughed or covered their mouths with their hands. I raised my hand to signify an affirmative response, and more than half the jurors raised their hands with me. Everyone looked around the courtroom at all the raised hands and we all laughed together. This single lighthearted question had accomplished exactly what I'd hoped it would. It eased all the tension that had built up in the room, helped me to relax and immediately connected me with the jury. A good start.

How many people, I then asked the jury, had looked over at my client sitting at the defense table and said to themselves, "I wonder what he did?" This time I didn't wait for anyone to raise their hands. I told them that Gerard, like all defendants, is cloaked with the presumption of innocence. Even having this thought cross their minds was incorrect. I asked them to all look at Gerard again and say to themselves, "There sits an innocent man." When I asked if anyone could not follow this principle, no one raised their hands. I asked a few more questions designed to get the jury to know Gerard and me a little, and then I began to focus on the question of witness credibility. "Should a law enforcement officer be given more credibility than any other witness?" I asked. I picked on a few jurors to tell me what they believed. In this way they were educating one another with their responses rather than simply having me lecture them. Since everyone had already promised the judge that they would not give a law enforcement officer's testimony any more weight than another witness's, I didn't expect anyone to say otherwise. But I needed to make this concept stick in their minds because it was going to be central to our defense. Having jurors state their responses out loud made it more personal.

Soon enough, however, one juror raised her hand, indicating that she would give more credibility to a witness who was an attorney than other witnesses. I instantly knew that no matter what else she said, we were going to strike her as a juror. But if I treated her with respect, this could be a great teaching moment for the rest of the jury panel. I asked her to explain. She stated that in her opinion an attorney had a higher responsibility to tell the truth than another witness. A simple truth. I was surprised by her answer—hadn't we all been raised on bad lawyer jokes? (What do you call a thousand lawyers buried at the bottom of the ocean? A good start.) But I gave her credit. Many people hide their true biases, particularly in front of a roomful of people they don't know, so I was thankful this juror was brave enough to raise her hand and state her honest belief. We had a discussion about why it was important to our judicial system that no witness's testimony be given more weight than another simply because of who they were or the line of work they did. I did not attack her. She was entitled to her opinion. And if anyone else now wanted to raise their hand, I did not want to dissuade them. The door had been opened. As we ended our conversation, I took the opportunity to inject a little humor and commended her for possibly being the only person in the entire courtroom who actually believed anything a lawyer said was truthful. Again, we all laughed together. She was stricken as a juror.

It took all day, but in the end we had our twelve jurors: seven male and five female, and two alternates. We were happy with the selection. We thought we had several jurors who were strong and would not be bullied by the majority into changing their minds simply because they were in the minority. There cannot be a guilty verdict if the jury is not unanimous. Most importantly, we felt we had some jurors who were not going to be swayed by the Kealohas' celebrity and positions of authority.

Judge Kobayashi adjourned the proceedings for the day and instructed that the trial would begin the next morning with opening statements and witnesses for the prosecution. I was relieved. After spending so much time and energy picking a jury, being "on" in front of so many people for so many hours, it came as a relief to be able to go home for the night, rest up and have just a little more time to get myself ready for the start of the second day of trial and the beginning of testimony. As we left the courtroom for the day, the mailboxes remained hidden under the table in their cardboard boxes, like ticking time bombs. ❖

CHAPTER 14

Trial, Day Two: *United States v. Gerard Puana*
Wednesday, December 3, 2014

When a juror walks into a federal courtroom in Hawai'i and is presented with prosecutors and their agents representing the United States of America, one can almost see the courtroom tilt in favor of the government before a word has ever been spoken. This impression is enhanced by the courtroom itself. When you think of a federal courtroom, think Washington, DC, with all those colossal white marble monuments and edifices. Washington, DC, was intentionally built by the Founding Fathers to impress foreign officials. Federal courtrooms are designed to convey that same message. They shout, "Something important happens in here!"

Hawai'i state courtrooms are mostly unadorned and small, having barely enough room to seat a jury. The federal courtrooms are at least four to six times the size of any state courtroom. They are clean, polished and brightly lit. The carpeting is white. The ceilings are thirty feet high, and the courtrooms seat more than ninety people in addition to the jury. The technology available for the presentation of evidence is second to none, with state-of-the-art toys that, if one knows how to use them, can be very effective in presenting your case to the jury. Prosecutors receive yearly specialized training on how to do just that. Even the walls of the courtroom are majestic, lined floor to ceiling with rare koa wood paneling. Hawai'i jurors know the value of koa, and there's plenty of it.

Federal judges are also generally viewed as more important and powerful than their state counterparts. They've been appointed by the president of the United States and confirmed by the United States Senate to serve for life. They make legal decisions that are often discussed in the local news media, and sometimes their rulings make national headlines. In the courtroom itself the judge sits several feet higher than everyone else, requiring everyone to look up at him or her. On the wall behind the judge is the great seal of the United States, the American bald eagle, wings flared, with arrows and an olive branch in its talons. The seal itself is several feet across. The judge is flanked by flags. On one side is the flag of the United States, with yellow frill lacing on the edges. On the other side stands the flag of the state of Hawaiʻi. If that isn't enough, in the courtroom for Gerard's trial there was a mural covering almost the entire wall behind the judge portraying the signing of the Constitution. Ben Franklin, Thomas Jefferson, Alexander Hamilton and George Washington all stared down at us as we addressed the court. The setting sternly intones, "Hey, jury. This is the real thing. Sit up. Pay attention. We *are* the federal government. And we have accused this defendant of committing a crime. Do your part, and justice will be served."

From the very moment the trial starts I try to capture the courtroom. To make it *my* courtroom. I want the jury liking me and paying attention to my case. Out of respect and deference to the jury, I always acknowledge them and say good morning as we are introduced each day. Surprisingly, many attorneys only acknowledge the judge, but it's the jury who will decide our client's fate. At sidebar conferences with the judge during the trial I make sure I'm facing the jury while conversing respectfully with the judge. I'm friendly with the courtroom staff during the breaks and even with the prosecutor. I always try to keep my interaction with the prosecutors professional. They're just doing their job, and juries respect them, so it will not further my case if I'm seen being disrespectful. Being considerate with everyone in this very adversarial setting eases the tension, including my own. And most importantly, I treat my clients with dignity and respect throughout the trial, which helps lessen any fear the jury may have of them simply because they are criminal defendants. I want them to see my client as a human being: a father, mother, son or daughter, an auntie or uncle, not a dangerous criminal. At the close of a case, during my final argument, I always apologize to the jury for my aggressiveness while cross-examining witnesses. I make the point that while it's my job to defend my client aggressively, they shouldn't hold it against my client, but only against me. A little humility goes a long way because there is usually no doubt that I may have been too aggressive for the liking of some jury members.

Through my first few cross-examinations I want the jury to see that things are not always as they first appear to be and that the government may not be presenting all the facts, only the evidence that best fits their case. I don't want the jury accepting the government's evidence at face value; I want them to learn to question the evidence presented to them by the prosecution as it comes in and not take it immediately as the truth. If I can get the jury to question the government's interpretation of the evidence of their own volition, I've won half the battle in leveling the playing field.

I do all these things because a prosecutor walks into the federal courtroom with a huge advantage. An assistant US attorney (AUSA) is not some fresh-faced just-out-of-law-school attorney. They are well educated, highly motivated and skilled attorneys with several years of legal practice behind them. Many are former judge's law clerks. Others come from large, well-respected private law firms. They are well dressed, polished, professional, with an American flag pinned to their lapel that signifies they represent the United States of America. Their agents, who are their investigators, are not beat cops, but well-seasoned and well-educated agents of the Federal Bureau of Investigations (FBI); Homeland Security (DHS); the Drug Enforcement Administration (DEA); members of the Secret Service; or Alcohol, Tobacco and Firearms Agency (ATF). Movies and TV shows have been made about these folks, and the jurors have seen these movies. They are the most respected law enforcement agents in the country. These agents are even given the title "special agents," but don't be fooled—all government investigative agents are given the title "special agents." Jurors don't know this little fact unless you point it out to them.

More importantly, government agents are highly trained and highly paid professional witnesses. Not only do they undergo extensive training in how to investigate crimes and document evidence; they're trained on how to testify as witnesses. They *practice* being a witness, so that they'll come across to a jury as being more believable than other witnesses. Agents testify in suits and ties. They fit and look the part. They look at the jury when answering an important question rather than at the attorney who asked the question. They smile only when appropriate. They address a defense attorney with respect. They do not use notes, so it looks like they are testifying from their own memory, rather than from just having read their reports moments before they took the stand. And they know how to handle exhibit binders and evidence without fumbling around, using laser pointers to great effect to highlight only the most incriminating evidence to the jury.

By contrast, defense witnesses are usually a defendant's family relations, or some innocent bystander who may have seen something useful to the defense. They are civilians. They are not polished or trained witnesses. They may not even own a suit. They are understandably nervous, most never having testified before or even been in a courtroom in their lives. Most importantly, they have never undergone cross-examination where their credibility is questioned and often become rattled.

But that doesn't mean the battle is lost before it even begins. All this show of power and importance suggests that the government, in presenting its case, should be beyond reproach. And that can be their Achilles heel. As United States Supreme Court justice Sutherland said in 1935:

> The United States Attorney is the representative not of an ordinary party to a controversy, but of a sovereignty whose obligation to govern impartially is as compelling as its obligation to govern at all; and whose interest, therefore, in a criminal prosecution is not that it shall win a case, but that justice shall be done. As such, he is in a peculiar and very definite sense the servant of the law, the twofold aim of which is that guilt shall not escape or innocence suffer. He may prosecute with earnestness and vigor—indeed, he should do so. But, while he may strike hard blows, he is not at liberty to strike foul ones. It is as much his duty to refrain from improper methods calculated to produce a wrongful conviction as it is to use every legitimate means to bring about a just one.

Every time during the trial that I can demonstrate that the government has cut corners, not fully investigated the case or presented evidence in a biased and unfair manner, the government's power and credibility is undermined a little more. Demystifying the prosecutor and their agents to a jury is essential in leveling the playing field and is often the key to getting a jury to be willing to examine the evidence in a more impartial manner. I always read Justice Sutherland's words to the jury in my closing argument because I believe this allows a jury the freedom to find a defendant not guilty without feeling they have let the government down in some way. This is particularly helpful when a jury likes the prosecutor in the trial. In Gerard's case, Justice Sutherland's admonition would be particularly relevant and important to highlight to the jury during my closing argument, as it neatly summed up our entire theory of the case as to why the jury should find Gerard not guilty.

But there would be no battle this day. No Mr. Osborne. Instead, assistant US attorney Thomas Brady appeared and notified the court that due to unforeseen medical reasons, Osborne was not able to be in court. Because the reason for his absence involved a medical condition, the exact medical problem affecting Osborne's nonappearance was only disclosed to Judge Kobayashi. The court excused the jury, and the trial was continued for one more day, to Thursday, December 4. Judge Kobayashi, however, instructed the government that the trial would commence on December 4 with or without Osborne. One way or another, she told the government, they should be prepared to conduct the trial, with a different attorney if necessary.

I've had false starts to a trial before. These sputtering starts can be advantageous. As much as one is prepared and anxious to proceed, I become much calmer when the trial restarts the next day, having already experienced the adrenalin rush that comes with being prepared and ready to deliver my opening statement. The fact that a brand-new prosecutor would be forced to try the case could work to our advantage. A false start also gives me one more day to fine-tune my opening and my initial cross, and perhaps get a better night's rest.

The mailboxes remained under the table, the clock still ticking. ❖

CHAPTER 15

Trial, Day Three: "What's Done is Done."
Thursday, December 4, 2014

We arrived in the courtroom the next morning. Again, no Osborne. As we took our seats prior to the jury coming into the courtroom, assistant US attorney Lawrence "Larry" Tong sat down at the government's table to stand in for him. Although Tong had been involved in the case from the beginning, he had only appeared in court a few times up until then. I didn't know how familiar he was with the case. He informed me he'd be taking Osborne's place as lead prosecutor. I knew he must have been up most of the night getting ready, reading documents and preparing his first couple of witnesses.

I considered Tong a "prosecutor's prosecutor." Like Osborne, he was a tried and tested prosecutor who knew his way around a courtroom. He was well spoken, polished, prepared and straightforward, and juries liked him. He spoke to them in a relaxed "Hey, I'm a local boy" style that Hawai'i juries found appealing. Much more jury-friendly than Osborne. I was not at all pleased to see that he had taken over the case. But given that he was being thrust into the trial at the last minute, I still thought we had gained an advantage.

I could tell I was right about the all-night jamming session when I saw AUSA Andrea Hattan sit down next to him as his second chair. I knew Hattan to be a meticulously prepared prosecutor who did not leave anything to chance. She did not like surprises. In the past, she had always appeared well groomed, sure of herself and her case. But not today. She had that "deer in the headlights" look, and her hair was disheveled. I could tell she was not pleased to have been thrown into this trial. I actually felt a little sorry for her. But only for a moment. She was still a prosecutor trying to convict Gerard.

The trial commenced as the courtroom deputy called the case to order:

"Criminal 13-00735 LEK, United States of America versus Gerard K. Puana. This case has been called for a jury trial. Counsel, please make your appearances for the record. Please speak into a microphone."

Judge Kobayashi addressed the jury, thanking them for "being bright-eyed and enthusiastic," and invited Tong to make his opening statement to the jury.

"This case is about the destruction and theft of a mailbox," he began. "We will show that on June 21, 2013, the defendant, Gerard Puana, the individual in the aloha shirt in the middle there, physically ripped a mailbox off of its pedestal and took it away." Tong informed the jury that the mailbox belonged to Katherine Kealoha, a city prosecutor, who was married to Louis Kealoha, the chief of the Honolulu Police Department. He gave a description of the mailbox which matched, unbeknownst to him, the false description given by Katherine Kealoha in her three statements to HPD and to postal inspector Brian Shaughnessy. Tong detailed how Niall Silva, an HPD technical officer, retrieved the surveillance video after having checked that everything on the recording device was working properly and the cameras were operational. I made a note to myself that Tong did not tell the jury *when* Officer Silva had been sent to the house. What you don't say in an opening statement is just as important as what you do say.

Tong told the jury that Katherine Kealoha, Louis Kealoha and Officer Bobby Nguyen would all testify that the person in the video surveillance footage stealing the mailbox was Gerard Puana. Tong, while admitting the video was not very clear, stated that all three were able to identify Gerard not only due to the fact that they had known him for many years, but specifically by the clothes he wore and his unique style of walking. Tong described it as "cocky—swinging his arms." Tong, concluding his opening statement, stated, "Ladies and gentlemen, the case should not take too long. We're all sharing that hope." I, however, did not share that hope at all. Tong wrapped up his remarks, as all prosecutors do, by urging the jury to find the defendant guilty:

At the conclusion, I'm sure you will conclude that a mailbox was destroyed, that the event was captured on tape, and the only issue for you to decide really is going to be did the defendant do it…. We submit to you that when we finish this case, you will consider the evidence and find the defendant, Gerard Puana, guilty of destroying and tearing down the mailbox.

It was now my turn to address the jury. An opening statement by the defense is very different from a prosecutor's opening statement and serves a different purpose. Because the government bears the burden of proving a defendant is guilty beyond a reasonable doubt, a prosecutor's opening statement is more of a road map of the evidence they are going to introduce that they believe will lead to a guilty verdict. The defense, on the other hand, has no legal obligation to prove anything. To get a not guilty verdict, all I had to was inject enough doubt to convince the jury the government had failed to meet its burden. I didn't have to prove Gerard was innocent. The burden of proof is always on the government, and I needed to be careful not to say anything that would shift that burden to us. If I promised something in my opening statement and failed to deliver on that promise, the jury could hold me accountable for that failure even though I didn't have the burden of proving anything.

While the general rule for a defense opening statement is to be more general and philosophical in nature, reminding the jury of the legal tenets of the burden of proof and reasonable doubt, there are always exceptions. Gerard's case was one of those exceptions. I had evidence that we fully believed would create a reasonable doubt. Damning evidence. Still, I had to be judicious as to what information I chose to disclose in my opening remarks to the jury, and therefore to the prosecution. While I was not going to lay out a detailed road map of our defense, I could make a few specific promises and live up to those promises. But under no circumstances did I want to disclose the existence of the two mailboxes. They would make their appearance in the trial only when they would have the most dramatic impact.

First, we decided to highlight the videotape surveillance footage itself because we believed it alone created reasonable doubt. While it seemingly proved that the mailbox had been taken and thus a crime committed, we also felt it provided the best evidence we had to convince the jury that it could not find beyond a reasonable doubt that it was Gerard who had taken the mailbox. We believed that when the jury viewed the actual video footage, rather than merely listening to government witnesses say it was Gerard, they would readily see that the grainy image in the videotape looked like someone much younger and more agile than Gerard.

A second piece of evidence we wanted to get right out to the jury was the "Rue the Day" letter written by Katherine, which supplied the motive for why three government witnesses would falsely identify Gerard as the thief. It was in her own words. Ugly words written to her then ninety-two-year-old grandmother. Reading out loud what Katherine had written would not only address why Katherine, Louis and Bobby Nguyen would falsely identify Gerard as the thief, but it also might instill in the jury a deep dislike for Katherine before she even took the witness stand.

I took a deep breath, introduced myself to the jury and immediately addressed the issue of the videotape.

"You're going to have an opportunity throughout this trial and, when you deliberate, to watch that video. And the government has to prove beyond a reasonable doubt that that is him [pointing to Gerard].

"The reason the government is calling Katherine Kealoha, Chief Louis Kealoha and Bobby Nguyen, all very close to each other, family members, is because you can't tell who's on that video.

"If you could tell who was on that video, you'll look at him [pointing to Gerard], you'll look at the video and it's over. They're calling them because you cannot [ID him from the video].

"There's an old saying that things aren't as they appear to be, and you, the jury, will hear from the first witness through the end that things are not the way they appear to be."

I refrained from telling the jury anything too specific. I explained in general the reverse mortgage transaction orchestrated by Katherine and how this nasty disagreement ended up with Gerard and Florence filing a civil lawsuit against Katherine, which was still pending in state court. There was a lot of money at stake, I explained, money that Gerard and his mother claimed Katherine had stolen from them. Gerard, I said, was being falsely identified as the thief by Katherine and Louis Kealoha in order to discredit his credibility in the civil case. I closed my opening statement with these words:

"From day one, the evidence will show the only person they went after was Mr. Puana. The only person they went after was the person who had the audacity to file a civil lawsuit against Katherine Kealoha. That's what this case is about. It's about Katherine Kealoha, it's about her reputation, it's about her job, it's about her license to practice law; that's what this case is about.

"So I leave you with these words from Katherine Kealoha, words that you're going to hear from her own mouth: 'How dare anyone make such malicious and false statements against me? I will prove that this is a horrible lie. Any person who repeats this lie should be damned ashamed of themselves for stating such crap. They will rue the day they decided to state these twisted lies.'"

The government objected, arguing my statement was argumentative, but it didn't matter. The jury had heard it loud and clear. As I sat down, I could tell from the juror's movements and whispers they were excited, and that was all I could have hoped for after opening statements.

The first witness the prosecution called was recently retired HPD officer Niall Silva. He stood and took the oath. I always pay close attention to a witness when they take the oath. I will remind them of this oath when I catch them not telling the truth and how they held up their right hand and swore to the court and to the jury they would not lie. Officer Silva stated he recently retired from the Honolulu Police Department and had worked for the department since 1988. His last assignment had been as a technician with the criminal intelligence unit. On the morning of June 22, 2013, he was assigned to recover a hard drive from a security camera located at the Kealoha residence in Kāhala. He arrived, he testified, at "around 9:00 a.m." Officer Silva detailed how he had checked the recording devices to make sure they were functioning properly, viewed the videotape footage with Officer Bobby Nguyen, removed the hard drive, inserted a new one and returned to his office at CIU with the recovered hard drive containing the footage of the theft. He was directed to make a video clip of half an hour before and after the theft, make one extra copy and some still shots. Officer Silva placed only those portions of the tape he had edited and the still shots he had made into his locked filing cabinet as evidence. The entire hard drive itself was not submitted as evidence.

I had a very limited opportunity at this point in his testimony to question Officer Silva about how he had obtained the surveillance video footage and how he had entered it into evidence. This line of inquiry has to do with the chain of custody of a piece of evidence, which must be proven in order to authenticate that a piece of evidence has not been tampered with from the moment it is seized to when it is used at trial. Normally, this line of questioning is not very fruitful or informative, but surprisingly, that was not the case here.

Silvert: How many hours of video are on the hard drive?
Silva: I don't know. Many hours.
Silvert: But you testified you saw it all?

Silva: Yeah.

Silvert: Could it have been days?

Silva: Oh, yeah. Yeah, you've got to sit there for hours and look through that.

Silvert: Is the hard drive in evidence—has the hard drive, has the chain of custody been preserved?

Silva: I don't believe so.

Silvert: So what we have here are just snippets of the hard drive, and the hard drive itself has been destroyed?

Silva: I'm not sure. I no longer work there.

Silvert: But you're not here today to introduce the hard drive as evidence?

Silva: No.

This testimony confirmed what we had long suspected. There was indeed a hard drive that existed that contained hours, even days, of videotape footage. More importantly, the hard drive might still be able to be obtained and viewed. For more than a year leading up to the trial we had tried through informal requests and then a court-issued subpoena to obtain this very same evidence, but HPD and Louis had all repeatedly sworn that no videotape footage existed other than the one hour of tape we had been provided. No one had ever admitted that the hard drive might *still* be located in the CIU offices themselves in the heart of the Honolulu Police Department building. We were barely an hour into the trial, and we had already learned of an entirely new lie committed by HPD, a lie that served to further support our claim that Gerard was being framed.

Tong returned to the podium to continue his examination and chose not to play the videotape footage to the jury during Silva's testimony. He simply had Silva authenticate it and enter it into evidence so that he could play it later via a different witness. Tong did, however, introduce, as Government Exhibit #7, the two HPD reports prepared and submitted by Silva. The first was the evidence or property report, the very same one we knew had been improperly altered by Silva. The second was a one-page report entitled HPD follow-up report. As Silva testified, each page of the reports was signed by Silva and contained the date and time he had prepared them. Tong had Silva explain what was written on each report and what it signified, and then offered them into evidence. I had no objection. I too wanted them in evidence.

It was now my turn to cross-examine Silva. Silva acknowledged that he was ordered to download only a portion of the entire hard drive. He also acknowledged that while there were six different cameras recording surveillance footage all preserved on the one hard drive, he chose only to download and preserve two of them. I asked him whether or not there was possibly a better videotape angle of the license plate of the car than the ones he preserved, such that the license plate number could have been read and traced back to the owner of the vehicle. In response Silva became combative and would not admit there was a better shot of the license plate, even though, as I pointed out, because of what he had done in only providing a selected portion of the videotape, we had no way of now knowing if there was, in fact, a better image of the license plate.

His responses and combative behavior were perfectly fine with me. I didn't expect him to crack under my questioning and agree with me that his actions were unacceptable. The jury could see it by his behavior on the stand. I was simply setting up my closing argument as to the importance of the missing hard drive and why it had either been intentionally destroyed, hidden or lost. As far as I was concerned, the more Silva defended himself, the more the jury would dislike him, and the more compelling my argument would be in the end.

I walked Silva through how and when he had been sent to the Kealoha residence. In particular, the forms that he had filled out now that they were in evidence. I did not need or want to question Silva as to how it was even possible for him to have been sent to the Kealoha residence at 8:59 a.m. to recover evidence before the crime was reported at 1:29 p.m. The fact that he had recovered the videotape surveillance footage at "0859 hours" was now in evidence through his own testimony and through his two written reports. There was no reason to give him any opportunity to try and explain away that jarring discrepancy. I simply needed to bide my time and hammer that point home during the closing argument.

But a central part of my cross-examination was about Government Exhibit #7—in particular the evidence or property report. Silva had sworn, under oath, that the evidence or property report submitted by the government as Exhibit #7 was true and accurate. We knew it was not, and now it was time to prove it to the jury.

I confronted Silva with our version of his report, Defense Exhibit JJJ, which was the altered form we had obtained from HPD. At first, Silva didn't understand why I was showing him the same form that had been marked as Government Exhibit #7, until I pointed out to him that he had changed the typed number "1" into a handwritten number "4." He now had no choice but to admit he had altered the form.

Silvert: So you used the same form and altered it, correct?
Silva: Yes, sir.

Now that he had admitted this fact, I confronted him head-on. I knew the jury wasn't going to buy whatever answers he gave about having altered the forms. This is one of those moments when you can ask a question without knowing or caring what the answer will be, because it simply doesn't matter. It's the question the jury will remember and accept as true. And they'd remember he'd lied to them under oath.

Silvert: And that's improper?
Silva: Excuse me?
Silvert: That's improper.
Silva: What is your point?
Silvert: It's not a point. Is it proper or improper to do that?

Silva paused a few seconds and glared at me for all to see. The courtroom was silent. He had been answering all my previous questions in a rapid-paced style, which made this pregnant pause even more noticeable. The heads of all the jury members were turned and looking at Silva. It was an important moment, and we all knew it. The first witness. Not even an hour into the trial. Finally, he answered, and his answer demonstrated his complete contempt for following the rules and procedure designed to preserve the integrity of evidence seized by police. More importantly, it demonstrated his own utter lack of remorse.

Silva: What's done is done, sir.

"What's done is done"? Bad answer. A really bad answer. No attempt at an explanation? No "I'm sorry. It was wrong to alter the form"? Silva's unapologetic response strayed way beyond the line of any possible acceptable and understandable answer. The words he used and the tone he delivered it in conveyed a get-over-it-nothing-to-see-here attitude that clearly didn't sit well with the jury, who were all glaring at him. Judge Kobayashi gave him a sideward glance. I saw several jurors turn and look away from him. Their reaction told me all I needed to know about what they now thought of his testimony. I responded sarcastically:

> Silvert: So be it. Doesn't matter you altered the form, you violated the policies of HPD, we don't care?

While the transcript makes it appear as if what I said was in the form of a question, it wasn't. By the intonation of my voice, it came across as a flat-out accusation rather than a question. And that is exactly what it was. I knew the jury wasn't going to hold the tone of my voice against me. The government objected, stating my question was "argumentative." The court sustained the objection. It didn't matter; the jury had gotten the message loud and clear. Was Silva's alteration of the report significant? Probably not, but that was beside the point. He didn't follow protocol, he'd lied and he didn't care. And that was the point. It was our first big step in showing the jury that HPD's investigation was designed with only one end in mind: the framing of Gerard Puana.

I had told the jury in my opening statement that we were going to show them that police forms and reports had been altered; evidence lost, misplaced or made up, and I had just made good on that promise with the government's very first witness. Better yet, I had done so by also proving that the evidence the government itself had put before them, in this case Government Exhibit #7, was, in fact, falsified. Moving forward, the jury now had to be leery of the evidence even the federal prosecutor presented to them. One witness in, and we were doing well—very well indeed. ❖

CHAPTER 16

A Kealoha Takes the Stand

The second government witness took the stand. To my surprise, it was Louis Kealoha. Although the government was free to call witnesses in any order they wished, we had all been led to believe that the next witness was going to be Katherine Kealoha. While I was prepared to cross Louis, something felt odd. Out of order. I had a gut feeling that Louis had asked the government, at the last minute, to call him to testify before his wife. I can't tell you exactly why I felt this way, but that's just how it felt. I had hoped to confront Katherine with the two mailboxes first before any other witness. But when things don't go as expected, one has to adapt. This was going to be one of those times. I was used to it. Trials never, ever go as planned.

Louis was attired in civilian clothes. He was not in his HPD chief's uniform adorned with all the medals and ribbons that go along with his title. Smart move. We had researched HPD rules and regulations and learned that it was against standard HPD procedures to appear in uniform in a court proceeding where your appearance was not in your official capacity. Since Louis was allegedly a "victim" in this case, it would have been improper for him to have appeared in uniform. In anticipation that Louis would wear his uniform, I had prepared a cross that would suggest to the jury that he had worn his uniform in an improper attempt to influence them in violation of his own HPD policies. Alas, he was in a civilian suit. Even without his uniform, his physical presence was commanding. He didn't need his uniform to tell you he was a person of authority.

Tong began his direct examination of Louis with questions designed to elicit Louis's law enforcement credentials and how he knew Gerard as the uncle of his wife, Katherine. All routine questions. I leaned back in my chair, one ear listening to the testimony while I was thinking about how to handle the mailbox situation. Should I cross him on the mailboxes and show him, and thus the government, our secret weapons still hidden under the table? Or should I hold off and wait until Katherine finally took the stand? Which would have the biggest impact upon the jury? What if the government changed its mind and never called Katherine to the stand? Then I'd have missed my chance entirely. I barely listened as Louis testified that he'd been in the Honolulu Police Department for thirty-two years: twelve years in a patrol division, then several years in the narcotics, criminal investigation and training divisions before becoming the chief of police five years earlier. He proudly testified that he had just been renewed, early, as the chief by the Honolulu Police Commission for a second five-year term.

Louis testified that he graduated in 1978 from Damien Memorial High School, a local religious-affiliated school and that he had a two-year associate's degree from Leeward Community College of the University of Hawai'i and a four-year degree in criminal justice and business administration from Wayland Baptist University. He went on to earn a graduate degree from Chaminade University, a local private college, in criminal justice, and a doctorate of education from the University of Southern California. While the chief listed off his impressive college and postgraduate educational achievements, if you live in Hawai'i you know the most important educational achievement Louis listed was where he went to high school. Where you went to high school tells everyone all they need to know about you. It tells who you know and whom you are politically connected to in the community. And in Hawai'i that is much more important than what college you went to.

Louis testified that he'd been married to his wife, Katherine, for sixteen years. He identified Gerard as Katherine's uncle, whom he had known for over thirty years since their days working out together at the same gym, even before Louis had joined the police department. Louis had also seen Gerard numerous times over the years before he married Katherine because Gerard worked as a security guard at the Aiea Shopping Center where Louis's mother had a restaurant. All this testimony was designed, of course, to lay the foundation for why Louis could readily identify Gerard as being the person in the grainy image in the videotape footage. But the government, through this testimony, was also laying an even more important foundation. The all-important "Hey, this guy here. He's local. He's one of you. His mother, she get one restaurant in Aiea. You may have eaten there. Good grinds. You can trust him."

To further build on how well Louis knew Gerard and to introduce the notion that Gerard knew his way around the Kealohas' Kāhala residence, Louis testified that Gerard had worked at the house for over two years helping Katherine's father, Gerard's brother, Rudy, remodel the house. All of this was nothing more than routine direct examination questions; I was hardly paying attention. Then things got interesting fast.

Tong asked Louis to give a few examples of times when Gerard would come over to the house "unexpectedly." I sat up in my chair and turned my full attention back to Louis's testimony. Although I didn't know what the answer would be, it was no accident that the government was asking this question. To me, the use of the word "unexpected" implied that Gerard had done something wrong. Moreover, because this was direct testimony, the government knew what Louis was about to say, so I knew it wasn't going to be good for us. Louis responded that there was a time when he and his daughter were swimming in their backyard pool when Gerard "suddenly" appeared. They were "startled." I leaned even further forward in my chair, at the ready to stand and object. I could sense that something improper was about to be insinuated about Gerard. Sure enough, the next words out of the chief's mouth were that they were "startled" because "the front gate—we have two front gates, one is a metal front gate and one is a—"

I sprang up; I wasn't about to let him finish his answer. "Objection, Your Honor, sidebar. 404(b)," I exclaimed.

The government and I walked up to the judge's bench for a private sidebar discussion out of the hearing of the witness and the jury. To ensure no one hears what is being discussed, white noise is broadcast throughout the courtroom. I told Judge Kobayashi that the government was attempting to introduce evidence of a prior "bad act," possibly a trespass or burglary, and that the government had failed to provide proper notice as required under Federal Rule of Criminal Procedure 404(b). Generally, if the government wishes to introduce a prior bad act of a defendant, which could be a prior conviction or simply any act that is relevant to the crime charged, the government must provide advance notice to the defense. This would have allowed me to file a legal challenge and have the court rule on its admissibility prior to trial. No such notice had been given, so I had had no opportunity to object.

The government argued they were simply trying to show how well Gerard knew his way around the property. They were not attempting, they claimed, to introduce any illegal or improper act on the part of

Gerard. I didn't buy Tong's reasoning at all. Over my objection the court allowed the testimony to be introduced for that purpose only, but Judge Kobayashi warned the government to be careful about crossing the line because Louis was, after all, a police officer and she did not want him testifying that Gerard had committed a crime by entering the property.

Louis, now having been permitted to answer, testified that they were "shocked because the front gate and the side gates were both locked." Now I was angry. This testimony had absolutely nothing to do with how well Gerard knew his way around the property. I had brought this exact point up at the sidebar that there should be no testimony about the gates being open or shut because that could only suggest that Gerard was trespassing. I objected again but was overruled again.

Louis continued, stating Gerard "looked startled, we looked startled. Gerard looked disheveled, he didn't have a shirt on, he was sweating profusely. And I also remember he had this cigarette in his mouth that wasn't lit, and it was bent up, like he had run into a wall or something." I had no idea what the relevance of this line of questioning was, other than to imply that Gerard, being high on something, trespassed on the Kealoha property scaring the heck out of Louis's daughter. But the court overruled my objections. My temperature continued to rise.

Louis was then asked to describe another time Gerard had come onto the property uninvited. I immediately objected, anticipating yet more improper testimony, but the court overruled my objection. But this time Louis only described an incident where Gerard drove into the driveway and asked to speak to Katherine, nothing more. I relaxed a bit, not being sure how this information was relevant or hurt us, but I did not think this was the answer the government expected. Tong moved on. I leaned back in my chair.

Finally, the questions turned to the day after the theft. Louis described how he woke up early on the morning of June 22 to go surfing. It was the weekend, sometime between 5:30 and 6:00 a.m. He loaded up his surfboard and proceeded to drive out of the driveway when he noticed the mailbox wasn't there. Louis stated he was "frustrated because of all the other incidents" that had happened at the house, so he decided to report it after he returned home and let Katherine know. According to Louis, he came home around 9:30 a.m. and spoke with Katherine. They agreed she would report the incident. Louis then gave a very general description of the mailbox and identified Government Exhibit #3 as being a photograph of the pedestal that Officer Rosskopf had taken after the mailbox had been removed. Tong asked Louis whether Katherine reported the theft as he had asked her to do. He responded, "Yes." I noticed that Tong was very careful not to ask Louis any questions about the mailbox itself or show him a photograph of the actual mailbox that had been stolen. Nor did he solicit what time Katherine actually called 911. I jotted down a note to make sure to point this out to the jury in closing argument. While I certainly intended to ask these questions on cross-examination of Louis, it would be equally important to remind the jury in closing that the government had not presented the whole truth to them when they had had the opportunity. Rather, as I would argue, I had to do it so that the jury could understand the whole truth.

Tong then asked Louis to explain what he meant earlier in his testimony about being "frustrated" due to earlier incidents at his residence. Louis described several events that had occurred over the last several years, where he claimed unknown people had yelled obscenities at their house and had even shot a pellet gun at their front door, breaking a window. Louis testified he was particularly concerned about that event because his daughter was inside the residence when it occurred, and her safety was an issue. Louis claimed he made a police report about it and that this was the reason HPD had installed cameras around the house for their protection. Ah, we finally got to the point. A long way to go to explain why cameras had been installed by HPD around the Kealoha residence, with just a hint that maybe Gerard was the person responsible for these various occurrences. Tong clarified, as he put it, "just to be fair," that Gerard was never "charged" with having committed any of these incidents. Louis agreed. I noticed, however, that Tong did not say Gerard wasn't a "suspect" in these cases, just that he hadn't been "charged." I did not believe for a second that Tong's choice of words was unintentional. It was very calculated.

We had already been aware of these allegations prior to trial because Louis had spoken about these incidents during a press conference. As a result, we had subpoenaed HPD records to obtain any and all police reports that had been filed by the Kealohas regarding these incidents. We found *no* police report regarding anyone having fired a pellet gun and having broken a window, much less having endangered the Kealohas' daughter. One would have thought that the chief of police would certainly have filed such a report, given the serious nature of the offense and that it occurred in a residential neighborhood where others could have been harmed. But no such report was ever made, despite Louis's testimony now, under oath, to the contrary. I was ready to bring this fact up on cross-examination to attack his credibility.

Tong next attempted to play the videotape footage of the theft that had been previously introduced through Silva's testimony but not shown to the jury. But for whatever reason, the government's tape didn't work correctly. It played at a very slow speed and kept skipping. Because I too wanted the videotape shown to the jury, I generously offered to play our copy of it for them. I would have never helped the government introduce a piece of evidence in any other case, but I wanted the jury to see the videotape perhaps even more than the prosecution did. I watched the jury intently as the videotape of the theft was played. I was relieved when I saw at the conclusion of the viewing that many members of the jury were looking at each other in disbelief and confusion. There were two local women on the jury, seated next to one another in the back row of the jury box, whom we were paying particular attention to. They were the type that we thought were not likely to take crap from anyone and would stand their ground and be a force to be reckoned with when the jury went to deliberate at the close of the case. I almost let out an audible sigh of relief when I saw them look at one another and throw up their hands in the universal "Say what?" gesture, shaking their heads "no" to one another. Adam and I looked at each other like we were doing a mental high-five. We knew we hadn't won the case yet, but we felt there was now no way this jury was going to come to a unanimous verdict of guilt. Sometimes, during a trial, something happens, and you just get that good feeling in the pit of your stomach. I had done enough trials to recognize and trust that feeling. We had just had that moment. But what happened next we did not anticipate.

I was leaning back in my chair, content with the jury's reaction to the videotape and feeling more relaxed and at ease than at any other point in the trial so far. The court had recently installed new chairs, and unless you locked them, they allowed you to lean all the way back, to the point where you were almost falling backwards. I had not locked my chair and was sitting way, way back.

Louis was testifying that he could positively identify Gerard as the person in the video by the cap and the white long-sleeved shirt that were worn. Then, out of nowhere, everything went to hell in a handbasket for the prosecution. Tong asked a simple question, expecting a yes or no answer. He got anything but.

Tong: All right. And are you able to compare the way the defendant appeared back at the time of the incident, June of 2013, to the present?

Kealoha: Well, he's picked up a lot of weight since that time. And I—how he looks in this video is how he looked when he was charged and convicted for breaking into his neighbor's house.

When I heard Louis's answer my blood pressure shot from zero to a hundred in an instant because his response was completely improper. It was, without a doubt, "bad act" evidence of the worst kind, using a prior conviction as a supposed point of reference for an identification. In addition, Gerard had *not* been "convicted" of any such a crime. But most importantly, it was the chief of police, a man who had thirty-two years of law enforcement service and a bunch of degrees, who had blurted this out in open court. This testimony was not only improper; it could not have been unintentional. Absolutely no way.

Tong was silent. As he would tell me later, he too was waiting for me to object. The entire courtroom was silent. It seemed like everyone was holding their collective breath. But I was leaned far back in the chair, and being the hefty person that I am, it wasn't easy for me to get to a standing position to object. It took me a few seconds. I slammed my hand on the table and shouted my objection. The sound of my hand slamming on the table echoed throughout the courtroom. It was a very impressive moment. No one seemed to notice that I had slammed my hand on the table partly in an effort to pull myself up.

All I could get out of my mouth was "Your Honor—" before Judge Kobayashi interrupted and immediately said that we needed to take a recess to discuss this testimony. Apparently Judge Kobayashi had also been waiting for me to object, as she didn't even need me to finish my objection. She knew what I was going to say and why. Judge Kobayashi ordered that the jury be dismissed before ruling on my objection but before she dismissed the jury, and without any request from me, she instructed the jury that they "need[ed] to disregard that last piece of testimony." She then instructed Louis that he was "not to testify about that unless you are specifically asked by the prosecutor." Louis, in what I could only interpret as an acknowledgement that he knew full well what he had done was wrong, offered his "apology" to the court and said he was "sorry." Why would he be "sorry" or "apologize" if he didn't know what he had said was seriously wrong? Now there was no doubt in my mind that he knew exactly what he had done.

After the jury had left the courtroom, I argued that given this grievous error, a mistrial had to be declared. There was no other option, I argued. The jury had been prejudiced and would be unable to keep this evidence out of their minds. The government argued that a curative instruction could be given, cautioning the jury not to consider this testimony, and the trial should continue. The court took a recess to decide.

* * *

The courtroom was abuzz while we waited for Judge Kobayashi to issue her ruling. Adam and I conferred with our colleagues about whether asking for a mistrial was the right move. Given how well we thought we had done up to that point in the trial, it was a possible option to simply agree to give a curative instruction and move forward. There was no right answer, just intuition. Spectators and members of the press in the courtroom were milling about and talking to one another, trying to understand what was going on but knowing something very, very wrong had happened. The government attorneys were also huddled together in one corner and, I'm sure, having the same conversation with their colleagues as we were having with ours. After approximately twenty minutes, Judge Kobayashi returned to the bench to announce her decision. The anticipation in the courtroom was palpable.

Judge Kobayashi delivered her ruling:

"So, counsel, before the recess, Mr. Silvert made a motion for a mistrial based on the testimony given by Louis Kealoha regarding Mr. Puana's arrest and conviction for burglary.

"Mr. Tong has argued that the curative instruction that the judge— that the court gave prior to recess was sufficient, or, if necessary, an additional cautionary instruction can be given to cure the prejudice.

"In doing a quick review, the court concludes that I have no choice but to grant the defendant's request for a mistrial. Instead of instructing the jury to disregard Louis's testimony and giving a strong curative instruction.

"Declaring a mistrial is appropriate only where a cautionary instruction is unlikely to cure the prejudicial effect of an error. This has been recognized by the Ninth Circuit and other circuits, in particular *Toolate v. Borg*, 828 F.2d 571, which is a 1987 Ninth Circuit case.

"In contemplation of the parties' position, given first the testimony with regard to a reference to Mr. Puana being arrested and convicted on a burglary charge, I find that the prejudice is too great to be overcome by a curative instruction because, one, it refers to a similar offense that's involved in this particular case.

"I also find specifically too that it was not elicited at all by Mr. Tong's questioning, that Mr. Tong's question, as we reviewed on the record prior to the recess, clearly related to Mr. Puana's physical appearance in the video and the basis for the witness's recognition of the person depicted in the video as being Mr. Puana. Wholly unsolicited, the witness gave testimony about an arrest and conviction.

"In determining whether or not there was—or there is a curative instruction to overcome the prejudice, the court considered various information that could be used for a curative instruction, but because of the nature of the charges in this case and the testimony given with regard to this prior arrest and conviction, coupled with the fact that the court ruled on this issue in a motion in limine, particularly relying on the fact that no 404(b) notice was given with regard to the conviction, and noting that it's early in the case, and Mr. Silvert did not mention in his opening statement any reference to whether or not Mr. Puana would be testifying....

"Therefore, the court concludes that there is no curative instruction that the court can give to overcome the prejudice of the testimony, and on this basis grants Mr. Silvert's motion for mistrial."

* * *

And with those words, the trial was unexpectedly and suddenly over. On the very first day of taking testimony. Before I had even the opportunity to cross-examine Louis, much less his wife, who sat sequestered in the trial witness room. There would be no verdict by the jury. The two mailboxes remained, unused and unseen, in cardboard boxes under our table. The members of the press all raced out to broadcast the news of what had occurred. I felt, without a doubt, that Louis had intentionally caused the mistrial. Katherine Kealoha, and in turn Louis, had simply too much to lose if she took the stand and I had the opportunity to cross-examine her under oath. They had too much to lose if I had had the opportunity to fully show to the jury, and thus the public, all the evidence of the frame-up we had uncovered. They had too much to lose if the jury came back with an acquittal.

My feeling that Louis intentionally caused the mistrial only grew more certain in a brief conversation I had with Tong in, of all places, the men's restroom as we waited for the court's decision. I could see that Tong was a bit shaken by the turn of events. I did not believe for a moment that that Tong had coached Louis to say what he said. No, Louis had done it all on his own. The fact that it was a complete surprise to Tong was written all over his face. I asked a simple question: "Larry, wasn't Katherine Kealoha supposed to be the second witness to testify?" No response. I followed up with more of a statement than a question: "I bet Louis, at the last second, asked you if he could testify first, claiming he was a busy man and needed to get in and out of the courtroom sooner, right?" Tong almost turned to respond but caught himself and didn't say anything. But he didn't deny it either. I took that as my answer. I had asked the question not only because I believed it to be true, but also because I wanted to see how Tong would answer. More importantly, if I was right, I wanted to let him know he had been played.

The day after the mistrial Gerard received an anonymous letter. It read, in part:

> Bro
> Did you see me there. We think he did it for you. Make sure you don't go down. He is stuck for now with that she-devil but not for long. She busted his balls for that mistake but we think that was the last straw for him. She-devil doesn't know. He got divorce attorney and wait for the end of christmas [sic] you will see.

Gerard did not know who it was from, although he thought it was a police officer. But neither of us believed it. We didn't think for a minute Louis had intentionally caused the mistrial out of some sense of desire to save Gerard. No, Louis was all in. He did it to save himself. He did it to save Katherine. He did it in the hopes that the case would just go away and no one, other than us, would ever learn of the evidence we had uncovered.

Years later, a different federal judge, in a much different setting, stated that Louis, in his opinion, had intentionally caused the mistrial but couldn't quite figure out why. The judge ventured that maybe Louis had a change of heart about what he had done and threw the trial to save Gerard. I never entertained this thought for an instant, and neither did Gerard.

But the case was not over. A mistrial simply meant that a new trial date was scheduled and the government would get a second chance to try and convict Gerard. The retrial was scheduled for April 28, 2015. With all that had happened and everything we had learned in one short trial day, we had a lot of work ahead of us. But it had certainly been one hell of a day. ❖

CHAPTER 17

The Decision

The day after the mistrial was declared, when the excitement of the moment had died down, it was now time to assess where we were. We had a retrial to prepare for, and we had learned valuable new information.

A review of retired Officer Silva's testimony revealed several critical new facts, the most important being that HPD lied to us in their responses to our subpoenas when they denied that more surveillance tape footage existed beyond the one hour they had provided to us. According to Silva's testimony, the entire hard drive containing hours, if not days of videotape could still be sitting in his locked filing cabinet in his former CIU office. We would be issuing our thirty-first subpoena, the thirteenth to HPD, to try and get it. We were convinced that whatever was on that video would help our case. Why else would HPD and CIU have gone to such great lengths to keep it from us? We also prepared a motion to have the court hold HPD and CIU in contempt for having lied in their previous responses to our subpoenas. The subpoenas issued to HPD were issued by the court's authority, and as such HPD had defied the order of a federal judge.

We believed the videotape footage might show someone prepping the mailbox to be "stolen." If so, this would prove it hadn't really been stolen but had been set up to be removed. There is no "theft" if you remove your own mailbox. The videotape might, as we suspected it would, contain better images of the vehicle, making it possible to identify the make and model, or even read the license plate. It could also prove that Katherine did not, as she had claimed, go to the mailbox on June 21 and retrieve "some mail" while placing "the rest" back in the mailbox. And now we questioned whether Louis had even left his house in the morning to go surfing as he had testified. The videotape could answer all these questions. It could be as important to us as the Nixon tapes were during the Watergate investigations. We were hoping the similarity ended there and they hadn't been "accidentally" erased, as occurred in Watergate.

Silva had testified that CIU officer Bobby Nguyen was present at the Kealoha residence when the hard drive was recovered and that he had viewed the footage and, apparently, identified Gerard as the thief. Silva had also testified that he was directed to make a short clip of the videotape footage and place that into evidence rather than the entire hard drive. Yet nowhere in Detective Akagi's closing report were any of these facts mentioned. Why not? Was Akagi more deeply involved in framing Puana than we thought? Or could it be that CIU and the Kealohas had all conspired to hide evidence even from Akagi? We'd need to dig deeper into these events and determine how best to use this information for the retrial. Certainly, this new information required more subpoenas to be issued to HPD. If Akagi wasn't involved, perhaps we could turn him into an ally. No one likes being made a patsy, particularly by their own fellow police officers, much less than by their own chief.

Next there was Louis's trial testimony to consider. We now knew how and why the government was going to claim the hazy image in the videotape footage was Gerard—by the manner and style of Gerard's walk and clothing. We would need to be better prepared to address this claim at the retrial. We also needed to learn much more about the incidents at the Kealohas' Kāhala residence that Louis had testified had allegedly occurred prior to the theft of the mailbox—incidents that we did not believe had actually occurred. We'd have to gather evidence to prove this to the jury. This would require more subpoenas and, if necessary, filing motions to try and keep this evidence out of the next trial. Otherwise, if this evidence was allowed to be introduced again without us countering the validity of these claims, the jury could simply infer that Gerard was the cause of those other incidents even though there was no actual proof of this. Juries have their own way of putting pieces of a puzzle together.

*   *   *

But all this might be irrelevant, depending on the outcome of a much more important decision we now had to make. Given the events of the trial, was it time to show our hand to the government and fully explain the evidence and the implications of the evidence we had gathered? And, if we did decide to show our evidence to the government, what should we ask for? How far were we willing to go in demanding justice? We had developed evidence that we believed proved not only Gerard's innocence but also suggested far-reaching corruption within HPD, spearheaded by its own chief, his prosecutor wife and members of the secretive CIU. Was obtaining a dismissal of the charges good enough? A dismissal would not mean Gerard was innocent. It would clear him of the charges, but it would not exonerate him. No, we decided a simple dismissal of the charges would not be enough after all he and Florence had been through. If we went to the government and took this chance, we wanted nothing less than his complete and absolute exoneration.

Given the events of the trial, we thought that at least some members of the prosecution team must have had a feeling that something was very wrong with their case. Louis was too well schooled in how to testify to have so brazenly caused the mistrial in the manner he had. If what I concluded from my restroom exchange with Tong was correct and Louis had, indeed, asked at the last minute to testify before his wife, we felt that Tong might have some uneasiness about the case. Hope springs eternal.

But going to the government at this stage of the case was fraught with danger. If our instincts were wrong, then disclosing our evidence to them now, before the retrial, would greatly damage Gerard's chances of getting an acquittal because we would lose the element of surprise. The government could shore up their case and have witnesses change their testimony to address our evidence. This was a troubling and difficult decision to make, further complicated by years of historical mistrust between the federal public defender office and, well, quite honestly, the entire law enforcement community. This "public defender versus every alphabet soup federal prosecutorial agency" conflict is natural given the nature of our work. We butt heads with agents, cops and prosecutors day after day, year after year, case after case. Not only in the courtroom, but on the phone, in meetings and informally in the halls of the federal building and courthouse. I have had more than my share of less-than-friendly encounters with federal agents and prosecutors, which had only further fueled my own personal distrust, a distrust I had before I even became a public defender.

Don't get me wrong. I don't believe that all prosecutors or all government agents can't be trusted. It is always an individual assessment that must be made. But my faith and trust must be earned. As a result of my thirty-six-year career in criminal defense work, I have found that many prosecutors became prosecutors for their own personal advancement or simply for the power it gives them. Being a prosecutor, more so than any other legal career, serves as a stepping-stone to either a judgeship, political office or partnership in some large law firm. But I've found having such power at a young age gives people a false sense of themselves. It's only natural for a prosecutor to believe that it's because of their own skills as a trial attorney that they were victorious, rather than acknowledging that they usually have the overwhelming weight of case law and evidence on their side from the start. Not to mention that the court is often in their corner as well, as in general judges have become more and more law and order–oriented by virtue of who is being appointed to the bench. Even so, I strongly believe in the goodness of individual people, including prosecutors. And even the most ardent prosecutor believes in their heart of hearts that they are serving justice. It's just their definition of justice that I take issue with. Put simply, we had to decide whether we trusted either Osborne or Tong.

We also had to consider whether the government, now more fully aware of our defense and able to adjust their strategy accordingly, might feel they were in a better position to win the case and thus not be open to our overtures at all. Although we had not called a single witness to the stand, I had made an opening statement and we had filed a witness list and exhibit list containing over ninety-four documents. The government would learn a lot about our defense from now having the time to take a closer look at these exhibits. Without a doubt, they would try to interview all of the witnesses we had put on our witness list, which meant they might learn about the two different mailboxes before the next trial by talking to Mr. Dryer and Mr. Slaugh. And that would mean no more ticking time bombs tucked under our courtroom tables.

Then there were the statistics to consider. Cold hard numbers. Less than 6 percent of all cases charged in federal court go to trial. And only a small percentage of those defendants who go to trial are found not guilty. That number plummets even further when there is a mistrial, exactly because the government has gained an insight into the defense and can better prepare their witnesses and plug the holes in their case before the retrial. While we still felt confident that we would ultimately get an acquittal, the odds had diminished. Although a lot could change between the first and second trials depending upon newly uncovered evidence, like obtaining the entire hard drive, the reality of these numbers were staring us in the face. And the government was well aware of these very same statistics.

What to do? For more than a week Peter Wolff; my investigators, Adam Choka and Kathleen Wright; and I debated this question for hours upon hours. Thinking about it kept me up at night. All of us had deep suspicions of the government. How much did they really know? How could they not have uncovered what we had? Were they really being misled by the Kealohas and by HPD? Or were they intentionally turning a blind eye to evidence that lay right in front of them due to their unyielding allegiance to and unquestioning faith in their fellow state law enforcement brethren? How much of their own egos had Tong or Osborne personally invested in their case?

We knew from court filings that Osborne fully believed in Gerard's guilt and Katherine's version of the events. In fact, Osborne had filed a motion specifically arguing that Gerard stole the mailbox because there were bank documents in the mailbox related to the civil lawsuit, documents he claimed Gerard had tried but failed to obtain through legal means. While this was completely false, Osborne did not seem to know this and had fully adopted Katherine's version of events. All one had to do, as we had done, was talk to the bank manager to learn that Gerard had obtained these very same bank records in early February of 2013 and thus had no reason to "steal" Katherine's mail on June 21 because he already had the records in his possession months earlier. But no one from the government had sought to verify what Katherine had claimed; they had just taken her at her word. We needed to consider all these factors and weigh the risks.

A final factor to consider was how willing the United States Attorney's Office would be to take the political fallout should it find our evidence persuasive and dismiss the case. We knew that the relationship between the United States Attorney's Office and HPD had deteriorated over the past several years. The two agencies were barely on speaking terms, and cases were not being referred from the state to the feds as was the norm. But this was happening behind the scenes, and the public was completely unaware of this feud between two law enforcement agencies that were supposed to be working together for the betterment of the community. A dismissal would be very public and would bring this dispute out into the open. It would be nothing less than a declaration of war between the Hawai'i United States Attorney's Office and HPD. There was no doubt a dismissal would cost the United States Attorney's Office dearly in terms of their relationship with all local law enforcement agencies, and we didn't know if either Tong or Osborne, or more importantly, Florence Nakakuni, the head of their office, was willing to pay this political price no matter what we showed them.

No, there was nothing simple or easy about this decision.

After much deliberation, we came to the conclusion that the Kealohas and HPD had colluded to hide the truth from the federal prosecutors. Given what we had uncovered and the desperate need of the Kealohas to have Gerard convicted and imprisoned for something, anything, we determined that, as unlikely a scenario as it was, the federal authorities *really* did not know they were being deceived by their state brethren. We came to this conclusion because we thought it would be difficult, if not downright impossible, for a federal prosecutor to believe that they would be intentionally lied to by state law enforcement officials on such a massive scale. By massive, I mean multiple false and misleading police reports being created and officers intentionally withholding information from federal prosecutors, not to mention the chief of police and his prosecutor wife outright lying to them. It was simply not a concept a federal prosecutor would entertain. It would go against all of their instincts. Our feeling that the feds had been lied to was aided by how Tong had made his opening statement and presented his evidence to the jury. He simply did not present his case as if he was aware the Kealohas and HPD were lying to him. He thought the evidence and testimony he was presenting was truthful. The fact that Tong had introduced Government Exhibit #7, Silva's reports, we believed, was further evidence that Tong didn't realize HPD was lying to him. A prosecutor would never knowingly submit an improperly altered document as evidence. Tong had looked as surprised as Silva, but for a different reason, when we had confronted Silva with his altered document.

This fact sealed it. We made our decision. We would reach out to the government. The ball would be in their court whether to take us up on our offer and hear us out.

We also decided that if we did meet with the government, we wanted both Osborne and Tong present. Osborne had returned to work, and even though it was still primarily his case, we were concerned that, as head of the entire criminal division of the Hawai'i United States Attorney's Office, he might be overly influenced by political concerns beyond our control. Tong would not have these same concerns. I had long suspected that the Kealohas, or people working on their behalf, had influenced the

United States Attorney's Office's decision to prosecute the case in the first instance. Early on in the case I had written several letters to Osborne demanding to know how the case had been accepted for prosecution and whether it had been taken as some sort of personal favor to the Kealohas. At the time I had written these letters, I was hoping that if there had been some sort of impropriety, it could get us a deal or perhaps make the government more willing to dismiss the case to avoid disclosure. Osborne had denied any such claim, but we had heard differently from several sources who claimed the United States Attorney's Office had taken the case as a quid pro quo to mend fences with HPD. If this allegation was true, I was concerned that Osborne simply had too much invested in the case to be open to viewing the case from our perspective. It was imperative to us that Tong take part in our meeting.

Tong, I believed, was the type of prosecutor who would not take kindly to being lied to by his own witnesses. While no prosecutor likes being misled, Tong, we thought, would be particularly incensed if he felt he was being played, even more so if that was being done by fellow law enforcement officers and a state prosecutor. As I said, Tong was a "prosecutor's prosecutor," and while he was rather strict and unbending in his views towards criminal defendants, a quality that had made him particularly difficult to negotiate with in prior cases I had had with him, we believed he'd bring that same attitude to bear on law enforcement officers who had purposely lied to him.

Now, what exactly did we want?

We wanted the world to know Gerard was innocent and had been framed—we wanted his complete exoneration. And we wanted to bring the fight to the Kealohas. Louis, the chief of the Honolulu Police Department, had tried to get an innocent man convicted. Katherine, a high-ranking prosecutor, had done the lion's share of the work to frame him. High-ranking state law enforcement officers had worked to frame him. Gerard had suffered embarrassment and humiliation—arrested in front of his girlfriend and his fellow church members. Handcuffed. Put in jail. All because, we believed, Katherine wanted to hide the fact that she had stolen hundreds of thousands of dollars from Gerard and his ninety-four-year-old mother, Florence. Her own grandmother! And worst of all, Florence had lost her family home because of what Katherine had done. It was clear that neither the Kealohas nor their state law enforcement allies cared about the rule of law, laws they were sworn to uphold. No, a dismissal was not good enough. We wanted Gerard exonerated, and we wanted the Kealohas investigated and prosecuted. A tall order, to say the least.

I contacted Tong to set up a meeting. I invited Osborne and Tong to our office, telling him that because we had prepared a PowerPoint presentation of our evidence and we had physical evidence to show them that was "too bulky" to carry down to their office, it was best to meet at my office. I did not tell him that the bulky items were the two mailboxes that the government still did not know existed. I had made no mention of them during the aborted trial, and we had made sure when we left the courtroom that the mailboxes remained hidden. If the government refused our offer, they still wouldn't know about them.

After several hours Tong called back and said they would be willing to hear us out. Adam prepared the PowerPoint presentation, as he knew the details, dates, places and names in the case better than I did. That admission will come as no surprise to anyone in my office. As an investigator, Adam was dogged. Smart. He remembered every little detail about the case. We had worked together on several previous trials—and had been fortunate enough to have gotten not guilty verdicts in all of them. He often made incredibly insightful points that I almost always incorporated into my cross-examination or closing arguments, and when I didn't, he let me know in no uncertain terms he was not happy with me! His distrust and dislike for all things prosecutorial was second to none. I trusted him implicitly. We often disagreed, argued and laughed when, inevitably, I misstated a fact or mispronounced a word that he called me out on and then proved he was right about. And we had a friendly running verbal battle about him being of Arab descent from New Jersey by way of Jordan, and my being of Jewish descent from New York City by way of Russia. We joked that we could be the model for an Arab–Israeli peace accord—or not, as people who witnessed our arguments would attest. At trial, I considered Adam my right-hand man and highly regarded his input.

Our presentation to the government was a tag team effort. I left the nitty-gritty details to Adam so I didn't get them all mixed up. Our presentation lasted for more than two hours. We dissected each police report and showed why it was either false or had omitted critically important information. Osborne interrupted us on many occasions to proclaim why some piece of evidence didn't mean what we thought it did or was unimportant. Several times we had to go back and show him the documents again to convince him that we were not making this stuff up.

For example, when Ms. Carrie Arakaki passed the polygraph examination stating no one had taken or used her car, but the HPD polygrapher had, nevertheless, written that the car had been stolen—Osborne denied that this was correct. So, we threw the polygrapher's report back up on the screen, highlighted the line and enlarged it, while I stood up and pointed at the words and read them out loud. We would repeat this procedure several more times during the course of the meeting.

The highlight of our presentation was, of course, the two mailboxes. We lifted the Gaines Manufacturing mailbox out of the cardboard box where it had remained since the trial and placed it on the conference table. We showed them Katherine's statements made under oath, as well as Detective Akagi's and Detective Garcia's reports, all of which described this exact mailbox as the one stolen from in front of the Kealoha residence. Tong had a puzzled look on his face. "Yes," I could see him thinking, "that's the mailbox that was stolen, just as described in the report. So?" Adam then lifted the Solar Group mailbox out of the second cardboard box where it had been hidden from view and placed it on the table. This was the moment of truth. Either they would now get on our side, or they never would.

I could sense Osborne and Tong waiting for an explanation. I let the visual sink in for a few seconds. We explained that it was, in fact, this second mailbox, the Solar Group mailbox, all white with a red flag, that had been in front of the Kealoha residence. It was this mailbox that had been "allegedly" stolen, not the Gaines Manufacturing two-toned and gray-flagged mailbox, as claimed. We laid out on the conference table all the photographs we had obtained from the Puana family showing the Solar Group mailbox in front of the house. We followed this up by putting Google Maps up on the screen, which showed the view of the Kealoha residence from June of 2013 with the Solar Group mailbox standing tall in front of the house. We didn't want them to think that the family photographs had been manipulated to show a different mailbox than that claimed by Katherine and HPD. We played the videotape surveillance footage and froze the video when it got to a good shot of the mailbox. As we all looked on in silence, there was no mistaking it. The mailbox in the videotape was the Solar Group mailbox sitting on our conference room table. No mistake about it at all.

I sympathized with Osborne. It was, after all, his case. He believed in it; he had worked on it for more than a year. But we were showing him his case from a very different perspective. It was hard for him to see the things he had either missed or overlooked because of his allegiance to his state law enforcement counterparts. Defensiveness is often expressed through anger and stubbornness. After about an hour, Osborne excused himself from the meeting. I hoped it was because he was disgusted by what he was learning. Tong stayed. Tong was paying close attention, taking notes and asking questions that we felt were appropriate, indicating he was listening. The fact that Tong chose to stay on when Osborne left the meeting was, we felt, a positive sign that we were making headway.

After Osborne had left, Adam and I huddled over the mailboxes with Tong as we pointed out the differences between them and again compared our new knowledge with Detective Akagi's closing report, Katherine's sworn statements and Detective Garcia's appraisal report. Throughout our presentation, we had repeatedly told Tong and Osborne that HPD and the Kealohas had lied to them and to federal agents. We wanted to make sure they kept hearing this refrain over and over again. We drove the point home with the mailboxes. Maybe, just maybe, we could get their blood boiling as ours had. But Tong was playing it cool, and Osborne had left.

At the conclusion of our presentation, Tong sat back and, after a few contemplative moments, looked up and simply asked us what we wanted. In that instant, with those few words having been spoken, I knew we had played our cards right. Now it was time to push the envelope. I told him we wanted the case dismissed "with prejudice," meaning it could never be prosecuted again. But before those words had barely left my mouth, I said we also wanted the United States Attorney's Office, his office, to refer the case to the FBI to investigate the unlawful conduct of the Kealohas and HPD. I knew he was prepared to hear that we wanted the case dismissed, but I don't think he was prepared for us demanding a full-scale FBI investigation of the Kealohas and HPD. I don't think he had ever heard a defense attorney make such a demand before. And we were making it.

He quickly responded that I could refer the case to the FBI myself if I wanted to. I knew I could. Anyone can contact the FBI and refer a case. But I also knew that if I referred the case, as a public defender, it would be viewed by the FBI as just another defense attorney crying over spilt milk, and the referral would be buried in the same warehouse as the Ark of the Covenant was at the end of the Indiana Jones movie. If the United States Attorney's Office itself referred the case, the FBI had to stand up and take notice. I pressed the issue. To sweeten the deal, I promised Tong that I would not disclose the evidence we uncovered to the press if his office agreed and referred the matter to the FBI for further investigation. But, I told him, if they did not refer the matter to the FBI, I was going to make a public statement, disclose all our evidence to the press and let the government deal with the public fallout. In light of what we had uncovered, I said, their failure to refer the case to the FBI would be viewed by the public as an attempt by federal authorities to shield HPD and the Kealohas from their own wrongdoings.

Tong thanked us and said the decision would take a few days. He would have to discuss it with the United States attorney for the District of Hawai'i, Florence Nakakuni. A decision like this, he said, could only be made by her. I fully understood, and with that we said our alohas.

Adam and I were silent for a while, taking in what had just happened, both doing a mental checklist to make sure we had covered everything. I'm sure Adam's "checklist" was more thorough than mine. After a few moments we looked at one another and, in unison, started talking at once. We felt the meeting had gone unexpectedly well. We felt good that we had, we believed, made the right call about Tong and Osborne. Still, neither of us were convinced of our powers of persuasion. Had we really done enough to convince the United States Attorney's Office to not only dismiss the case but to refer it to the FBI? We were both too cynical to believe Gerard would get the full measure of justice he deserved, but only time would tell. It was going to be a long few days and Tong had not given us a specific timetable. All we could do now was wait and hope. Gerard was optimistic; after all, he knew he was innocent and fully expected that the government, now illuminated with our facts, would come to the same conclusion.

The next day our hopes were raised when Tong asked us to make a copy of our PowerPoint presentation so he could show it to his boss, Florence Nakakuni. This was a good sign. A very good sign. It indicated that Tong was true to his word. He would present our evidence in detail, not just a summary, to the head of the United States Attorney's Office. He could have been blowing smoke when he had left the meeting, but we had faith in Tong, and so far he was proving us right. Radio silence, however, followed for the next several days. We waited, playing mind games with ourselves, debating whether no news was good news. Then, to our amazement, it was over.

My phone rang. It was a call from Tong. I waited for just a second to compose myself before I answered. Without fanfare, he informed me that he had made a presentation to Ms. Nakakuni and that she had spent the weekend mulling over her decision. She had, just moments earlier, notified Tong that he was authorized to dismiss the case, with prejudice. But more importantly, Tong told me she had authorized her office to refer the case to the FBI. Tong said the government would be filing an order with the court shortly. I was ecstatic but tried to calm my voice. I thanked him for his willingness to listen to our presentation of the evidence with an open mind, but as I hung up the phone I could hardly contain my excitement.

I called Adam and Kate into Peter Wolff's office and told them the news. We were elated and a bit shocked. None of us had ever imagined such an outcome when Gerard first sat in my office in early July 2013. Almost a year and a half had passed since then. A lot had happened. The mood in the room was one of great satisfaction. The case against Gerard was being dropped, forever. All the hard work our office had done had paid off. Gerard's steadfastness in the face of tremendous odds had been vindicated. The Kealohas and HPD officers, the people who were the real criminals in this case, at least in our eyes, were going to be the subject of an FBI investigation. And for some of us, particularly in my case, there was a heartwarming sense that the criminal justice system, every now and then, actually works. I felt like the Grinch whose heart had grown three sizes,

I called Gerard. He choked up and broke down in tears upon hearing the news. I could only imagine the weight that was lifted off his shoulders. He thanked us profusely and I, in turn, thanked him for having had the fortitude and the willpower to stand tall and take on such powerful people and institutions. I thanked him for not having taken the easy way out and sought out some sort of plea deal just to get it over with. I asked him to share this news with his mother, Florence, now ninety-five, who also had been through so much and lost so much. I assured him we were not done, and that we were going to see this through to the very end, together. "Amen, my brother," he replied.

On December 16, 2014, Judge Kobayashi signed the dismissal order filed by the government. It was short and to the point:

ORDER FOR DISMISSAL

Pursuant to Rule 48(a) of the Federal Rules of Criminal Procedure and by leave of court endorsed hereon, the United States Attorney for the District of Hawai'i hereby dismisses the Indictment filed on July 11, 2013 against GERARD K. PUANA in the interest of justice, with prejudice.

In light of all the local publicity the case had received and the shocking conclusion, I prepared a written statement to read to the press. Normally I make some notes for myself or just wing it, but this felt too important. Also, since I had promised not to disclose the evidence we had uncovered to the public, I had to be careful what I said. The dismissal order did not say anything about the fact that the United States Attorney's Office was referring the case to the FBI. But we wanted to make that point crystal clear to the press. It would demonstrate that the case against Gerard was not simply being dismissed due to some procedural reason, but because there were indications of serious misconduct on the part of the Kealohas and HPD, misconduct that warranted further investigation. Investigation by the FBI, no less!

I had one overriding goal in mind as I prepared my press release, and that was to keep the pressure on the FBI to move forward with their investigation. My heart might have grown three sizes, but I was not stupid. As it turned out, I couldn't have been more correct in my concerns about their willingness to proceed. I just didn't expect to be so right so quickly.

Prior to the news conference, I had informed the press that the referral to the FBI came from the United States Attorney's Office. I had done this so they would have time to confirm this fact before airing it on the news. No one was going to simply take my word for it; it had to be verified. But right before the press conference, I was called by several members of the press who told me that the FBI spokesperson was denying that the United States Attorney's Office had made the referral. Rather, the FBI spokesperson was claiming it came from me. I was furious and disappointed. My heart shrank a size, maybe two. I saw this as yet another attempt by a law enforcement officer to belittle the significance of the dismissal order and the referral, in order to save whatever working relationship the FBI still had with HPD. It also infuriated me that an FBI spokesperson would take it upon himself to misstate a directive that came from the United States Attorney's Office.

I immediately called the FBI spokesperson and confronted him with his misstatement. He did not deny it. Rather, in an "aw shucks" kind of tone, he defended himself by saying it really didn't matter who referred the case, so why was I "so irate." I told him in no uncertain words that he damned well knew why it mattered. Why else, I told him, did he say it came from me and not the United States Attorney's Office, a fact he just admitted to me he knew to be true, if it didn't matter? To say the least, this is a very sanitized version of what I said. I demanded that he call each and every member of the press he had spoken to and clear up this "misunderstanding," or I'd make sure the news story would be as much about him and how the FBI was already trying to cover up for HPD as it was about the case.

He made the calls, and his little stunt resulted in an unintended benefit. I had promised the government that I would not specify who within the United States Attorney's Office had made the referral. There might have been a political price to pay if the name of the specific AUSA was made public. I would simply say that their Office, in general, had made the referral. As it turned out, the FBI spokesperson, when calling back the press, specifically named AUSA Les Osborne as the prosecutor who referred the matter to the FBI. The fact that it was now public that Osborne, the head of the criminal division of the United States Attorney's Office, had made the referral made it even more significant. It was turning out to be a very good day after all.

I did my best in front of the press and cameras to stick to my prepared statement:

December 16, 2014
STATEMENT TO THE MEDIA

About two weeks ago there was a mistrial in the federal criminal prosecution against my client, Gerard Puana. After that occurred, my client and I decided to put our faith and trust in the integrity of the United States Attorney's Office and a meeting took place with the federal prosecutors where the evidence we had uncovered in this case was presented to them. I am pleased to announce that after that discussion and based upon further internal deliberations and inquiry, the United States Attorney's Office has filed an order to dismiss the charges against Mr. Puana effective immediately and with prejudice, meaning that this criminal prosecution is over once and for all. My client, Mr. Puana, is extremely pleased that this ordeal is now over.

In addition, it is my understanding that the United States Attorney's Office has referred the matter to the FBI for further investigation into how this case was handled by HPD and others. As I stated in my opening statement to the jury, Mr. Puana was innocent of these charges from the outset.

Because there is now a pending federal investigation into these matters, Mr. Puana and I have agreed that we should not discuss the underlying facts of this case with the public to allow the FBI to conduct its investigation in the manner they deem appropriate. I want to thank the United States Attorney's Office for allowing us to present our side of the story to them and for filing the order to dismiss. In addition, I want to thank the United States Attorney's Office for referring this matter to the FBI as we believe that further investigation of the matter is warranted.

Finally, we ask the members of the Honolulu Police Commission, which is reportedly meeting with Chief Kealoha tomorrow, to uphold their obligation to the public and to conduct their own investigation into this matter and related matters. We ask that this inquiry, as well as any others that are done by appropriate entities, be done openly and transparently so that there can be meaningful accountability to the public. *Mahalo.*

If ever there was a time when I could have literally "dropped the mike" and not looked foolish, this was that moment. I did it anyway, if only in my mind.

Years later postal inspector Brian Shaughnessy would testify that he had told Tong that he recommended against prosecuting the case against Gerard, saying the "case was a loser." Nevertheless, after consulting with his office, which could only mean with Osborne and/or Flo Nakakuni, Tong instructed Shaughnessy that the decision had been made to prosecute the case and that he should "write up charges." Osborne himself would later tell the press that in thirty-nine years as a prosecutor he'd "never seen anything like this case," where law enforcement officers worked in concert to frame an innocent man. As Osborne said, "It's such an outlandish concept that it didn't even cross my mind that I was being duped." It was only after our meeting that he knew he had a "moral and ethical obligation to dismiss the charges."

These statements by Shaughnessy and Osborne validated that our uneasiness in reaching out to Osborne and Tong had been entirely justified and that, had we not played our cards exactly right, the case would not have been dismissed. These statements also demonstrated just how difficult it must have been for Osborne and Tong to hear and accept what we told them during our meeting. But most importantly, they proved that when confronted with the truth, despite their loyalty to law enforcement and their own personal investment in the case, in the end both stood up for justice and did the right thing. Justice had won out. My heart grew back a size or two. ❖

ACT II

CHAPTER 18

Time to Meet the FBI

"Hey, look who's at the door. It's the FBI." It's usually a bad day in the life of one of my clients when the FBI is knocking on their front door. The FBI normally greets my clients with weapons drawn, wearing flak jackets with "FBI" emblazoned across the front. And that's the good part. After that it's the arrest, body search, handcuffs, interrogation and imprisonment. FBI agents and federal defenders often butt heads with one another in and out of the courtroom. We routinely challenge the legality of the searches they conduct and attack their credibility on the witness stand. Needless to say, this does not create a friendly relationship, and sometimes it gets personal. Alleging that an agent violated the Constitution, whether through negligence or incompetence or, worse, with intent, does not win you friends. There are no softball games between our offices. We don't share a beer together. I had done my fair share of discrediting FBI agents over the years and had developed a reputation as being a less-than-friendly, but I hoped worthy, adversary.

January 14, 2015. It was time to meet the FBI. The FBI could not ignore the United States attorney's referral to investigate Gerard's case. We were going to have our opportunity to present the evidence we had gathered to the FBI and hopefully convince them to launch a large-scale corruption investigation into the Kealohas. We knew that the deep law enforcement ties between the FBI and HPD would make the FBI skeptical of our claims. After all, we were asking them to investigate people they worked alongside on a daily basis—HPD officers who trained with the FBI, who played softball with them and shared a beer or two with them. While the meeting was private, given the publicity of the trial and the unusual dismissal with prejudice by the United States Attorney's Office, the press wanted to know if and when we were going to meet with the FBI. After consulting with the United States attorney and getting her approval, I had told the press that we were meeting with the FBI and when. Not groundbreaking news, I thought, given the circumstances, but the FBI usually likes to conduct their investigations discreetly. Well, not this time. I wanted transparency. I wanted the public to know so it would make it more difficult for the FBI to do a slipshod investigation or, worse, to bury it altogether.

The meeting took place at our office. This was *our* ball game, and it would be played on *our* home turf. Our office is located in the Federal Building in downtown Honolulu, across from the federal courthouse. The office has a small waiting room consisting of two used chairs and a broken-down sofa. There's a magazine rack containing an eclectic display of magazines, from children's books to environmental magazines on the preservation of endangered wildlife or the effects of global warming. No expensive koa wood lines our walls like the United States Attorney's Office downstairs. No bulletproof glass. No cameras peering down on you from the ceilings, not even hidden ones. Our conference room? A used conference table given to us as a hand-me-down from some judge's chambers and a mishmash of chairs—most, but not all, still able to recline without tipping you over. No state-of-the-art technology to display our evidence, only a computer and a screen we had set up against the wall. But it was our home field, rough and rocky as it was, with plenty of character. I had thought about buying fake cameras to put up on the conference room ceiling to make the agents feel more at home, but we nixed that attempt at humor given the seriousness of the matter and because the agents probably wouldn't even get the joke.

Two FBI agents showed up, Agents Jeffrey Felman and Matthew McDonald. Adam was prepared to present our PowerPoint presentation, which he had updated and fine-tuned with more exacting details, since these were investigative agents who were trained to pay attention to detail. We had extra binders to give to the agents containing all the paper evidence we had gathered, yellow highlighting to clearly show the inconsistent statements and omissions in the various police reports. Adam and I had spent a lot of time discussing how we wanted to present our evidence so that it would have the most effect. We knew we were only going to have one shot. We placed the two mailboxes on the conference table before they arrived. We needed to grab their attention immediately, and there was no longer any shock value to be gained by hiding them. We were apprehensive but excited. We'd never been in this position before, presenting evidence to the FBI rather than being on the receiving end. It felt a bit surreal going into the meeting. It soon got a lot more surreal.

Upon entering the conference room, the agents would not even shake our hands. Instead, they ignored us and gruffly sat down. Then Agent McDonald spoke—not words of greeting but of aggression and annoyance. He let us know in no uncertain terms that he was not happy to be here and that "the FBI did not appreciate [me] talking to the press and everyone knowing what they were doing." That was, he protested angrily, "not how they worked," and "the FBI's schedule was not to be a matter of public knowledge." I was initially taken aback by his comments. I had expected a more polite greeting. I responded rather defensively. I explained that I had spoken with the United States attorney Florence Nakakuni before I made my statements to the press and she had no problem with what I had disclosed. In fact, I had been careful about what I had said exactly because I wanted to make sure I didn't unwittingly ruffle anyone's feathers at such a critical juncture in the case. I was trying to live up to my end of the bargain and put the evidence in the hands of the FBI rather than go public. I thought I was playing nicely with the government, which, for people who knew me, was a big, big step. But obviously not a big enough step for Agent McDonald.

His demeanor made it clear we were not on good terms with one another and not likely to become friends. I guess we wouldn't be grabbing any beers later! He responded angrily that he didn't care what the United States attorney had told me—"the FBI doesn't work for the United States attorney." That was enough for me. My olive-branch holding was over. I didn't like playing nice with the FBI to begin with, and now Agent McDonald's attitude allowed me to respond in kind. I knew exactly what he was doing. He was trying to regain home field advantage, on our turf no less.

But I wasn't going to allow it. I'd been defensive, but now I was angry. While the FBI is a separate entity from the United States Attorney's Office, both offices work under the umbrella of the Department of Justice, and as far as I was concerned, they were in one big bed together. Playing nice didn't seem to matter to Agent McDonald, so my gloves came off. "I, too, don't work for the United States Attorney's Office," I responded, and I reminded him, in case he'd forgotten, that I didn't work for the FBI or the DOJ either. Gesturing to the door, I told him he was free to leave.

There was a moment of silence between us. He was weighing his options. He could stay and hear us out, knowing we didn't care about his status as an FBI agent, and deal with our lack of deference to him, or he could leave. I knew in actuality he had no real choice. He couldn't walk out. Not after a referral from the United States Attorney's Office. He knew I'd go right to the press and tell them that the FBI had simply walked out of the meeting. He had to at least hear us out. After a few moments of silence, he simply said, in a not-so-friendly tone, "Get on with it." So we did.

I was sure Agent McDonald didn't believe we had any evidence that could be taken seriously. Just another defense attempt to smear the good names of law enforcement agents with some wacky, unsubstantiated conspiracy theory. He'd heard it before. Agents McDonald and Felman, we thought, must have drawn the short end of the straw and were forced to come to our office to hear us out, but that didn't mean they had to like it. They had made that perfectly clear. I'm sure they were thinking that after meeting with us they could get back to the real business of catching criminals. While I had hoped for a better start to our relationship, it was not to be. Now I wanted him to eat his words.

*　*　*

We didn't know how much they'd been told. So we made our presentation as if they knew nothing. We walked them through Katherine's sworn statements claiming it was a Gaines mailbox that had been stolen from in front of her residence with a value of $380. We showed them Detective Akagi's report and how it matched, to a tee, the description contained on the Gaines website. We put up on the screen Detective Garcia's appraisal report that confirmed that the mailbox was, indeed, a Gaines mailbox valued at $375, used. I could see they were stealing glances at the two mailboxes placed before them on the table as we presented this evidence. Curiosity would work in our favor to keep their attention. Finally, one agent commented that, so far, we were only proving what they already knew, but I could tell they were beginning to suspect that something was going to go sideways soon. So we went sideways.

We showed the agents the photographs we had gathered from the Puana family and the Google Map images of the mailbox, the Solar Group mailbox, that had really been in front of the Kealohas' Kāhala residence. Now the agents understood why two mailboxes were on the conference table. These photographs proved that it was the second mailbox on the table, the Solar Group mailbox, that was stolen. We told them that one thing was for sure: no Gaines mailbox had been taken because no Gaines mailbox ever stood in front of the Kealohas' house. We had long ago come to the conclusion that the entire theft had been staged, and we wanted to convince the agents of this truth, or at least the possibility of this truth. We explained the testimony that Mr. Dryer and Mr. Slaugh had been prepared to give regarding the differences between the two mailboxes. We described, point by point, the distinguishing features between the two mailboxes so that the agents understood it was not simply an innocent mistake to have misidentified the mailboxes for one other.

Now the two agents were looking interested. We all stood up to take a closer look at the two mailboxes as we went over the distinguishing features: the different roofs; the two-toned color of the Gaines mailbox as opposed to the uniform color of the Solar Group mailbox; the red flag versus the gray flag; the fact that the pedestal in the crime scene photo, the one manufactured only by the Solar Group mailbox company, was clearly the pedestal in the photograph taken by Officers Rosskopf and Jurison, and lastly the noticeable weight difference between the two mailboxes. Excitement filled the room as it dawned on the two agents just how significant this was in proving that Gerard had been set up by the Kealohas and HPD. "Who lies about the kind of mailbox they have?" I rhetorically asked them.

We saved the best for last. It was time to show the agents the one piece of evidence in the crime scene photograph of the pedestal that we felt proved beyond a doubt that the entire theft was staged. We displayed the photograph of the pedestal and zoomed in on the top of the ¾" rod. The agents could now see the nut that had been placed several inches down from the top of the metal rod. We explained that Mr. Dryer had told us that no nut was supposed to be in that location. According to him, we told them, the mailbox could not have been removed as shown in the videotape surveillance without the rod either snapping in two or coming off at the base of the assembly. And, if that had happened, the mailbox would still be attached to the rod as it was carried away. But that was not what had happened. The rod had remained attached to the pedestal, not to the mailbox. I rhetorically asked the agents if it was still considered a "theft" if you steal your own mailbox?

To drive our point home, we disassembled the pedestal and put it back together, piece by piece, which we did on our hands and knees on the floor. The agents were on the floor with us as we assembled the Solar Group mailbox to its pedestal. When properly assembled, the entire unit tightens as the mailbox turns and screws securely onto the rod that runs from the mailbox down through the three pieces of the pedestal and into the base plate. Each turn tightens the pieces of the pedestal until the entire unit is solid from top to bottom. After we put the mailbox on the pedestal and assembled the unit as it was designed, we pulled on the mailbox. It didn't move an inch. No way that baby was coming off. You'd need a saw to separate the rod from the mailbox. And no saw was used in the taking of the mailbox.

We then took the mailbox off the pedestal and placed a nut on the metal rod in the same location as depicted in the crime scene photo. This time, when we placed the mailbox on top, it could only screw on a few turns before it hit the nut and could not tighten any further. The structure was not solid, but the mailbox didn't fall off. The mailbox just sat on the nut. We pulled again on the mailbox. Because it had taken a few turns on the rod before hitting the nut, it didn't lift straight off. It couldn't. It did, however, lift off if pulled at an angle. The exact same angle as shown in the videotape surveillance footage, slightly off to one side. The agents were now all in. Everyone was excited. It was like solving a puzzle. They got it. They understood what this meant. We could see that they were experiencing the "aha" moment that we had experienced months earlier, the sweet realization when it all clicks into place. It was a thrill when we had felt it, and it was exciting to see the agents experiencing it too.

We ended this part of our presentation by driving home the point that the Kealohas had lied about the make and value of the mailbox to ensure Gerard was charged with a felony rather than a misdemeanor offense under state law. They did this, we told them, because of the civil suit pending against Katherine. Another piece of the puzzle fell into place for the agents. There was no question the agents realized the significance of this fact, as they were well schooled in how a felony could be used to discredit a witness.

After this demonstration, the meeting became a much friendlier, smoother discussion as we walked the agents through all of the lies, inconsistencies and omissions we had uncovered. We made sure to point out that CIU officer Silva claimed he had recovered the hard drive from the Kealoha residence at 8:59 a.m., even though Katherine didn't call 911 until 1:29 p.m. We also discussed several leads we had uncovered during our investigation regarding other questionable activities by the Kealohas, which, for one reason or another, we had elected not to pursue when preparing for Gerard's trial. With limited resources and time, we only pursued evidence we felt would be useful and admissible at trial, but now we showed the agents everything we had found that we thought might be worth their time to follow up on.

One interesting fact we had uncovered was that on May 14, 2014, almost a year after Gerard's arrest, John Haina and Michael Cusumano, the two sergeants who had been in charge of CRU District 6—the police squad that had arrested Gerard—were named sergeants of the year by HPD. We learned that they were surfing pals of Louis and both served on the board of SHOPO, the police union, which had deviated from its normal practice and openly lobbied and supported Louis to become chief. We were also told that neither had been selected by the selection committee to receive the award but that either Louis or deputy chief McCauley had overridden the picks made by the selection committee and had named Haina and Cusumano as the winners. After we had been given this information by administrative personnel at HPD in emails, HPD tried to "take it back" by telling us that they shouldn't have released this information to us. It was a little too late for that. We had their emails to prove what they had told us.

We boxed up all our binders and gave them to the agents. We also gave them the two mailboxes. I would miss them. After a rough beginning to the meeting, we felt that the rest of the meeting had gone rather well, and we were optimistic, until we came to the conclusion of the meeting. Trust was still lacking between us. A three-hour meeting does not heal old wounds easily. I was still very much concerned that the FBI, or some high-level official, would squash the investigation. We fully understood that we were putting the FBI in a difficult position. We needed to keep the pressure on, and we wanted to maintain the upper hand. And I wanted to remind them whose field they were playing on.

I asked Agent McDonald how long he thought it would take to investigate the case. "No idea," he responded. Not good enough. I could already envision growing old and gray while the "investigation" lingered on, being told, "Don't worry, Mr. Silvert, it's moving along. Call back next year and we'll let you know." No, I was not going to let that happen.

"I'll give you three months," I told Agent McDonald. Somehow the agents were able to combine a look of disapproval and shock at the same time. I don't think anyone, other than their bosses, had dared give them a time limit; certainly never a defense attorney.

Agent McDonald responded with indignation, saying that it was now in "their hands" and it would take them as long as necessary.

"No," I responded. We might have turned the evidence over to them, but we were not going to lose control. I reminded the agents that we had already done more than a year's worth of investigation and compiled a ton of evidence for them, which gave them a tremendous head start, including critical witness interviews and statements. Using my best NCIS Agent Gibbs impersonation, I told them all they had to do was "put some suspects in a room and get them talking."

I knew this was an understatement of what needed to be done, but it certainly felt good saying it. Agent McDonald's dander was up. He was not going to be spoken to like this, certainly not by a defense attorney. But I wasn't about to let up, and I drove my point home before he could speak by playing my trump card. I told the agents that if I didn't see clear signs that the investigation was moving forward in three months' time, I would hold a press conference and release the evidence we had uncovered to the public. We would also publicly question why the FBI was sitting on it.

Agent McDonald, with a look of "no, you can't do that" on his face, said, "No, you can't do that." I reminded the agents that the evidence, in this case, was not theirs, but ours. This was not the usual situation, where the FBI had been the ones who had uncovered the evidence and could keep the investigation to themselves. *We* had compiled the evidence, and *we* were not going to play by *their* rules. I was hoping, through my antics, to convince him that I was a loose cannon and if he wanted to keep any control over the situation he was going to have to try and meet my demands.

At this point Agent Felman, in his role as the "good cop," stepped in. Agent Felman did not challenge my position but simply asked if we would wait four months before making a decision. He promised that at the end of four months they would contact us and give us a progress report. He assured me that if there were issues, they would have an open and honest discussion with us. I agreed. We shook hands this time, as they left the conference room with all of *our* evidence.

* * *

April came. Silence. Several more weeks passed. Nothing. Crickets. That was enough. I hadn't been bluffing. I would go public if necessary. On April 24 I called Agent McDonald. No answer. No return call. Five days later, I called again, and this time he answered. I asked about the status of the investigation. "I'm not at liberty to discuss with you the status of an ongoing FBI investigation," he said. I reminded him of our agreement. Agent McDonald maintained his position and his tone, indicating he was back in full FBI imperial mode. He thought, sitting in his nice office in the fortified FBI building in Kapolei, that he was back in control. That was not going to happen. I told him that unless someone in authority called me to tell me what was going on, I was calling a press conference the next day. Then I hung up. No reason to keep playing nice at this point since it sounded to me as if the investigation had been buried. I began to imagine my two mailboxes in a crate in the back of that Indiana Jones warehouse. Adam and I felt let down. Sure, we could go to the press and hope it would put public and political pressure on the FBI to explain their actions, but if the decision had already been made to bury the case, we could be at the end of the line. Little did we know that Agent McDonald actually was a "good cop." I had misread him.

Three minutes later I received a call from someone named Michael Wheat. He had a deep, authoritative voice. He identified himself as an assistant US attorney from the San Diego, California, office. He informed me that he was the special prosecutor assigned to the case. Although he worked for the San Diego office, he had been handpicked by then attorney general Eric Holder to investigate and prosecute this case. He reported only to the attorney general. He had, in essence, the same title and legal authority as special prosecutor Robert Mueller, who had been assigned to investigate Russia's alleged involvement in the 2016 presidential election, but without all the manpower. Wheat told me that he intended to "run this case to the ground" no matter where it led. I let those words sink in. *Run it to the ground!* Sounded damn good to me.

Wheat had been given the assignment because the FBI and the Hawai'i United States Attorney's Office had requested that an outside prosecutor be appointed, given all the possible conflicts of interest that could arise if the Honolulu office handled the investigation. This is standard procedure when a conflict of interest or the appearance of one could exist, as when conducting an investigation into people or organizations with which the local United States Attorney's Office interacts on a regular basis, such as the Honolulu Police Department and the City and County Prosecutor's Office in this case. Mr. Wheat assured me that not only was there an active investigation underway; it was vigorously moving forward. To further reassure us, Mr. Wheat asked that we meet and that I hold off talking to the press. I agreed.

I hung up the phone, a little stunned by the conversation. But in a good way. A very good way. I quickly informed Adam about the call. This short conversation with Mr. Wheat landed on us like a bombshell. Adam and I had experienced our fair share of cover-ups of police misconduct over the years, yet here we were. We went instantly from feeling we were being dissed by the FBI to total jubilation. We couldn't believe the investigation of the Kealohas and HPD was being taken seriously and was proceeding, that it was really happening and that Gerard and Florence might one day be vindicated.

"Run it to the ground," Wheat had said. And he sounded just like the type of guy who was going to do just that. ❖

CHAPTER 19

"It's a Sunny Day"

The time had come to meet Michael Wheat face-to-face. The principal purpose of the meeting for Wheat was to assess Gerard's credibility for himself. The principal purpose for us was to assess Wheat's credibility. It was July 23, 2015. It had been two months since I first spoke with Wheat on the telephone after having threatened the FBI that I would go public if I didn't feel the investigation was being taken seriously. We'd kept quiet so far. Now we were going to have the opportunity to get a feel for where things stood. Adam and I were still skeptical, but this was the next logical step in the process, so we'd agreed to go to the lion's den, the FBI office in Kapolei.

Kapolei is a planned community designed to become Oʻahu's "second city" to relieve Honolulu of being the focal point of government and jobs. It's still a work in progress. The FBI was the first and largest federal agency to take advantage of the large tracts of open land in Kapolei to build their very own offices. And that's where we were headed, against the flow of traffic.

The FBI building is an impressive fortress, surrounded by walls and fences, with armed guards at the entrance. United States flags flutter in the wind. Even after we passed through the initial security screening, we had to pass through locked doors and additional security clearances to go from one corridor to the next. Cameras stared down at us from every angle, recording our every move.

We were eventually ushered into a nondescript conference room. A recording device sat precisely in the center of a way-too-large conference table, cameras again in each corner of the room peering down at us. We knew each word would be monitored by some other humorless agent in another room. It was, to say the least, an intimidating home-field advantage.

Prior to meeting with Wheat, Adam, being the ever vigilant and inquisitive person that he was, did some research to help us figure out just who this "special prosecutor" was. Was he to be taken seriously, or had he taken the case just to get free trips to Hawai'i? We learned that Wheat had been a prosecutor for some thirty years in the San Diego United States Attorney's Office and had handled a variety of important criminal prosecutions, from drug smuggling and human trafficking cases to major corruption investigations. The case that drew our attention, however, was Wheat's public corruption prosecution in 2005 of the acting mayor of San Diego and several county councilmen. Wheat had obtained convictions against several of these powerful politicians for performing political favors for a local strip club owner who was donating to their campaigns. The case was known in San Diego as "Strippergate." To gain more personal insight into Wheat's character, we also called several defense attorneys in San Diego who had dealt with him. They all said he was a hardworking career prosecutor who could be trusted. No-nonsense and a straight shooter. We were heartened by Wheat's prosecutorial pedigree, but that didn't mean that he wasn't going to succumb to Hawai'i's beauty and end up just taking a mid-career hiatus. We would soon see.

Wheat was waiting for us in the conference room. He was wearing a white dress shirt, but I immediately noticed he wasn't wearing a tie. I liked that. I took it as a good sign that he wasn't a total stuffed shirt. Wheat introduced himself and the two FBI agents in the room. Fresh faces. They sat on one side while we sat across from them on the other side. Several folders were on the table between us. After a few pleasantries, Wheat got right to business. He told us that he was completely familiar with the evidence we had uncovered and that their own investigation was underway and had been for some months now.

Wheat crossed over to our side of the table, another good sign, and opened up several of the folders and started asking Gerard detailed questions elaborating on some facts Wheat wanted to know more about. Gerard would answer and Wheat would nod his head in satisfaction. Or Wheat would ask for a more detailed explanation, building upon the facts that Gerard had already supplied. This exchange lasted for about a half an hour, but it spoke volumes to us. First, I recognized that some of the dialogue between Wheat and Gerard was simply designed to test Gerard's credibility, in that Wheat would ask questions that he knew the answer to just to see if Gerard gave the correct response. Wheat's nodding head and follow-up questions indicated to me that Gerard was doing just fine. But more importantly, this conversation demonstrated that Wheat was on it. He knew his facts. He knew details. He was not bullshitting us when he said he was completely familiar with the evidence. As Adam would later point out to me with a smile, Wheat didn't need an agent, or Adam, to correct him or remind him of the facts and dates; he knew them all. Wheat had also pronounced all the Hawaiian words correctly, as Adam made sure to tell me with a smile that was slightly wider than the first. I was duly impressed by Wheat's performance, which I also thought was one of Wheat's objectives, since he knew we would have to build trust between us in order for his investigation to move forward with our cooperation.

And then it came. That unexpected moment. Wheat, in a rather matter-of-fact tone, stood up and said they were now ready to give Gerard a polygraph test and that he should follow the agent into another room to get started. This caught me by complete surprise. I knew that at some point Gerard would take a polygraph examination, but I thought that would be after we were prepared and had negotiated the questions and the format. Certainly not during our very first meeting. At least, that was my thinking. I always tried to control, as much as I could, the conditions under which one of my clients took a polygraph, knowing how quickly it could become an interrogation session. Most importantly, while the case against Gerard had been dismissed, and while I certainly believed he didn't commit the crime, how did I know for sure? There was a big difference between my belief that Gerard hadn't stolen the mailbox and Gerard actually passing a polygraph examination. I believed he was innocent. I believed he was framed. But how could I know for sure? In my mind, the difference between my belief and Gerard passing a polygraph was the size of the Grand Canyon.

I looked at Gerard. He showed no signs of hesitation at all. He didn't even bother to check with me; he just said, "Let's do it, bro," then got up and walked out of the room with the agent. That left Adam and me in the room with Wheat and gave us a chance to talk about the case privately. We didn't necessarily trust one another yet, and talking about the case was the safest way to get to know one another. But Wheat was not about to disclose, at least not openly, his investigation or any new evidence the FBI had gathered. And Adam and I wanted to know. We played a cat and mouse game, talking about different pieces of evidence with Wheat and trying to glean new information from the discussion. For my part, I wanted to assure myself that Wheat understood each piece of evidence we had uncovered, its importance and how the pieces interconnected with one another. This was particularly important in terms of understanding who each HPD police officer was, in which department within HPD they worked and how they were connected to either Louis or Katherine Kealoha. It became clear through our discussion that Wheat not only knew most of the connections we had learned about, but he had also made his own discoveries that went far beyond our knowledge.

Whenever I asked Wheat whether he had made a particular connection and understood its significance, if it was based upon information we had already provided to the FBI we would engage in a discussion about it. However, when I sensed he knew more and asked him about it, he simply smiled and said, "It's a sunny day, isn't it?" And that became his catchphrase from then on. Whenever I wanted to make sure Wheat was following up on a lead or had made a connection between different pieces of evidence, he'd simply say, "It's a sunny day, isn't it?" and I would know he was hot on the trail.

After about an hour Gerard returned. The FBI agent told us he had passed the polygraph examination. No deception whatsoever. He had specifically been asked if he stole the mailbox or if someone else had stolen the mailbox for him. "No" had been his truthful response.

I let out a sigh, hoping no one heard or saw it. It would certainly not look good for Gerard to see his own defense attorney let out a sigh of relief. But Wheat saw it and simply said, "Did you have any doubt? We knew he was going to pass."

I asked Wheat how he could possibly have known for sure? Gerard had no clear alibi. Gerard said he was home all night, but his friend who was visiting from out of town had been asleep in the upstairs bedroom and had gone to bed well before the time the mailbox was stolen. We couldn't prove Gerard's whereabouts on the night of June 21, 2013. So how could Wheat be so sure? Unless, we realized, the FBI had already developed evidence that proved to their satisfaction Gerard could not have committed the crime! Maybe they had done cellular tower tracking of his phone? All Wheat said in response to my probing questions was, "It's a sunny day, isn't it?" I could tell by the fact that Wheat's grin grew a bit wider that he was having fun playing with this mouse. I would see that same grin again years later.

Gerard took it all in stride. He knew he didn't do it. He didn't even sense that the polygraph examination could have been a trap.

Later, back at our office, Adam and I met to digest and discuss what had just transpired. We were both relieved and extremely happy that

Gerard had passed the polygraph. That was a big moment. We had been working on the case since July 2013. Now, more than two years later, having endured many of our friends and colleagues telling us that we were just "conspiracy nuts" like Mel Gibson in the movie *Conspiracy Theory*, the FBI and a special prosecutor not only believed our story but appeared to be well on their way to putting together a case. Adam conveyed my own sentiments when he blurted out that Wheat was "a fucking prosecutor!" And that was meant, for the first time in our lives, as a compliment. We needed "a fucking prosecutor" on our side. We went over each conversation, trying to squeeze out what new piece of evidence the FBI might have uncovered from the cryptic but meaningful "It's a sunny day" replies Wheat had made. We knew the FBI had resources and investigative abilities far beyond our limited resources. But Wheat's statement that he had no doubt that Gerard would pass the polygraph examination was the one event of the day we kept going back to because it implied so much. It meant not only did they know Gerard did not steal the mailbox, but they also believed someone else did. Wheat and the FBI had come to the same conclusion we had, that there had been a conspiracy to frame an innocent man. The questions now were who exactly these people were and whether Wheat could uncover enough evidence to prove it.

The realization that the case was now really out of our hands was bittersweet. We had gotten exactly what we had asked for. We had wanted a serious, take-no-prisoners, damn-the-political-consequences investigation, and it appeared that was going to happen. It was now up to Wheat. Only time would tell whether our initial assessment of him would be proven right or whether our cynicism about the system would, once again, sadly, be proven true,

Years later, I asked Wheat why he had taken the case in the first place. He told me it was because he had seen other corruption investigations wither on the vine and die from inaction, and he wanted to make sure this investigation didn't suffer the same fate. Over the next several years, as his investigation went on and on and on, I came to thoroughly enjoy being told by Wheat "It's a sunny day" over and over again as he uncovered more and more evidence. When he started responding by saying, "It's a *very* sunny day," I knew that something was about to happen. And it did, in ways far beyond anything Adam, Gerard or I could have imagined back in July of 2013 when Gerard sat in my office and declared, to our disbelief, that he was framed. There was no disbelief now. It was truly going to be "a very sunny day." ❖

CHAPTER 20

The Long Wait

T o investigate the events surrounding Gerard's arrest and prosecution, the first grand jury was empaneled in September of 2015, less than two months after we had first met Wheat and Gerard had successfully passed his polygraph examination. While the grand jury process is secretive, in that neither the grand jurors themselves nor the prosecutors are allowed to disclose what is testified, witnesses who appear before the grand jury are not themselves sworn to secrecy and are free to discuss their testimony with whomever they like. Any member of the public can wait outside the grand jury room and watch who enters. In some big metropolitan cities, Mexican cartels and organized crime figures hire people to do just this to see if there are any ongoing investigations into their illegal activities and, more importantly, who may be ratting them out. Not so in Hawai'i. The only people watching outside the grand jury room were members of the press.

As Wheat's investigation developed and became more far-reaching, Lynn Kawano of Hawaii News Now, and sometimes Nick Grube of Civil Beat and Jennifer Sinco Kelleher of the Associated Press, began to sit outside the entrance to the grand jury room watching who came and went. They sat uncomfortably on the hard, white Italian marble floor of the federal courthouse waiting for Wheat and his witnesses to parade before them. Chief judge Michael J. Seabright finally took pity on them and had a wooden bench set up so they wouldn't have to sit on the floor. No soft cushions, but it was better than journalists sitting on the floor, laptops, lunch bags and water bottles strewn about. That was too unsightly for the federal courthouse, not to mention making scratches on the brand-new marble floor.

I—The Offensive

After the mistrial and the dismissal of Gerard's case, the Kealohas and their allies went on the offensive. In February of 2015 Katherine won the civil case brought by Gerard and Florence regarding the reverse mortgage and Katherine's alleged mishandling of funds. This likely served to further embolden the Kealohas. Florence and Gerard had hired their own attorney for the civil case, and while we had shared information with him, he had made his own decisions as to how he presented the evidence in that case. Just as we'd predicted, Katherine tried to introduce evidence in the civil case that Gerard had stolen her mailbox, even though he was never convicted. The state court judge didn't allow it. But even without this evidence, the jury ruled in Katherine's favor. By all accounts, when Katherine took the stand, she won over the jury. Unfortunately, the false statements she made in the mailbox case that we had uncovered were not used against her. It appeared to have been a very one-sided affair, with the jury believing everything Katherine testified to under oath. The jury found Katherine to be a credible witness and found in favor of Katherine and against Gerard and Florence Puana. Katherine was awarded $658,787.66 in punitive damages, with another $18,523.41 in costs plus attorney fees.

This was a devastating blow to Gerard but even more so for Florence, who now had not only lost her home but owed Katherine hundreds of thousands of dollars. Worse, the verdict strongly suggested that everything Florence and Gerard had alleged about Katherine's conduct was a lie. That Florence and Gerard were simply besmirching Katherine's good name to cover up for their own financial failings. Gerard could not believe the jury didn't see through Katherine's lies. But I knew that juries are often unpredictable and that a trial can be a crapshoot. If a jury believes one important witness, it can choose to ignore all the other evidence suggesting otherwise. It isn't right and it doesn't seem fair, but it happens more often than one would like to believe.

We were appalled that Katherine had been able to con the state jury. What made things worse was that even if Katherine was ever charged and convicted of framing Gerard, it was hard to see, in legal terms, how the verdict in the civil case would be overturned. Her framing of Gerard did not mean the verdict in the civil case was legally wrong and would be reversed. It did not mean that Katherine had necessarily done anything improper in how she had conducted the reverse mortgage deal. The only thing we could hope for was to bring Katherine to justice and have the world see her for what she really was, a criminal and a con artist. Now it was not only about vindicating Gerard; it was also about vindicating Florence, a ninety-five-year-old grandmother whose own granddaughter had stolen everything she had, including her dignity. I personally felt a great deal of responsibility to bring the Kealohas to justice for what they had done to Gerard and Florence, but that responsibility now rested entirely on the shoulders of Wheat and the FBI. My job was to assist in any way I could to keep their investigation moving forward. I was confident that, through Wheat's investigation, Katherine would eventually be exposed as the liar she really was.

As part of their continuing offensive, over the course of the next several years the Kealohas filed three civil suits against the City and County of Honolulu Ethics Commission, in particular attacking its executive director, Chuck Totto, and his investigator, retired HPD captain Letha DeCaires. Totto and DeCaires were pursuing fifteen separate ethical violation investigations against the Kealohas. The Kealohas alleged that Totto and DeCaires were maliciously and falsely pursuing investigations against them for personal or political reasons and should be disqualified and removed from the investigations. If the Kealohas were successful in having Totto and DeCaires removed, they knew it would kill the investigations. Unfortunately, they were indeed successful yet again.

City and County managing director Roy Amemiya refused to renew investigator DeCaires's contract in September 2015, forcing her to retire and leaving the Ethics Commission with no investigators. Mayor Caldwell appointed three former state judges to the commission in March 2016, and along with the other members of the commission, they immediately imposed strict limitations on Totto's activities as executive director, in part due to the complaints made by the Kealohas. On June 15, 2016, Totto resigned, stating he couldn't effectively work under the newly imposed conditions. This left all of the Ethics Commission's multiple investigations into the Kealohas unresolved, a status that astonishingly remains to this very day, more than five years later, with no explanation from the Ethics Commission as to why.

Luckily, before Totto and DeCaires were removed from their positions at the Ethics Commission, they had unknowingly uncovered an important lie perpetrated by Louis. On September 24, 2014, Louis had told the press that he had turned the mailbox investigation over to McCauley, his deputy chief of police, and that she had turned the case over to the CIU. DeCaires, as part of the investigation into potential ethical violations by the Kealohas, deposed McCauley on May 28, 2015, five months after Gerard's trial. McCauley testified, under oath, that Louis had *not* put her in charge of the investigation and, in fact, had never even told her about the mailbox theft until weeks later. McCauley testified that in June of 2013 she wasn't even in the United States. She was in France, on vacation, with no contact number—a fact that Louis had to have known, considering she was his deputy chief of police. McCauley didn't learn of the mailbox theft until she returned home several weeks later. We didn't know this fact in December 2014 when we went to trial, but we had subpoenaed McCauley to be one of our witnesses, intending to question her about Louis's statement to the press that he had contacted her and told her about the mailbox theft on the evening of June 21. I've wondered to this day what she would have said on the stand. We'll never know. I can only imagine the impact her testimony would have had on the jury.

On the public relations front, in his capacity as chief of police, in April 2016 Louis authorized the Honolulu Police Department to hire a private PR firm at a cost of $100,000 to improve HPD's image. Or was the $100,000 of taxpayers' money to improve *his* image? Then, KHON television news, a Fox News affiliate, aired a three-part interview with the Kealohas starting on April 27, 2016. The Kealohas were interviewed sitting in the kitchen of their home, dressed in matching red-flowered aloha-print outfits. The interviewer, Gina Mangieri, wore similar red attire. The kitchen was spotless, as if never used. A collection of all-white porcelain dolls lined the kitchen cabinets behind the Kealohas as they spoke, creating an eerie image as Katherine vehemently proclaimed that the couple had never used their positions for personal gain or for a vendetta, as that would be "totally unethical." Katherine further declared that she was extremely confident that the allegations were unfounded and that the attacks against her and her husband were racially motivated because they were Hawaiian, a theme the Kealohas would carry forward in their defense for years to come. Katherine asserted that if she had done anything wrong, she'd resign, but she doubted she or her husband would ever be indicted. The Kealohas' newly hired criminal defense attorney, Myles Breiner, however, contradicted Katherine's assertion, stating to the press that the Kealohas fully expected to be indicted because prosecutors could "indict a dead horse," calling the federal grand jury proceedings a "dog and pony show" designed to intimidate witnesses.

The Honolulu Police Commission, the civilian oversight organization that has the power to hire and fire the chief of police, continued to fully support Louis despite calls from the public that it was not taking the allegations against Chief Kealoha seriously enough. The commission refused to conduct any investigation into the allegations, saying it had "asked" Chief Kealoha if everything was all right, to which Louis simply assured them there was nothing to any of the allegations. That appeared to be the extent of the inquiry by the public's principal oversight commission. This was the same commission that had renewed Louis's term one year earlier than was required and had given him the highest ratings possible for his leadership of HPD. Honolulu mayor Caldwell, who appointed the police commissioners, also continued to express his full confidence in the Police Commission's handling of the situation, agreeing that no action should be taken unless Chief Kealoha was indicted.

Nick Grube of Civil Beat interviewed Katherine at the same time that she made her KHON television appearance. Katherine proclaimed that "the one thing that I have on my side are facts, and that's the one thing people are going to have a damn hard time disputing." In a stunning statement, Katherine, a state prosecutor for most of her legal career, told Grube:

> I've lived my entire life going into law, being in justice, believing in the system, believing that the system is good and it works. And I can tell you firsthand that I feel like our system doesn't work. If people think I'm a hypocrite for saying it now, then so be it because I just didn't see it before.

At the time Katherine made this statement she was still actively serving as a prosecutor, arresting and convicting defendants as head of the Career Offender Unit of the Prosecuting Attorney's Office. I did think she was a "hypocrite." It was hard to see it any other way.

City and County prosecuting attorney Keith Kaneshiro, Katherine's boss, and HPD deputy chief of police McCauley, Chief Kealoha's second-in-charge, both testified before the federal grand jury for the first time on May 19, 2016. Over the course of the year, both would go on to make multiple appearances before the grand jury. Kaneshiro, a day after his initial appearance before the grand jury, appeared on local TV news bashing special prosecutor Wheat for his handling of the federal grand jury, claiming that the investigation was nothing more than a "fishing expedition." Kaneshiro, continuing his verbal assault, stated he was "appalled by what's going on in the federal grand jury" and it had "spiraled out of control, it is a circus. It is a parade…which is unfair, not impartial, and it defies all principles of justice in our criminal justice system." Kaneshiro refused to comply with a subpoena requiring him to turn over documents relating to Katherine and filed a motion to quash the subpoena. His motion was denied.

Soon after, Kaneshiro, on behalf of his office, and Myles Breiner, on behalf of the Kealohas, filed motions seeking to disqualify Wheat as the prosecutor and to dismiss the grand jury proceedings in their entirety on the basis that they were being conducted improperly and in a biased manner. The Kealohas were trying to employ the same strategy they had successfully employed against Totto and DeCaires in the Ethics Commission investigation. This time, however, this strategy failed, as the Kealohas were now dealing with a federal judge appointed for life and a special prosecutor assigned specifically to investigate them by the United States attorney general, not volunteer commissioners appointed by a mayor. The motions were denied. I was later told that the federal judge, in denying the motions, actually yelled at the attorneys for Kaneshiro and the Kealohas, saying that the motions were frivolous. Kaneshiro's refusal to cooperate voluntarily with the grand jury investigation and his very public attacks against Wheat and the FBI were unprecedented. I questioned why Kaneshiro would be taking such inexplicable legal positions in defense of Katherine Kealoha, positions that I knew had no basis in the law and would effectively jeopardize any further working relationship between federal and City and County of Honolulu law enforcement agencies.

If that were not enough, Katherine, on June 22, 2016, wrote a letter to Kaneshiro that she later released to the public. In it, Katherine claimed that any reasonable person, "after a careful review" of the allegations being made against her and her husband, would conclude they were total *shibai*, lies. She further asserted that the federal trial against Gerard had been bungled by incompetent United States attorneys who would have been fired had they worked in the prosecutor's office. A state prosecutor attacking a federal prosecutor, a more powerful colleague, broke new territory. As a defense attorney, watching this play out simply brought a smile to my face, as I knew who was going to win this battle.

II—The Tide Begins to Turn

Mayor Caldwell, in the face of mounting criticism over the failure of the Police Commission to take action as well as his own unwillingness to step in, appointed Loretta Sheehan as a new commissioner on June 3, 2016. Sheehan was a former City and County deputy prosecutor and assistant US attorney before she entered private civil practice in a prestigious local law firm. She was well respected, and her appointment was lauded by the community. Prior to her appointment, the commission did not have a single member who had practiced criminal law or who had any law enforcement background whatsoever. All the sitting commissioners were either in tourism, the restaurant and entertainment industries or private business. All had one thing in common: significant political connections. The commission's chairman, Ron Taketa, was head of the Hawai'i Regional Council of Carpenters, one of the largest construction trade groups in Hawai'i, whose union was instrumental in Mayor Caldwell's re-election. Sheehan soon became an outspoken critic of the Police Commission's handling of its oversight duties and openly questioned Louis during the commission's monthly meetings, a hitherto unknown occurrence. Police commission meetings, broadcast live on Civil Beat's webpage, became must-see internet TV. Needless to say, Sheehan's refreshing style and attitude, although popular with the general public, was not warmly received by her fellow commissioners, who preferred to conduct most of their business in secret executive sessions.

Bill Harrison, a local prominent defense attorney, was hired to represent now retired CIU officer Niall Silva. On September 8, 2016, he acknowledged that Silva had received a "target letter" from the FBI on August 31. Silva was the first person known to have received a target letter, but he would not be the last. A "target," according to the *United States Attorneys' Manual*, is a person whom a prosecutor has substantial evidence linking to the commission of a crime and who, in the judgement of the prosecutor, is a possible defendant. A target letter does not have to be issued by a prosecutor before they can arrest or charge a defendant. It acts as an invitation to a defendant to get a lawyer and to enter into talks with the prosecutor to resolve their potential criminal liability without the formal necessity of being indicted by the grand jury. Breiner, the Kealohas' attorney, on the other hand, told the press that the issuance of the target letter merely indicated that the feds were having a hard time getting people to implicate the Kealohas and were simply employing "pressure tactics."

Gerard testified before the grand jury on September 22, 2016. While a grand jury witness has the right to an attorney, that attorney (in this case me) cannot go into the grand jury room with their client. If Gerard wanted to talk to me during his testimony, he had to first ask to consult with me before answering a particular question, leave the room, speak with me and return alone to answer the question based upon the advice I had given him. I sat in the grand jury waiting room doing just that, waiting. Gerard never came out to speak with me, though I hadn't really expected him to. When he finally emerged from the grand jury room, he simply grinned at me and said, "All good." Wheat came out and gave me the thumbs-up signal. No need to tell me "It's a sunny day." I already knew it was.

III—The Ball Starts Rolling

On December 15, 2016, Silva entered a guilty plea to conspiracy to obstruct justice. He was the first person officially charged in the case and the first to admit there was a conspiracy to frame Gerard. It was a breakthrough moment in Wheat's investigation. Although the co-conspirators were left "unnamed" in his charging document and plea agreement, a common practice when evidence is still being developed against other individuals, the facts describing the conspiracy made it clear *who* these "unnamed co-conspirators" were. One was clearly Katherine Kealoha. Another was Bobby Nguyen. Adam and I were in the courtroom as Silva pleaded guilty, as were Police Commissioner Sheehan and newly appointed commissioner Steve Levinson, a former Hawaiʻi Supreme Court judge. Standing before federal magistrate judge Kevin Chang, Silva admitted that he lied under oath at Gerard's trial, since *he never even went* to the Kealoha residence to retrieve the videotape surveillance footage on the morning of June 22. It was Bobby Nguyen who went to the house, retrieved the hard drive and brought it to CIU. Silva admitted that the paperwork he prepared certifying that he had retrieved the hard drive and checked that the videotape equipment was functioning properly, as he had testified at Gerard's trial under oath, was entirely fabricated.

Silva also admitted that he had been instructed by his CIU supervisor, CIU lieutenant and later acting CIU captain Derek Hahn, to omit that it was Bobby who had retrieved the hard drive and instead to write that he had done it. Hahn had been handpicked and promoted by Louis to work in CIU. Silva stated that before and after his trial testimony he was in contact with Bobby to inform him that he had "stuck to the story." This was a clear violation of a court order that prohibits witnesses from talking to one another during trial. Discussion between witnesses who have not yet testified is prohibited precisely so that a witness does not alter their testimony to match what another witness has already testified to. Further, Silva claimed it was Hahn who had instructed him to copy only a portion of the videotape and place only that edited portion into evidence, rather than the entire videotape hard drive.

In an astounding revelation, the FBI would later discover that while we were in the process of obtaining and serving our subpoena to obtain the hard drive in mid-2014, CIU technicians had started the process of videotaping over the *entire* hard drive so that all of the video footage of the mailbox, before and after the one hour that we had been given, was destroyed. The camera was intentionally left on as it filmed the ceiling of the CIU office in the heart of HPD headquarters for six full days. Videotaping over the hard drive, as opposed to simply erasing the footage, made it impossible to recover the underlying original footage. It appears that CIU anticipated we would be seeking a subpoena after we had made several informal requests inquiring whether there was more videotape evidence than what we had been given. CIU's actions ensured we would never get that evidence.

Silva was asked what he thought when he saw Gerard in the flesh for the first time at Gerard's trial, and Silva testified, "I was very upset because when I saw Gerard Puana, who was the supposed suspect…like, that is not him in the video cuz he is one thick guy, no neck. The guy in the video is like scrawny. It was like no way it was him, and my heart sank." When asked why his heart sank, he replied, "I perpetuated a lie, and it was against somebody who wasn't guilty." Perhaps his heart did sink, but it hadn't prevented Silva from lying throughout his testimony in Gerard's trial, as he sat looking at the man whom he supposedly then knew hadn't committed the crime. I didn't feel sorry for him, not one bit.

As Silva was leaving the courtroom, he abruptly turned towards us to shake my hand. When Silva first reached out his hand, I took a step backward because I wasn't sure of his intentions. After all, he'd just pleaded guilty and was facing jail time because of our actions. As he shook my hand, he told us he was "sorry" for not telling us the truth earlier on. Adam interjected, telling Silva that he had, on several occasions, tried to interview him prior to Gerard's trial but Silva had repeatedly refused to talk with him. Adam pointed out to Silva that he could have "told us the truth" then. Silva responded with a blank stare and simply turned and walked out of the courtroom.

"What the heck was that?" Adam said, turning to me. I was speechless. I had never before been thanked by a person who just pled guilty to a crime that we had helped uncover and expose. It was, once again, another first for us in this very, very strange case.

A few days after Silva pled guilty, Louis received a target letter of his own from Wheat. On December 19 Louis placed himself on restrictive paid leave but did not step down as chief.

On January 6, 2017, due to mounting criticism that Louis had not been forced to resign and was still being paid by the City and County of Honolulu taxpayers despite receiving a target letter, Louis negotiated his retirement with the Police Commission. Through his civil attorney, Kevin Sumida, Louis received a $250,000 cash buyout and, because he was allowed to retire in good standing, he was also entitled to receive his full pension benefits, worth $150,000 per year. Roughly $9,700 a month after taxes. Had Louis not been allowed to retire in good standing, he would not have received any pension monies at all. Multiply $150,000 by ten or twenty years, and it would result in a savings of millions of dollars to the taxpayers of the City and County of Honolulu. The agreement, however, did require that Louis pay back the cash buyout of $250,000 if he was convicted of a felony offense within six years. There were no provisions in the agreement to ensure that Louis could not file for bankruptcy and eliminate this obligation entirely. Only police commissioner Loretta Sheehan voted against the agreement. Sheehan demanded that Chief Kealoha be dismissed "for cause," with no cash buyout. When Sheehan pressed for changes to the agreement, she was told by Donna Leong, the head civil attorney of the City's Corporation Counsel, and by Max Sword, the chair of the Police Commission, that the deal was not negotiable. It was a done deal.

In response to public outrage over the terms of the agreement, including from some members of the City and County of Honolulu City Council, Max Sword pointedly told the City Council to stay out of it. Donna Leong stood alongside Chairman Sword in defense of the agreement. Later, Ms. Leong would receive a target letter from the FBI, allegedly for misconduct in how the $250,000 was paid out of city funds. It was only after Lynn Kawano of Hawaii News Now aired the fact that Leong had received a target letter a week earlier that Mayor Caldwell placed her on paid leave.

In spite of all these events, on January 3, 2017, Kaneshiro placed Katherine in charge of a newly created unit in his office tasked with going after criminals who targeted tourists. The mayor announced that he intended to talk with Kaneshiro regarding Katherine's status as a prosecutor, to which Kaneshiro responded that he didn't work for the mayor and that it was none of the mayor's business how he conducted his office. Sound familiar?

In an unprecedented move, on January 13, 2017, the FBI, armed with federal search warrants, raided Katherine's and Kaneshiro's offices. They seized documents and computers relating to Katherine's alleged illegal activities. Simultaneously, and in coordination with the search of Kaneshiro's office, FBI agents raided the Frank Fasi Municipal Building in downtown Honolulu and seized backup computers for the Honolulu Police Department. It was not known what the FBI was looking for or why such evidence was suspected to be at these locations. However, the fact that the FBI believed it was necessary to obtain search warrants and conduct surprise raids on fellow law enforcement offices suggested that this extreme measure was done out of fear that evidence might be tampered with. These unannounced raids indicated that the relationship between the FBI and Wheat, on the one hand, and HPD and Kaneshiro, on the other, had gone from frosty to bitterly ice cold. This determined effort to get at the truth was far beyond anything I could have imagined would be politically possible, and it appeared to me that Wheat and the FBI were taking no prisoners. Wheat was being true to his word—he was "running it to the ground." ❖

CHAPTER 21

Indicted...and So Much More

Ten months later, on October 19, 2017, it finally happened. The front page of the *Honolulu Star-Advertiser*, in three-inch capital letters, proclaimed simply, "INDICTED." In the foreground, behind that one explosive word, taking up the entire top fold of the newspaper, was a photograph of Katherine and Louis Kealoha wearing matching aloha attire and flower lei as they walked away from the federal courthouse, arm in arm, after having been arraigned and released on bond on conspiracy charges to obstruct justice and to violate Gerard's civil rights. Lei are traditionally worn to celebrate festive occasions, not for being criminally indicted. The picture of the Kealohas leaving the courthouse wearing lei, waving and smiling to the assembled press, was not well received by the public.

CIU officers Derek Hahn, Bobby Nguyen, Gordon Shiraishi and Daniel Sellers, all named as co-conspirators with the Kealohas, had been arrested over the course of several days leading up to the arrest and arraignment of the Kealohas themselves. It was a momentous step in the case. United States attorney Alana Robinson, the head of Wheat's office, flew in from San Diego and held a press conference on the courthouse steps. Flanked by a team of deputy US attorneys; Wheat, the Hawaiʻi FBI special agent in charge; and acting HPD chief Cary Okimoto; Robinson stated:

> This is just the beginning…. The 20-count indictment describes a complex web of fraud, deception and obstruction by a husband-and-wife team so desperate to fund their lifestyle and maintain their self-professed status as Honolulu's power couple that they swindled hundreds of thousands of dollars from banks, credit unions and some of the most vulnerable members of the

community.… But the most troubling aspect of this case is the way these powerful defendants allegedly manipulated the justice system for their own purposes.… The Kealohas used their considerable power and influence as public officials to launch a secret campaign to cover up their financial crimes and to discredit their victims with the help of a few friends from [the] elite Criminal Intelligence Unit.

FBI agent in charge Paul Delacourt added that "what [the indictment] makes clear is this is far more than a case about a stolen mailbox."

The forty-two-page indictment alleged that the members of the conspiracy used their law enforcement positions to frame Gerard in order to cover up financial crimes committed by the Kealohas that Gerard's civil lawsuit might have exposed, just as we had alleged at Gerard's trial. But the FBI had also been able to piece together text messages and phone calls between some of the co-conspirators that showed them communicating with each other at critical points in the conspiracy. And Silva, a member of the conspiracy, was cooperating with the investigation.

These sensational charges included allegations that in 2011, Katherine, along with Bobby Nguyen, unlawfully entered Gerard's residence, after

Left to right: Defendants Gordon Shiraishi, Derek Hahn,
Bobby Nguyen and Daniel Sellers

he was arrested for unlawful entry into his neighbor's house, and stole over $25,000 in cash, along with other personal items, from Gerard's home office. In order to silence Gerard and cover up her theft, Katherine told family members that they should not bail Gerard out of jail and should have no contact with him because he was a drug addict. Gerard was not a drug addict. He spent seventy-one days in jail before his family would even accept a phone call from him and bail him out.

Louis and Katherine were also indicted on bank fraud charges for falsifying information on several bank loans. Katherine was separately charged with identity theft for illegally using the identity of a female police officer to further her bank fraud scheme. These charges included additional allegations that Katherine had stolen another $167,000 from a trust fund belonging to Ransen and Ariana Taito, Katherine's niece and nephew. The trust fund had been established for Ransen and his sister when they were ten and twelve years old from a medical malpractice lawsuit involving their deceased father. It was to be disbursed when they turned eighteen. Katherine was a co-trustee, along with attorney and co-trustee Jim Bickerton. Katherine not only stole and spent all the monies from the trust fund over an eight-year period, but she also claimed the trust fund monies as her own and altered bank records in order to inflate her personal net worth to obtain personal bank loans. When the Taitos came of age, Katherine falsely told them that she had given all the money to their drug-addicted mother and, if they told this to anyone, their mother would go to jail. Katherine convinced both Ransen and his sister to falsify documents that Katherine had prepared and to lie to Wheat's grand jury to testify that they had, in fact, received the monies owed to them from the trust. Katherine even hired the Taitos an attorney, Jacob Delaplane, to represent them when they went before the grand jury. Delaplane was a former deputy prosecutor who worked directly under

Katherine and had been involved in the prosecution of a gambling case that ended up being dismissed, twice, by a state court judge for prosecutorial misconduct allegedly committed by Katherine. It is not believed Delaplane knew of Katherine's criminal behavior concerning the Taitos.

But this story gets even stranger. When the Taitos turned eighteen, co-trustee Jim Bickerton inquired of Katherine as to the status of the funds. As co-trustee, he was legally required to ensure the monies were properly disbursed. In response, Katherine's secretary, Alison Lee Wong, left phone messages assuring Bickerton that all was well and the monies had been disbursed to the Taitos. But there was one problem. Alison Lee Wong *was not a real person*. The government alleged that Katherine had created Alison Lee Wong out of thin air. Alison Lee Wong was an alias. The FBI discovered that Katherine had ordered and received a notary stamp in the name of Alison Lee Wong so she, meaning Alison Lee Wong, could notarize any document Katherine desired. Using this false persona, Alison Lee Wong notarized a number of false documents created by Katherine and served as an intermediary to fend off adverse inquiries questioning Katherine's conduct. Alison Lee Wong even wrote a character letter to the Hawai'i Legislature in support of Katherine's nomination as director of the Office of Environmental and Quality Control. To portray Alison Lee Wong as a real person, Katherine even created a fake Facebook page under the name Alison Lee Wong and sent emails to various people acting as if Alison Lee Wong had met them at some social function. Everyone agreed that we all needed a "friend" like Alison Lee Wong, and some people joked that T-shirts should be made in her honor. People had already been making homemade mailboxes with the name "Kealoha" written on them as Halloween costumes, so why not an Alison Lee Wong costume?

On October 25, 2017, the Honolulu Police Commission announced the appointment of Major Susan Ballard as Honolulu's eleventh police chief and the first woman to lead the department. Ballard, a thirty-two-year veteran of the police department, promised to bring more transparency and to restore trust and faith in the Department.

Then, unexpectedly, the US marshal retired on November 13, 2017. No specific reasons were given for his retirement. There were rumors he had provided improper special treatment to Kaneshiro and deputy chief of police McCauley when he had allowed them to use the secured underground parking entrance to the federal courthouse to avoid being photographed. Even though they were in a car with tinted windows and entered the garage through a side entrance to the courthouse, Lynn Kawano of Hawaii News Now had been there and was able to video them being driven into the garage. The driver? The US marshal himself. Six o'clock news!

On December 4, 2017, exactly three years to the day that Gerard's trial ended, City and County chief deputy Chasid Sapolu of the Honolulu Department of the Prosecuting Attorney was served with a target letter and went on leave. It's not clear what his alleged misconduct may have been. Growing suspicion that Kaneshiro had also received a target letter was neither confirmed nor denied by him or his office's spokesperson. Kaneshiro would continue to lead and run his office because, as an elected public official, it was unknown who in government, if anyone, had the authority to remove him other than through an impeachment process or an election.

A month later, on January 5, 2018, Ransen Taito, the nephew who had his trust monies stolen by Katherine, pleaded guilty to lying to the grand jury on Katherine's behalf. The deal allowed his sister to go free. Like retired HPD officer Silva, he too agreed to testify for the government against Katherine. His guilty plea seemed unjust to many, as it was Katherine who had convinced him to lie after stealing all his money. Fittingly, in January 2021 the government dismissed all charges against him in the interest of justice. It was the right thing to do.

Indicted on multiple counts and without access to any more stolen monies, on March 20, 2018, the Kealohas defaulted on the mortgage of their Hawai'i Kai residence and were sued by Hawaii Central Federal Credit Union. The government also filed forfeiture proceedings against this property, with any recovered monies earmarked to pay back the victims of the Kealohas' fraud. The government seized the residence on October 11, 2018.

In another twist, Big Island fireman Jesse Ebersole was charged on July 9, 2018, with conspiracy to obstruct justice for lying to the grand jury on behalf of Katherine Kealoha. Here was yet another person who agreed to lie on Katherine's behalf, under oath, to the grand jury. In the time-honored tradition of "follow the money," the FBI had discovered that large sums of money stolen by Katherine, over $20,000, were spent on hotels, airfare and car payments for Ebersole. As it turns out, from approximately 2009 through 2015, he was having an affair with her. It's said that the worst thing a police officer's spouse can do is have an affair with a fireman, and Ebersole was a pretty good-looking fireman. She convinced him to lie about their relationship to the grand jury and, once again, hired an attorney to represent him. Ebersole did, in fact, lie to the grand jury and to federal agents when questioned about the nature of his relationship with Katherine, and he too got caught in lies trying to cover for her. Watching this on the nightly news left me wondering what spell Katherine had over so many people that they would put themselves in criminal jeopardy for her. On July 12, 2018, Ebersole pleaded guilty as charged and agreed to cooperate…and tell the truth.

Amid these new and lurid allegations, Katherine finally resigned her position as a prosecutor on September 17, 2018. Her boss, Kaneshiro, did not force her resignation. Then things went from lurid to bizarre.

In an indictment that seemingly came out of left field, Wheat charged Katherine yet again on February 7, 2019, this time with drug conspiracy. Her co-conspirator was her brother, Rudy Puana, a Big Island doctor. These charges alleged that Rudy Puana issued falsified opioid prescriptions in exchange for cash and cocaine. Katherine was alleged to have used her position as prosecutor to misdirect police investigations that might have led to the uncovering of his illegal activities. It was also alleged that she used cocaine while serving as prosecutor and even distributed cocaine to another person. The word "hypocrite" did not come close to describing Katherine.

Four days later Daniel Sellers, one of the four CIU officers charged in the original conspiracy indictment, who was an ex-boyfriend of Katherine's before she met and married Louis, pleaded guilty to minor charges. Sellers admitted that he improperly shared classified information with Katherine regarding the make and model of Gerard's car during the mailbox investigation. This was new information to us and had not been disclosed by HPD in any official report when we were preparing Gerard's defense. Had we known about it, this information would certainly have helped us in our argument that Gerard was being framed.

As political tensions mounted over Kaneshiro's continued refusal to acknowledge whether he had or had not received a target letter, on February 12, 2019, newly appointed Hawai'i state attorney general Clare Connors filed a petition with the Hawai'i Supreme Court seeking Kaneshiro's immediate removal and the suspension of his license to practice law, stating that this was an extraordinary situation. Susan Ballard, the new chief of police, openly supported the petition, expressing her concern that Kaneshiro should not be part of any high-level security briefings given that he might soon become a criminal defendant.

At a press conference on February 12, 2019, Bill McCorriston, Kaneshiro's newly hired attorney, confirmed for the first time, despite the months of silence by his own client, that Kaneshiro had received a target letter. Despite this admission, Kaneshiro continued to refuse to step down and prepared to respond to the attorney general's petition to the Hawai'i Supreme Court. However, on March 7, the day Kaneshiro was to respond to the petition, he placed himself on a paid leave of absence and left his office in the charge of his handpicked successor. As a result, state attorney general Connors did not go forward with her petition. An impeachment petition, however, was circulated by members of the public to permanently remove Kaneshiro from office. Kaneshiro successfully blocked the impeachment petition from moving forward through court challenges until his term in office naturally expired in November 2020 and a new City and County prosecutor, Steve Alm, was elected. Kaneshiro had been able to stay on paid leave for more than a year and a half.

The Kealohas tried one last time to go on the offensive, making their last and most desperate attack to influence the public. As their trial neared, on March 25, 2019, Louis's lawyer, Rustam Barbee, wrote a letter on behalf of the Kealohas to the dean of the William S. Richardson School of Law at the University of Hawai'i. He argued that law professor Ken Lawson, who was acting as a legal commentator for the Hawaii News Now television station and who was also the director of the Hawaii Innocence Project, should "refrain from public comment opining on the guilt of pretrial defendants" or be "fired." Barbee argued that Lawson, due to his positions as head of the Innocence Project and as law professor, was acting unethically in making pretrial statements that seemed to favor the government and presume the guilt of the Kealohas. The letter was not well received by the public or members of the legal community, and the ACLU spoke out in defense of Lawson's right to free speech. Lawson himself responded to the letter, saying that "he would not be bullied," nor would he "shut up." Lawson explained that this was a "teaching moment for everyone on the island," and that the letter was nothing but another attempt by the Kealohas to silence their critics. Lawson was neither silenced nor fired by the law school.

Neither my boss, Peter Wolff, nor I received a similar letter. But unbeknownst to us, similar allegations of unethical conduct from an unknown source, this time leveled against me, appeared to have also been made to the Ninth Circuit Committee that oversees the selection and retention of the federal public defenders within the Ninth Circuit.

In March 2019, the same time Lawson had received his letter, the Ninth Circuit was seeking input on Peter Wolff's continued retention as the Hawai'i federal defender, a process undertaken every four years. Wolff had been retained for six prior terms up to this point without a hitch and was seeking one more four-year term before retiring. We would only learn much later that these allegations would be taken seriously by the Ninth Circuit Committee and, this time, have their intended effect.

Throughout this long wait, Lynn Kawano and Nick Grube had been dogged in their coverage of these events. Both knew the facts inside and out and got them right, a feat not often accomplished by other reporters. They both had been doubted and criticized for their commitment to the story over the years. Both had been warned that they should not publicly question the credibility of the Kealohas. They had put their reputations on the line. But each had worked diligently and often reported events before they even became officially known. Through their reporting they represented, in every sense, the best the world of journalism had to offer. Not only did their efforts expose corruption as it was happening; they significantly contributed to the public's understanding of what the Kealohas had really done and, unfortunately, how the state and local government agencies had all failed the community. Most importantly, their stories served to exonerate Gerard.

*　*　*

On May 13, 2019, after months and months of delays, the long-anticipated trial of the Kealohas and the remaining three co-defendant CIU officers began. Over a thousand jury questionnaires had been sent to prospective jurors due to the publicity the case, and 413 potential jurors appeared for the first day of jury selection. Because the federal courthouse could not accommodate such a large number of people, presiding chief judge Michael J. Seabright moved jury selection to the Neal S. Blaisdell Center, a venue usually reserved for concerts, large trade shows and graduation ceremonies. After opening remarks by Judge Seabright, the prospective jurors spent an hour answering a thirteen-page questionnaire that sought details about their personal backgrounds and their views on the defendants. The jury selection process continued over the course of the week, with opening statements scheduled to begin on May 22.

It was now time to put the Kealohas on trial. The most important corruption trial in Hawai'i state history was about to commence. ❖

CHAPTER 22

Witness Number 37

The trial lasted nineteen days. Seventy-six witnesses testified. Sixty-one witnesses were called by the government, fifteen by the defense. None of the five defendants elected to testify on their own behalf. I was the thirty-seventh witness to testify in the trial that had come to be known as "The Mailbox Case."

Despite my role in having initiated the prosecution and turning everything over to the FBI, I didn't consider myself to be a critical witness. Gerard's and Florence's testimony was far more important than mine. The testimony by the government agents regarding forensic evidence, texts, phone calls and email correspondence between the Kealohas and their co-defendants was more important. Silva's testimony was far more important. But because the public knew who I was and the role I had played in exposing the Kealohas, my testimony was one of the more anticipated moments in the prosecution's case. It was finally my turn to testify on May 31, 2019, seven trial days after the trial had begun.

As I entered the courtroom to take the witness stand, I could see that the courtroom was packed. Members of the press filled their reserved seats in the first and second rows of the courtroom. Since filming and photography are not permitted in federal courtrooms, the press had been granted permission to use computers and their phones to blog and tweet, but no live shots of the proceedings were allowed. Courtroom artists were brought in to provide sketches for the nightly newscasts. Some sketches were, shall we say, amusing. Throughout the trial there was nightly coverage on all the local news stations, providing a witness-by-witness account of the proceedings. Due to the publicity a second courtroom had been fitted with monitors so that the overflow crowd could watch if they couldn't get into the trial courtroom itself.

This was the first time I had seen this done for a trial in my thirty-three years practicing in federal court in Hawai'i.

Because of the witness exclusion rule, I had not been allowed inside the courtroom, so that my testimony would not be influenced by the testimony of any other witness. I only knew how things were progressing by watching the local news or from my office co-workers telling me who was on the stand. As I walked to the stand, I looked at the jury watching me approach. I knew they were already sizing me up. First impressions are important. Wheat had made sure to tell me how he wanted me dressed. I wore a jacket and tie, not aloha attire. I even trimmed my beard for the occasion. I tried to channel my inner "special agent" look, hard for me since I have more of a Columbo look. I knew the jury had already been told who I was and that I represented Gerard. I'd heard that Wheat had explained my role to the jury in his opening statement and had described me as "tenacious." I wondered what the jury was thinking as I walked past them and took the witness stand to take the oath. I hoped I looked "tenacious."

A witness is supposed to recount relevant things they saw, heard or did that help prove or disprove the charges against the defendants on trial. My investigation was not relevant to the facts and evidence being presented to the jury in this trial. I had not been a witness to what the defendants had done; I had only uncovered some of what they had done.

The charges in the trial were related to obstruction of justice and conspiracy, facts and evidence mostly unknown to me at the time of Gerard's trial. I didn't know Officer Silva had lied in his report and under oath at Gerard's trial about having never actually gone to the Kealoha residence to retrieve the surveillance tape. I didn't know that the surveillance tape had been recorded over by HPD, so that the original video was unrecoverable. I didn't know that this had been done intentionally within hours of my having sought a subpoena to obtain those tapes. I didn't know about the text messages and phone calls between the defendants as they schemed to frame Gerard and then cover it up. I wasn't present in the grand jury or with the FBI when some of the defendants allegedly lied to them.

I was, however, a witness to Louis having lied, under oath, at Gerard's trial when he said it was Gerard who stole the mailbox. Prior to trial I'd met several times with Wheat to discuss what he wanted me to testify about. Essentially it boiled down to two specific and relevant events. The first was to discuss and introduce photographs of the two different mailboxes. The second was to read to the jury the trial transcript of Louis's testimony in Gerard's trial. That testimony was relevant because the government had specifically alleged, as part of the conspiracy in the indictment, that Louis had committed perjury when he testified that the person who stole the mailbox was Gerard. Wheat decided that I would play the part of Tong, the AUSA who had done the direct examination of Louis, and Wheat would play the role of Louis. We would read the trial transcript of Louis's testimony to the jury. Easy enough. But I knew that my limited testimony was going to be a disappointment to many people who were expecting fireworks.

Wheat had reminded me that lawyers do not usually make good witnesses and to make sure I didn't testify like a lawyer. He didn't explain what he meant, but I interpreted it to mean, "Don't be a self-centered, egotistical ass; just answer my questions." I had seen lawyers testify before, and I'm pretty sure my understanding of Wheat's comment was spot-on. My wife had told me the same thing in a much more loving way, so I'd been forewarned by a higher authority!

Wheat called me the night before I was to testify to say there had been a slight change of plan. After briefly reviewing the two limited areas I was going to testify about, Wheat ended the conversation by casually saying that after I had testified about those two issues, he was going to have me testify about our investigation and what we had uncovered. All of it.

It took a second for this to register. He was essentially telling me that he was now proposing that I testify for hours about matters we had never gone over. Yes, it was information that I knew and that I had been discussing with him for years, but that was during the process of assisting him with his investigation, not testifying. I told him that I didn't see the relevance of such testimony and that it would be objected to. My investigation, in my opinion, was not relevant evidence. Wheat simply responded, "Well, we'll see how far we get," and hung up. That was it. No further trial preparation at all. Just "we'll see how far we get."

Because I was a witness, Wheat was not allowed to tell me what other witnesses had testified about. I knew Wheat had presented his "theory of the case" to the jury in his opening statement, which was that Katherine, along with her co-defendant law enforcement officers and Louis, had framed Gerard to discredit him in the civil case that was then pending in state court. And I knew Wheat had already put on several witnesses to testify about the reverse mortgage deal contrived by Katherine. I also knew that Wheat had presented witnesses to prove that Katherine and HPD had lied about the make and value of the mailbox and why this fact was significant. And I knew Gerard himself had already testified. But I didn't know the specifics or how this testimony had been received by the jury.

It was in this state of limited information that I approached the witness stand and was sworn in. What immediately struck me as I took the oath was the view of the courtroom itself. As an attorney, I always sit facing the judge, the witness and the jury. Other than opposing counsel and courtroom staff, no one else stands in my line of sight. The gallery, which usually consists of a few interested onlookers, perhaps the defendant's family, and attorneys biding their time while they wait for their own hearings, is behind me. I'm usually so focused on what's happening in front of me that I rarely pay any attention to the people behind me. During recesses I may take a moment to look around, but when the trial starts up again my focus is back on what's in front of me. Now, when I took the witness stand and turned to take the oath, I was facing the entire courtroom and able to see everyone. Everyone. And they were looking back at me.

It took me a moment to take it all in. All the people in the gallery, whom I had been able to ignore and put out of my mind when I was the trial attorney, could now not be ignored. I recognized most of the people in the gallery. They were not strangers. There were members of the press in the front row, all of whom had interviewed me numerous times over the years leading up to the trial, fingers on their laptops and phones ready to summarize and tweet out my testimony. Most of the people from my office were there. They weren't going to miss this show for the world. There were many civil attorneys and some state officials who were in the courtroom, simply intrigued by the trial. Over the years, one way or another, I'd met them all. There were court staff members who were taking in as much of the trial as their time permitted. I knew they were more than a little amused to see me as a witness for the prosecution. And there were several assistant US attorneys in attendance waiting to see me get cross-examined. Some of the people in the gallery were smiling in support. Others, I imagined, were smiling to see me get a taste of my own medicine. I quickly realized that I was not going to be able to shut them out of my mind while I testified. My nervousness grew.

I was also looking down at everyone from my vantage point in the witness box. I hadn't accounted for that perspective. The witness stand is the second-highest point in the courtroom. Only the judge sits slightly higher. I noticed that I was looking down at the attorneys who were questioning me. I could see the tops of their heads. I was even looking down at the jury who were seated to my left and appeared to me to be way, way too close for comfort. And everyone was looking up at me. This is not the way a person has a normal conversation. While it may give a judge a sense of power, it only gave me a sense of unease.

The witness stand itself surprised me with its simplicity. There was really nothing to it. A chair placed in the middle of a wooden box. A microphone sitting before me. A computer monitor to one side. Nothing else. Nowhere to put your elbows. The chair wasn't comfortable, just a chair. A chair I would sit in for five hours. I was disappointed; I thought it would feel grander.

Wheat began his questioning, and I could tell in my first few answers that my nervousness was showing. I was speaking too fast. As I had come to understand and appreciate living in Hawai'i, I had worked hard on talking more slowly in court. Not because people in Hawai'i couldn't understand me when I spoke faster, but because it is culturally considered rude to speak rapidly. But more importantly, if one talks a

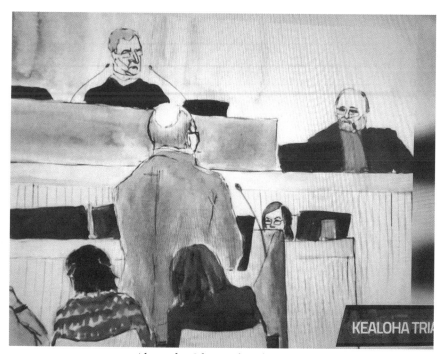

Alexander Silvert takes the stand.

little slower one can be better understood and more clearly heard—not a minor point if you're a trial attorney trying to get a jury to hear and understand you. But now my nerves were getting the better of me, and I was answering questions too rapidly. During the first recess, Wheat asked the court to remind me to speak more slowly. I felt like a child being reprimanded by the principal. But it helped me gather myself for the next round of questions.

When it came time to read the trial transcript of Louis's 2014 testimony, Wheat informed the court of his intention to have me play the role of AUSA Larry Tong while he played the role of Louis. I don't know why, but I couldn't resist turning to Judge Seabright to say, "And that, Your Honor, is the first time I've ever been asked to play a prosecutor." I'd appeared before Judge Seabright many times and knew he would be amused, even though I wasn't supposed to speak directly to the court. He knew better than most how out of character it was for me to ever even play at being a prosecutor. He smiled ever so slightly, but he wasn't about to let me read Tong's testimony. Judge Seabright nixed Wheat's suggestion and ordered that his law clerk read Tong's questions as put to Louis during Gerard's trial, while Judge Seabright himself read the part of the judge.

I stepped down from the witness stand and stood by a wall on one side of the gallery. While everyone else in the gallery and the jury listened intently to the reading of the transcript, I took the time to take it all in. After all, I'd heard it before. Now I had the unique opportunity to simply watch. It was surreal, like an out-of-body experience. Reporters were typing away. People were giving one another passing glances or whispering to one other. Finally, the crucial testimony was read, when Louis, at Gerard's trial some four and a half years earlier in December of 2014, pointed to Gerard sitting next to me at the defense table and said, "That's him. He stole our mailbox." No hesitation at all. No words indicating any doubt. Not a second thought that he was, at that very moment, trying to get an innocent man, his family relative no less, convicted and sent to jail for a crime he did not commit. The jury, I noticed, was listening intently throughout the reading of Louis's testimony. I looked around the room one last time before I retook the witness stand. "Fascinating," as Spock would say.

By now I was calm. It was like the second half of a ball game. I knew what to expect. Wheat was on a roll. He quickly finished going over the last subject we'd planned on covering during my testimony. Then Wheat took a breath, looked straight at me and, as he promised, started asking me questions about my investigation "just to see how far we would get." No one objected. I was permitted to testify to whatever area of my investigation Wheat wanted to ask about. We hadn't discussed what I was going to testify about, so I tried to follow his lead, anticipating where he wanted me to go. It was like a dance. He would lead, I would follow, or at least try to. Several times I didn't understand his lead, and I knew right away that I hadn't given the answer he was hoping for. Not a wrong answer, just not the one Wheat wanted. But as a witness you don't get to speak up and try to answer the question again just because you didn't get it right the first time. I knew if he really wanted a different answer, he would ask the same question, but in a slightly different manner. That would tell me he was looking for something other than what I had said. But I was disappointed in myself for not getting it "right" as we went along. I was trying to learn and keep up with the dance steps. As my testimony went on, I got better at it.

At one point Wheat asked me to discuss the Hawai'i state theft statute to explain to the jury the distinction between a felony theft (requiring a theft of an item with a value over $300) and a misdemeanor theft (a value under $300). Louis's attorney, Rustam Barbee, objected, saying that since I was not an attorney licensed by the state of Hawai'i, I shouldn't be allowed to answer the question. Barbee knew that his objection would be overruled. After all, I'd been a practicing attorney for over thirty-three years. I was licensed in the Commonwealth of Pennsylvania, two federal district courts, two federal courts of appeals and the Supreme Court of the United States, which certainly made me "qualified" to read and interpret a Hawai'i state theft statute. I'd known Barbee from when he'd first moved to Hawai'i from Wisconsin and worked in my office with me, so he was very familiar with my legal background. But what Barbee was really trying to do by making the objection was to point out to the jury that I wasn't "one of them." I wasn't local. He was a licensed Hawai'i attorney; I was not. I was an outsider accusing his local Hawaiian client of misdeeds. He was playing the local hometown card. Somewhat ironic, given he too wasn't born and raised in Hawai'i.

I turned to look at Judge Seabright for his response, and I could see he was furious. It's not uncommon for the defense to play the hometown card when out-of-town attorneys come to Hawai'i to litigate a case. But it has to be done subtly. You have to make sure the jury isn't going to be offended by this tactic, which means they already have to be sympathetic to you and to your client. And you have to use this card against the right witness. I was the wrong witness. I wasn't an outsider. I could instantly tell by the jury's reaction that it was not well received. Judge Seabright certainly made no effort to hide his displeasure. After all, the jury knew I had represented Gerard, a local boy through and through, and had allegedly uncovered a massive conspiracy to frame an innocent man and steal hundreds of thousands of dollars from his mother. Moreover, up to this point in my testimony it was clear the jury was listening to me. They weren't turning away. They weren't bored or irritated. They weren't shifting in their seats. These would all be signs that a jury didn't like or believe a witness. No, they'd all been paying close attention as I testified; some had even smiled at me. The objection fell flat, and I believe it hurt Barbee's credibility with the jury. I answered the question.

When Wheat finished, I'd already been testifying for more than three hours. It was finally time for cross-examination. During Wheat's direct questioning, the only two people I could really see at the defense table were Katherine and her attorney, Cynthia Kagiwada. While Wheat was standing at the podium, I couldn't see Louis or his counsel behind him. The defense tables had been formed into an L, with the Kealohas and their attorneys seated at the defense table facing forward towards the judge, while the other three defendants and their counsel sat at tables to their left facing the jury. I could only see the other three lawyers and their clients if I leaned forward. During my testimony I watched as Katherine stared at me and sometimes, when she thought my answer was favorable to her, nodded her head in approval. I didn't know why she was nodding, because I didn't feel any of my answers were particularly helpful to her. I noticed that her attorney was taking copious notes on a yellow legal pad and appeared to have several different-colored markers that she used to underline or circle things she had studiously written down as I testified. I was sure I was going to face a lengthy cross from her. Given all her note-taking, I didn't doubt she had many things to question me about.

But it never happened. Only a handful of questions came my way when she questioned me. She asked if I still represented Gerard. She seemed caught off guard when I said I still did, even though his trial was over and his case had been dismissed with prejudice. She asked me in what manner I still represented him, breaking the cardinal rule of cross-examination to never ask a question you don't know the answer to. And while I don't subscribe to this rule as an absolute, in this case it proved to be dead right. I replied that my office now represented Gerard as…a victim. Having me remind the jury, by reason of her own question, that Gerard was a real live victim of her client's criminal misconduct did not help her case.

Ms. Kagiwada then asked whether, given this fact, I had a "vested interest" in the outcome of the trial. I took this question to mean whether I had a financial interest in the outcome of the case, as a civil attorney might if they won a case and got paid a percentage. I responded no. As a public defender, I got paid a salary and nothing more. Winning or losing a case may be a matter of professional pride and justice being served, but it is not a payday. As a public defender, I cannot accept any monetary remuneration in any form from a client. In response to a further question, I added that while I did not have a financial interest in the case, I did hope the defendants would be found guilty and Gerard would "win." And despite her copious notes, that was it. She sat down. I was surprised, to say the least. I had been wondering whether she had a hidden sledgehammer under all those notes.

Each defense attorney took their turn. Each time the attorneys introduced themselves, it was a bit awkward since we were no strangers to one another. I felt like saying, "Hi, Rus," or "Hi, Birney," but refrained from doing so, although I did grin to myself as I gave the more formal and appropriate response: "Good afternoon, Mr. Barbee;" "Good afternoon, Mr. Bervar." Each attorney probed and jabbed, trying to make points that they thought helped their case. Sometimes, when you can't attack a witness head-on, you have to skirt around the edges or simply try to undermine their credibility.

Barbee, Louis's attorney, tried to make the point that Louis had not technically lied on the witness stand during Gerard's trial when he had testified that Gerard had been "convicted" of "breaking into his neighbor's house." He correctly stated that Gerard had pled guilty in March of 2013 to that charge and, at least at that moment in time, Gerard was in fact "convicted." He reminded me that it was not until several months later, in June 2013, that the state court had converted his guilty plea into a DANC plea, thereby setting aside and vacating the conviction. Thus, Barbee pointed, Gerard was, at one time, convicted, just as Louis claimed. True enough. But by the time of Gerard's trial in December of 2014 when Louis testified, Gerard was, in every legal sense, not convicted because his request for a DANC plea had been accepted by the state court. There could be no question that Louis knew this fact because in September 2013 Katherine had tried to get the state judge to reverse his decision. She'd been unsuccessful in yet another attempt to get a felony conviction against Gerard. But if anyone understood the legal significance and meaning of a DANC plea, it was Louis. I knew Wheat and his team would make these facts absolutely clear to the jury in their closing argument.

Birney Bervar was up next. He represented Derek Hahn, who was retired HPD officer Niall Silva's CIU supervisor. Hahn had allegedly instructed Silva to falsify his reports regarding the videotape surveillance footage and to hide the hard drive when we had subpoenaed it—facts we did not know in 2014 but discovered through the FBI during their investigation. Bervar walked me through the dates I had asked the court to issue the subpoena to HPD for the videotape as opposed to when we had actually served that subpoena on HPD. He pointed out that although I had filed our papers with the court requesting a subpoena for the videotape evidence several days earlier, we had in fact not served the subpoena on HPD until a day *after* the surveillance footage had already begun to be taped over by CIU technicians. Bervar's questioning was designed to suggest to the jury that the taping over of the videotape surveillance footage was a matter of routine practice and not done nefariously in response to our subpoena. The problem was, no matter when we served the subpoena on HPD, HPD knew I was attempting to obtain more videotape footage from all my informal requests to the government and from my subpoena to Louis himself. Under any circumstances, the hard drive should never have been altered or deleted, as it constituted evidence in an ongoing prosecution. HPD was specifically trained in how to properly preserve evidence when there was a pending prosecution. Again, I was confident this fact would not be lost on the jury.

Another attorney made a mistake, and it was evident to everyone as it was happening. He asked me if I knew whether the mailbox and pedestal had been properly assembled. I answered that I knew it had originally been properly installed because Gerard had told me he had helped build it and it was put together properly. Not letting this go, he asked me if I had later learned that the mailbox pedestal had simply been "improperly assembled." The question suggested human error, no sinister intent. I answered by saying that while it might be *his* opinion that it was not properly assembled, it was not my opinion. I knew if he kept pushing me, I would have to testify that, according to what Mr. Dryer, the representative of Solar Group, had told me, the mailbox had been intentionally rigged to come off. I had withheld giving this answer only because I didn't want to hurt the entire defense team simply because one attorney had asked the wrong question. I'd been in that position before, and I felt it was a matter of professional courtesy to refrain if I could. But he persisted.

I tried one last time to wave him off of this line of questioning and even asked him if he was requiring me to answer his question. I looked at Wheat. He wouldn't look at me. You know that feeling you get when someone is intentionally not looking at you? You can just tell. He had that look. Instead, Wheat was looking directly at the defense attorney. Wheat had a huge Cheshire Cat grin on his face. Ear to ear. The same smile I'd seen years earlier when Gerard had passed the polygraph examination. He knew what my answer was going to be. I saw the attorney look around for a second, not quite sure why I was questioning him, and then turn back to me and say, "Yes, you do." I had done all I could. Then I explained that Mr. Dryer had told me that the specific placement of the nut on the rod allowed the mailbox to be removed in the very manner seen on the videotape, and *only* because of the placement of the nut in that specific location could the mailbox have been removed as it was. I concluded by saying, "So you say it wasn't properly assembled. I take a little different view of that."

The last defense attorney to question me was Lars Isaacson, who represented Gordon Shiraishi. Shiraishi was a supervisor in CIU and a friend of Louis. The government claimed that he lied to the FBI about the timing of a phone call he claimed he received from Louis that might have explained why the surveillance tape had been retrieved from the Kealoha residence before Katherine called 911. His name hadn't surfaced at all during our investigation of Gerard's case in 2014. This lie, according to the government, had occurred in response to FBI questioning long after Gerard's trial was over. Therefore, during my entire direct testimony I had never said anything about Shiraishi, as I hadn't even been aware he existed during our investigation of the case in 2013 and 2014.

Sometimes the best defense is not to cross-examine a witness at all, even if you can impeach them or you want to solidify an answer you like. Sometimes it's just better to walk away. I have found that this is one of the hardest things for a defense attorney to learn: not to talk! I've learned the hard truth of this lesson on more than one occasion. I once won a motion to suppress, and my client's freedom, by not asking any questions. None. I still remember how hard that was. I stood up to cross-examine, but my gut was telling me to sit down. I hesitantly told the judge I had no questions and sat down. I questioned my decision until the moment the judge ruled in my favor. It was a great learning experience. First, that I should trust my gut more, and second, to humbly acknowledge that my brilliant cross-examination skills do not necessarily win cases as much as I would like to think they do.

Isaacson had obviously learned the same lesson. Although he did ask me a handful of questions, they all essentially pointed out that I did not mention his client's name during my direct testimony, and then he sat down. Good move. It's always a good move to point out to the jury the complete absence of evidence against your client.

Wheat asked several clarification questions, and I was done. No one had brought a sledgehammer. I felt relieved.

* * *

Ten days after I testified, on June 20, the testimonial stage of the trial ended. Closing arguments began on June 25 and ended in the early afternoon of the next day. At 1:50 p.m. the jury began its deliberations. The next day, at approximately 3:30 p.m., the jury completed its work. It had reached a verdict. It had taken less than nine hours over the course of two days for the jury to decide the case. Not a long time considering the length of the trial, the complexity of the charges and the fact that they had to reach a verdict on each of the counts for each of the five defendants. As it turned out, the jury had been the one holding the sledgehammer all along. ❖

ACT III

CHAPTER 23

The Verdict

T he word spread like wildfire. The speed and timing of the verdict caught us all by surprise. It was late Thursday afternoon. The jury had been deliberating less than nine hours. Some of that time would have been used to go over the jury instructions, read the indictment and fill out the multipage verdict form. Thus, the deliberations on whether the defendants were guilty or not guilty had taken even less time. Given the lateness of the day, everyone assumed the jury would return on Friday. There had been one jury note sent to the court during their deliberations. That note, submitted by the jury on the morning of June 26, soon after closing arguments, simply asked if they could have more supplies, a list of trial exhibits and a timeline of events. The court provided all requested items except for the timeline of events, as no such document had been introduced into evidence. Other than that, nothing more from the jury. Nothing until now, when they notified the court they had reached a unanimous verdict on all counts.

Everyone descended and congregated outside the courtroom. But no one could get in. It was locked. The court always requires lawyers and their clients, the defendants, to be within fifteen minutes of the courthouse. The defendants and their lawyers in this case were all present and waiting in the witness rooms, away from the eyes of the public and press. But the courtroom doors remained closed. No one could enter. This was unusual. Normally, it's the judge, whose chambers are located immediately behind the courtroom, who is waiting impatiently for the parties to appear. No one wants to keep a jury waiting, particularly when it has returned a verdict late in the afternoon.

There were a good thirty to forty people milling around outside the courtroom door. Small groups of two to four people formed, then dispersed, and new groups formed. Everyone was on edge, some with the excitement that comes with the anticipation of a verdict, others, like myself, simply nervous. The speed of the verdict had us all guessing. If you've done many jury trials, you sometimes get a feel for what the verdict will be, particularly if the evidence is overwhelming. But often it's just a guessing game. I thought I knew what the outcome would be, but the speed and timing of the verdict created an added measure of uncertainty. Did a quick verdict mean the evidence was overwhelming? Did it mean the jury simply didn't believe there was enough evidence to convict beyond a reasonable doubt? Everyone was speculating. Many who had sat through the entire trial felt the evidence of guilt was clear and that the defense had done little to offer any explanation to rebut the government's proof. Others who had only seen bits and pieces of the trial, like myself, were less convinced. It was a complicated case. There was no smoking gun. Everything was circumstantial. No one testified that the Kealohas actually framed Gerard. No one testified that the Kealohas arranged to have their mailbox taken. No mailbox was ever recovered, nor was the car used in the theft found, much less the driver. Much of the government's case was based upon proving that the Kealohas had a strong motive and that the numerous phone and text messages between the co-conspirators, coupled with all the lies, suggested they were working in concert at critical times in the case. There were bits and pieces here and there, but was it enough to overcome reasonable doubt? That was the million-dollar question, and that's what worried me.

One of Katherine Kealoha's attorneys, who had only recently joined her defense team a few days before the trial ended and thus had not been in the courtroom throughout the trial, made a point of telling anyone and everyone who would listen that the quick verdict could only mean one thing and one thing only: that Katherine was not guilty. No doubt about it. Write it down. No one responded. It was a ridiculous statement to make. We were all a bit taken aback by his brazenness. But his confidence did have me worried.

I was also struggling with my own internal battle. I was rooting for a guilty verdict. I had never, ever, done that before. But I wanted a guilty verdict for Gerard. I wanted a guilty verdict for Florence. I wanted a guilty verdict for justice so that a clear message would be sent out that dirty cops and dirty prosecutors would not be allowed to get away with framing an innocent man. And I believe strongly in the concept of reasonable doubt. It is all that separates us from mob rule, from the Wild West days of lawless posses hanging suspects from an old oak tree. If the verdict was not guilty, could I live with that? This was no longer simply an intellectual exercise for me; this was personal. In this particular case, I doubted I could accept a not guilty verdict.

Finally, the courtroom doors were unlocked, but we were still not allowed to enter. We were instructed to wait until the defendants and the attorneys entered the courtroom first. The jury had its own entrance and would be led in separately once everyone was settled. As the defendants walked through the hall in a line to enter the courtroom, we parted like the Red Sea. Everyone stopped talking. The silence made the scene surreal, like watching someone being led to the gallows. Then we all entered the courtroom and took our seats, but the unsettling silence persisted. Waiting for the jury to be shuttled into a courtroom to render its verdict is always an awkward time for everyone. You make small talk. You set up your paperwork just like you want it. Then you move it around and set it up just like you want it again. You reassure your client, smile, pace a little. And this is just my reaction as the attorney; I can only imagine what a defendant must feel knowing their fate is decided and they're moments away from hearing it. Will you be led out of the courtroom in handcuffs, or are you going to have breakfast with your family tomorrow? Once, one of my clients literally almost had a heart attack, he was so anxious. When his not guilty verdict was read, he let out an audible gasp that came from the pit of his stomach, put his head down and started weeping uncontrollably.

The jury came in and took their seats. More speculation. Were the jurors looking at the defendants? Were they glaring? Smiling? Smiling at whom? Were their arms crossed or relaxed at their sides? I've had juries that purposely did not look at anyone so as not to give anything away as they entered the courtroom. Others come in with smiles. If a juror smiles at you or your client as they take their seats, wow, what a feeling. It almost always means they have found your client not guilty. People don't like to judge. They don't like to be the ones who put someone behind bars. They'll do it, for sure, but it is not a good feeling. If they are smiling and chitchatting it means they are feeling good about themselves. That's usually a not guilty, unless the crime and the defendant are particularly appalling. Then it's not. Everyone in the gallery looked at the jury trying to get some clue, discern some "look," see some furtive gesture that would indicate which way the jury was leaning. I didn't see anything that told me what to expect. But they weren't smiling at the defendants, and there was no chitchat.

Finally, Judge Seabright came out and asked the foreperson of the jury to rise and state whether the jury had reached a unanimous verdict. Another moment to speculate, but only for an instant. It is sometimes very telling who the foreperson is on a jury. A foreperson, depending upon their personality, can often use their leadership position to sway less strong-minded jurors. Since I had not been present during most of the trial and didn't really know anything about the jury members, who the foreperson was in this case didn't particularly signify anything to me. But I'm sure the lawyers in the case were making immediate assumptions when they saw the foreperson rise. It's a guessing game we all play.

The deputy clerk retrieved the sealed envelope in which the verdict forms had been placed and handed it, unopened, to Judge Seabright. The sound of Judge Seabright opening the envelope, removing the verdict forms and leafing through them one by one resonated throughout the courtroom. He made no facial expression. Nothing to indicate the verdicts he had just read. I think judges go to judge school to learn how to do this. I'm not too sure if I ever were a judge that I could keep a straight face. He handed them to the deputy clerk and asked her to read the verdicts out loud. The defendants all rose.

"As to count one, Conspiracy, the jury finds the defendant, Katherine Kealoha, guilty."

Katherine gave no reaction. We waited for the next shoe to drop.

"As to count one, Conspiracy, the jury finds the defendant, Louis Kealoha, guilty."

Louis, upon the reading of his verdict on count one, the first of five more to come, slumped his shoulders and dropped his head. As one reporter put it, it looked like the "life was sucked out of him." There was a moment of silence as everyone took in the significance of what had just been read out loud. Then, all at once, the sounds of computer keys began as reporters hurriedly rushed to get the news out to their editors and to the public. People began to whisper to their neighbors. I couldn't help but picture the scene from the movie *His Girl Friday*, starring Cary Grant and Rosalind Russell, where, upon hearing the guilty verdict in a murder trial, all the reporters raced out of the courtroom to call their newsrooms, back in the days when there were only pay phones available. But now the sounds of computer keys or cell phones clattered away as their words were immediately sent out via the Internet.

The deputy clerk continued on:

"As to count one, Conspiracy, the jury finds the defendant, Derek

Hahn, guilty.… As to count one, Conspiracy, the jury finds the defendant, Bobby Nguyen, guilty.… As to count one, Conspiracy, the jury finds the defendant, Gordon Shiraishi, not guilty."

Even though the verdicts on the five remaining counts had not yet been read, it was a foregone conclusion. Katherine Kealoha, Louis Kealoha, Derek Hahn and Bobby Nguyen would be found guilty on all counts related to their joint actions. They would be found not guilty, as would Shiraishi, on all counts that directly related to their alleged jointly taken actions with Shiraishi. Shiraishi would walk away a free man. But not the others. The jury had spoken. Loud and clear. Both by the judgement they had rendered and by the speed with which it had been done, they had put an end to the corrupting influence and power of the Kealohas. Emphatically. With a sledgehammer.

The jurors sat solemnly throughout the reading of the verdicts. No smiles. No whispering to one another. Each juror was then polled individually to ensure that each guilty verdict correctly reflected their individual judgements. Sixteen times a "Yes" response echoed in each of our ears. Sixteen times each "Yes" rang in the ears of Katherine and Louis Kealoha, as if to say, "Yes. You. You are guilty of framing an innocent man." Judge Seabright thanked the jurors for their service and told them the press would likely wish to speak to them but that it was their decision whether or not to talk to members of the press. With that, they were led out of the courtroom, their service as jurors and to the court having been completed.

Judge Seabright set separate dates for sentencing for each defendant for October, putting Katherine's sentencing hearing first, to be followed by Louis's, and then Hahn's and Nguyen's the following day. Sentencing reports had to be prepared by the United States probation department for each defendant and objections by the lawyers filed and argued prior to each defendant appearing in court at their sentencing hearing. All this takes time, which is why the court set the sentencing hearings so far ahead. The court inquired whether there were any motions by the government regarding any of the defendants' bail status. Up to now, all the defendants had been released on bail conditions. Wheat rose and asked that Katherine, and only Katherine, be immediately remanded into custody pending sentencing. The government had on several occasions prior to trial made motions to have Katherine detained. Each motion had been denied. But it was different this time. The presumption of innocence no longer applied. The court did not immediately rule on the motion by the government but set a hearing for Katherine for ten o'clock the next morning and adjourned for the day. Because the government had only asked that Katherine be detained and none of the other defendants, only Katherine had to return to court for the hearing. Katherine was free for at least one more day. It was almost five o'clock in the afternoon. It had been a momentous day.

The culmination of six years of work. Six years of hoping that justice would be served. Six years to get Gerard exonerated, and now, vindicated. A momentous day indeed. ❖

CHAPTER 24

Breaking News

As I came out of the courthouse the press were everywhere, easily thirty or more reporters with microphones and cameras at the ready. Tripods were set up on the lower concourse to do one-on-one interviews, and cameramen with handheld cameras were following their assigned reporters to catch statements on the fly as defendants or newsworthy people exited the courthouse. The print news reporters from the Associated Press and the *Honolulu Star-Advertiser*, with their photographers, were also waiting. For over an hour the television stations went live, cutting into their regular scheduled lineup with "breaking news." It was, to say the least, a chaotic scene as the reporters and their crews pivoted every time a defendant or juror came out the courthouse doors. It was like watching a school of fish dart around. Everyone was commenting upon the speed of the verdict and the message this sent. Ken Lawson, Hawaii News Now legal analyst, who had attended every day of the trial, remarked that it meant that the jury had "got it" even before closing arguments were made. Victor Bakke, an attorney who had also been providing legal analysis throughout the case, said that the speed of the verdict and the acquittal of Shiraishi meant the jury had paid attention to the evidence and that "the government had gotten what they came for."

I was one of the first ones to emerge and was immediately beset by a throng of reporters. I commented on how surprised I was with the speed of the verdict in such a complicated case, but that it meant that the jury had to have had a gut feeling that the Kealohas were guilty before they started deliberating. On behalf of Gerard and Florence Puana, I said the verdict gave them a great sense of satisfaction and vindication that their story was at long last believed, and the speed and quickness of the verdict sent a strong message to law enforcement that if you abuse your position of trust as an officer of the law, you will be held accountable.

I called Gerard to tell him the news. He broke down in tears, hardly able to speak. When he was able to compose himself, Gerard expressed his gratitude to me and my staff, as well as to Wheat's team for everything we had all done to clear his name and to bring justice for his family. I asked Gerard if his mother knew about the verdict yet. Gerard told me she was having a "bad day" and was not conscious, but he would tell her at the first opportunity. I soon received a text message from the Puana family asking me to read a statement to the press on their behalf. While holding back tears, I read:

> We find no joy or comfort in the outcome of the "Mailbox Trial." Our families' losses have been tremendous. Florence's home will never be restored to her. The years of humiliation, heartache, tears and sorrow inflicted on Florence, Gerard and our family won't be assuaged or erased. Some family relationships have been completely, perhaps forever severed, while others still remain tenuous. Yet through it all, our 'ohana has survived strong and united. We will eventually recover as we continue to look after each other. We'll keep the faith with our sights on the future [and] leave the past in the past while hoping and praying for happier tomorrows.
>
> Our family is extremely indebted and extend a sincere *mahalo nui loa* to the US Department of Justice, their attorneys and investigators; the entire federal public defender office, and our family attorneys for their confidence, tenacity and relentless pursuit of justice. We thank all our extended family, friends, clergy, doctors, nurses and medical personnel who have prayed for us, provided care, kindness, counsel and guidance over the past 7 years. We salute those members of the news media who diligently, objectively and fearlessly reported the facts and stood firm in the truth. We are most grateful as well to all the jurors who took time from their busy lives to serve on this jury; to listen intently to the evidence presented in this difficult and complicated case and commit themselves to upholding the truth and veracity of the law.
>
> May God bless each and every one of you.

A fitting, thoughtful statement. I don't know if I could have been so gentle or kind with my choice of words had I been subjected to the ordeal that Gerard and Florence had endured since 2009.

Finally, several of the defendants came out of the courthouse to run the gauntlet of the press. There would be no side door escape hatch this time. Shiraishi and his attorney came out first, choosing not to make any statement. That made sense. He had been found not guilty. No reason to hide, but bad form to gloat when fellow officers who served under him had just been found guilty of committing crimes. Then Derek Hahn came out, followed soon thereafter by Bobby Nguyen. Again, no statements to the press. Each bowed their heads slightly and avoided eye contact. Bobby's attorney put his hand on his back to comfort him as they walked away, cameras filming their every step. But no Kealohas. Several members of the press re-entered the courthouse to find out where they were, fearing they had somehow been able to slip out some side exit. Not this time. No courthouse security officer was going to make that mistake. The Kealohas were simply trying to wait out the press. But the courthouse was closing, and they were finally forced to show themselves. This time there were no lei. Katherine emerged first with her attorneys and refused to talk to the press, making her way silently down the courthouse steps with a stone-cold expression on her face. No eye contact with anyone. Katherine Kealoha's co-counsel, Earle Partington, who had so brashly predicted a not guilty verdict, said, "I'm afraid the government smear of Katherine Kealoha was very effective."

Louis emerged next, slightly behind Katherine. There was no hand-holding or walking side by side this time. While Louis at first said he was not going to make a comment, after taking a few steps he stopped, turned to the reporters and, facing the cameras, said, "There's still a lot to take in… I just want to thank everybody, especially the community, for the love and support. That's all I have to say." No acceptance of responsibility for his actions. No apology to Gerard or Florence. Louis turned and walked away with his attorney but did not try to catch up to his wife, who was ten to twenty feet ahead of him. Louis walked alone, head bowed as the cameramen filmed every second of the Kealohas' departure down the courthouse sidewalk and up Mililani Way. We were all wondering exactly which "community" Louis was thanking for their support. Legal analyst Ken Lawson, who was visibly upset by what Louis had said, commented that Louis was acting like a "crybaby criminal" and that he should take the verdict "like a man."

United States attorney Robert Brewer for the Southern District of California, the new head of Wheat's San Diego office, issued a statement:

The Kealohas' extraordinary greed inspired astonishing corruption. The audacity of this couple to use the power vested in them as law enforcement officials to fund a lavish lifestyle and satisfy their personal vendettas was unconscionable. These two were supposed to be the good guys. They were supposed to enforce the law—not break it. Instead, they broke the community's faith in a monumental way. This city has been harmed by their deception and greed, but the jury has spoken, and it has loudly said NO to corruption. NO to abuse of power. NO to special treatment. NO to injustice.

As we've often seen, the cover-up was worse than the original crime. The most troubling aspect of this case was the way these powerful defendants manipulated the justice system for their own purposes.

Some members of the jury had come out before the Kealohas but did not speak to the press. Several would later be interviewed on television and provide insight into their deliberations. But at this moment, they appeared relieved and relaxed. Some smiled broadly. One juror even took a bow. About nine months later, I had the opportunity to speak to one of the jurors. My first question was about the speed of the verdict. He told me that when the jury had first gotten into the deliberation room, they had immediately taken a vote as to each defendant just to see "where they stood." As to Katherine and Bobby Nguyen, they all voted guilty. As to Gordon Shiraishi, they all voted not guilty. As a result, he said, the only discussions they had concerned Louis Kealoha and Derek Hahn. Two members of the jury were concerned whether there was sufficient evidence to convict them beyond a reasonable doubt. No one believed that the defense had offered any evidence or argument that either was not guilty; the only issue was whether the government had met its burden of proof. The jury examined two specific pieces of evidence that ultimately convinced these two jurors to vote for guilt. The first was Louis's testimony at Gerard's trial in 2014. The jury all decided that there was absolutely no way anyone could tell that the person in the videotape surveillance footage was Gerard. In reviewing Louis's testimony from the trial, they wanted to see if Louis had hesitated in any way in stating that it was Gerard in the video. He had not.

The other evidence they discussed was the pattern of phone calls between the co-defendants that the government had introduced during the trial. In the course of its investigation, the government had obtained the cell phone records of each of the defendants and had mapped out on a chart the pattern of phone calls between them. These phone calls and text messages showed that at critical times during the conspiracy, Katherine, Louis, Derek and Bobby all had multiple communications with one another. At other times, there was almost no communication between the four of them. That evidence sealed the deal.

The juror also told me that they knew when they were coming out to render their decision that it was going to be an historic moment in Hawai'i history. As they lined up to enter the courtroom, they told each other, "Okay, this is it. This is history." They had agreed that when they filed into the courtroom no one would look at any of the defendants. They didn't want any defendant thinking by some furtive look or glance that they were not guilty.

I asked if any of them were scared, a question I had been asked myself many times before. He told me some of them were. They felt there could be some sort of retribution by the Kealohas or others on their behalf. But they were determined to do their civic duty. I was heartened to hear that they had done their duty in spite of their fear.

Throughout the day and the days to follow, news commentators offered their opinions. Lee Cataluna, then a columnist for the *Honolulu Star-Advertiser*, wrote that "the truly disturbing core of all the Kealohas' malfeasance is knowing that the Honolulu Police Department, our police department, was used to settle someone's personal score. What must happen now, what is critical—more critical than just about any other threat facing our community—is a fierce and fearless examination of all parts of the City agencies that allowed two high-powered, incredibly corrupt and not very sophisticated people to misuse public resources so egregiously for so long. Also crucial is the question of why it didn't bother anyone on the inside enough to find the guts to say something when they saw something."

Police Commission chair and former assistant US attorney Loretta Sheehan, reacting to the jury's verdict, told the *Honolulu Star-Advertiser*:

The jury heard the evidence and made a decision. Their decision was swift and definite. The jury has spoken and the integrity of the criminal justice system has been preserved. In regard to HPD, my sense is that they want to put this behind them, that they are tired of the shadow of Kealoha that has hung over their department. I can understand them wanting to move past this.

But respectfully, I disagree. We should be talking about what happened with Chief Kealoha, and what happened in the CIU, and what happened with this small band of individuals for a long, long time. This is not something we should try to move away from quickly. We should be talking about it, examining it, and figuring out ways to make sure that this never happens again.... I think we have to work hard to ask difficult questions, to ask uncomfortable questions. We have to feel free to offer constructive criticism. We have to be free to point out when we think there's a better way of doing things. There has to be give and take between the Police Department and the Police Commission.

And there has to be transparency. As the *Washington Post* says, "democracy dies in darkness." And they're right. And so that's what we have to do. We have to shine the light on what's happening at the Police Department. Because the police officers, all the way up to the police chief, are public servants.

Apparently these sentiments were not shared by many of the people in positions of power in Hawai'i local government. Susan Ballard, Louis's successor as chief of the Honolulu Police Department, issued a statement on behalf of HPD distancing the actions of the Kealohas from the department: "The damage caused by this small group of individuals hurt both the community and the department. But the men and women of the HPD have been working hard this past year and a half to restore HPD's reputation and the public's trust. We are moving forward and are committed to making sure that Honolulu continues to be one of the safest cities in the nation."

Mayor Caldwell, picking up the theme, issued a short and pointed statement, saying, "The jury has reached a verdict and I respect the process and their decision. It's time to move on." He added that he was "not one to look back, if there are problems, tackle those and move forward." It appeared that the political establishment was already attempting to persuade public opinion to "move on" without committing to any change. As the defenders of the status quo would repeatedly say in the days and months to follow, the actions of the Kealohas were those of "just a few bad apples" that had been eliminated from the batch. The rest of the apples were just fine. Of course, no one in either the state or local government had done a single thing to take out these bad apples. In fact, those that had the authority to do so, like the Police Commission, had repeatedly refused to investigate the allegations against the Kealohas. And those who tried had been removed from their jobs or, as in the case of Gerard, arrested, imprisoned and prosecuted.

The next day, June 28, Katherine returned to the courtroom on the government's motion to revoke her bail. Now the presumption of innocence no longer applied. Katherine was accompanied only by her lawyers. Louis was nowhere to be seen. Everyone in the courtroom knew what was coming. Katherine knew what was coming. The government made its request to detain Katherine pending sentencing, arguing she was a "walking crime spree" and could not be trusted not to try and obstruct justice yet again, just as she had done by framing Gerard and by convincing the Taitos and Ebersole to lie to the grand jury on her behalf. Katherine showed no emotion as she sat at the defense table, hands on her chin, looking straight ahead but not at the judge. She knew that she was not going to be leaving the courthouse the same way she had entered it. No support letter from Alison Lee Wong was going to save her now. Alison Lee Wong, to paraphrase the song, had caught the last train out of Clarksville.

Judge Seabright agreed with the government and ordered Katherine's bail revoked, saying that Katherine was a "corrupting influence" and "obstruction was her bread and butter." Judge Seabright also cited Katherine's "determined and consistent effort to have an innocent man incarcerated," a crime for which she was now convicted. Katherine said nothing, showing little if any emotion. The sound of the gavel rang throughout the courtroom as Judge Seabright left the bench. Katherine rose and was led away by two US marshals through a side door that led to an elevator and then directly into the marshals' courthouse cellblock. Katherine would never again be in court wearing aloha attire or greeting the press wearing a lei. No, those days were over. Katherine's next appearance in court would be in a white prison jumpsuit.

Months later, on October 22, 2019, in a plea deal to avoid additional jail time and the need for two more trials, Louis and Katherine each pleaded guilty to the bank fraud charges related to their false statements on several bank loan applications they had submitted to obtain additional monies to fund their lavish lifestyles. Katherine also pleaded guilty to providing misleading information to police investigators who were looking into her brother's alleged illegal opioid prescription scheme.

All charges would be consolidated for sentencing. After the guilty pleas, Wheat made his first and only appearance before the press, stating:

> Today another page is turned in the long saga that has plagued this community for some time. Today's pleas will bring some vindication for the additional victims of the Kealohas' fraud and will allow us to move on to continue our investigation.

Yes, Wheat's corruption investigation was continuing on. There was still work to be done. Several people had received target letters that were still outstanding, namely City and County prosecutor Keith Kaneshiro and Donna Leong, the head civil attorney for the City. Katherine's brother's trial was still to come. And it appeared certain that there would be more indictments to come. Wheat's investigation had not yet run to ground.

And as for the whereabouts of the mailbox and the identity of the person who stole it? Those are mysteries still to be solved. ❖

CHAPTER 25

Voldemort

I am frequently asked if Gerard or anyone on my team ever felt in danger or harassed by law enforcement or friends of the Kealohas. As straightforward as that question seems, it's difficult to answer. Can I point to a specific instance where I could prove harassment or retaliation? No. Did someone come up to me and make a direct threat? No. But sometimes intimidation, retaliation or the thought that you are in danger is more about the feeling of being scared, the feeling that something is about to happen, than something actually happening. I'm talking about that feeling you get that someone is watching you, and when you turn around you see a person look away. You have absolutely no proof that it was anything more than just a coincidence, but you just can't shake the feeling. Eventually, you convince yourself it's all right, but you still keep peeking out of the corner of your eye to try and catch the person looking at you again. Living with that feeling for over seven years is a little unnerving.

It was a feeling Gerard knew all too well. Gerard's answer to this question was an emphatic "Yes." For Gerard, that back-of-the-neck, prickly-hair sensation had already proven to be true. He didn't need any further police encounters to heighten his sense of danger. During the years following the announcement that the Kealohas were under investigation, Gerard had several minor run-ins with HPD officers, which only further fueled his fear that he was being watched, followed and retaliated against. Several times he was stopped by a patrol car for traffic infractions that became much more than the usual admonition of "Here's your citation, be more careful driving next time." Gerard was even pulled over when he was driving to the federal courthouse for the first day of the Kealoha trial. If this wasn't enough of a coincidence, it was where and when he was pulled over that made the traffic stop even more suspicious.

Gerard was driving towards Honolulu on Nimitz Highway during the morning rush hour commute when he was pulled over. Nimitz Highway is one of the most congested streets on O'ahu during the morning rush hour. It is one of only two main thoroughfares into Honolulu. That's like getting a speeding ticket in midtown Manhattan during rush hour. It's just not possible, until it happens. Before he was pulled over Gerard, who was always on alert, had noticed a patrol car following him for several miles, switching lanes with him as he drove towards Honolulu. All he could do was slam his hands onto the steering wheel as the siren went on and pull his car off to the side.

Constant fear and anxiety can take their toll. And they had for Gerard. Because of what he had endured, for long periods of time Gerard had been afraid to go out and had become a recluse in his own home. He kept his window shades drawn, and when he did venture out his head was like a swivel on a stick, constantly looking to see who was around, expecting to be arrested or harassed for something, anything, at any moment. At my urging he finally sought professional help and was diagnosed with, among other things, PTSD. I've always wondered what a psychiatrist says to alleviate a person's "paranoid delusions" when, in fact, there is no delusion at all!

I was told by one reporter who covered the story that he had been told by HPD police officers who were friendly to him that "they could no longer protect him." But that is his story to tell and I did not learn of this until after the Kealohas were already convicted and incarcerated.

Brian, the first investigator assigned to the case in my office, told me years after the fact that early on in the case when he came out of his house to go to work one morning, he found a knife plunged into his front yard. Not by the curb, but in the middle of his yard. Just sticking there, straight up. Buried up to the hilt. He didn't see anyone do it. There was no note attached. It was just there. A warning? The case had only just recently started making the news, and his home was in a neighborhood where a lot of police officers also lived. It was the timing that made him believe it wasn't just some drunken guy passing by his house who had randomly plunged a knife into the ground. It could have been anyone's front lawn. But it wasn't. It was his. Brian didn't tell me about it at the time because he didn't know who had done it or why. But later he told me he had the prickly-hair thing going on after he found the knife. "Prickly hair" may not be a legal standard, but it should be, somewhere above proof by preponderance of the evidence and right below proof beyond a reasonable doubt.

I knew from past experience that it's not above law enforcement to use their authority to get even for some perceived slight or affront you may have caused them. There's nothing new or profound about this fact, except when it happens to you. Many years ago, when I first moved to Hawai'i, I represented a client who was charged with money laundering. My client was a right wing tax protester who had been getting under the IRS's skin for years for not paying taxes and for creating a business to educate others about why they too should not pay taxes. He believed that paying taxes was voluntary and often appeared on local talk shows openly advocating his position. Under federal law, if a person truly has a "good faith belief" that paying taxes is voluntary, they cannot be convicted for failing to pay taxes. The IRS hadn't been able to touch him. I successfully argued to a jury that the IRS had set my client up in a money laundering scheme due to his political views. In other words, they had intentionally entrapped him for a crime he wouldn't otherwise have committed but for their actions. Within months of the not guilty verdict, I was audited by the IRS for several years in a row. It had never happened before, never happened again. Luckily for me, as my wife did our tax returns, we had slightly overpaid our taxes for most of the years they audited us, so we actually got money back! Ha!

When we began to investigate the Kealohas in earnest, I checked our cars to make sure the registrations and safety inspection stickers were all up to date. Turns out my safety inspection was five months overdue, so I got that taken care of immediately. I called my son and told him to do the same. Whenever we drove, we made sure our seat belts were always on and I tried, I said *tried*, to stay within the speed limit. Hard to do for an old cab driver from NYC. But there was no reason to give a police officer any justification to pull me over and "make something happen." Too many of my clients had told me stories of how cops had planted guns or drugs on them. I never believed them, and I knew no one was going to believe me either if I told that story to a lawyer.

Throughout the case there was lurking a dark and foreboding figure who was always present in the back of our thoughts. That menacing dark person was thought to have connections to Katherine. We jokingly referred to him as "he whose name cannot be spoken," a reference to Voldemort of *Harry Potter* fame. It was meant as a joke, but sometimes not. Even today my wife and I stick to this mantra and don't speak this person's real name lest our fears manifest themselves into reality. Superstitious? Yes. But better safe than sorry.

During our investigation into Katherine's past history we uncovered the fact that she had been involved in multiple business ventures. They seemed completely innocuous at first. A real estate venture here, a solar company there, a financial hui here. Business partners came and went. But one name stood out. He was rumored to be a local mafia figure. He was a person whom many of my clients had told me was very dangerous and violent. I had heard the same from federal agents. It was said he had thugs working for him and had had a professional sports personality beaten up at his nightclub. To this day, if I come across a story in the paper referring to "he whose name cannot be spoken," I'll simply say "Voldemort," and my wife knows exactly who I'm talking about.

It seemed that every month we would learn new information that made the connection between Katherine and this Voldemort fellow stronger. At first it was hard to believe that Katherine, a high-level county prosecutor, a person who was head of the Career Offender Unit, could possibly be a friend or business associate of a suspected under-world crime figure. But the more we learned about Katherine's character and personality, the more we thought it was possible. When we finally got the FBI to investigate the Kealohas, the thought that Katherine might take matters into her own hands and "call" upon her friend was always in the back of our minds. It never happened, but that didn't stop us from being wary of strangers or out-of-place cars in our neighborhood, didn't stop us from closing window shades so no one could get a clear look into our house. After the Kealohas were convicted, Voldemort himself was charged with murder. To this day we have no specific evidence that Katherine really had any direct connection to this person, but the mere suspicion that she did was enough to keep us on our toes.

My wife also experienced a similar incident to Brian's, an incident that just didn't feel like a coincidence. It was December of 2016, and it had just become public that Louis had received a target letter from Wheat, the first indication that the Kealohas were about to be charged with crimes. I hadn't gotten home yet. It had just turned dark, and she was on the phone with a friend when she noticed a police car parked across the street from our residence. It was a regular blue-and-white squad car, not an unmarked police vehicle. The officer just sat there in his car, doing nothing as far as she could tell. He wasn't on his radio. He wasn't looking around. He was just sitting in his car. Right across from our house. We live in a very safe residential neighborhood. Police cars only come around when they have been called. They never patrol our neighborhood, much less park their vehicle on the side of the street. And never before had a police car parked directly across from our house.

My wife wanted to let him know she knew he was there, just in case. She went out into our carport where he could see her and see that she was on the phone, talking. Her friend on the phone, a former state judge like my wife, told her to write down the license plate number of the police car, but before she was able to get in position to see the license plate, the officer drove off. It left her a bit unnerved, even though there was nothing to support the assumption that the officer was doing anything wrong. It was just the timing of the whole thing. After what Gerard had been through, we couldn't help thinking that this was some form of intimidation.

And I'd be remiss not to mention the bees. Yes, bees. Instruments of terror. Maybe not one of the seven plagues, but still, a lot of bees. And again, it was the timing thing. It was the day the Kealohas were arraigned for their indictment, October 19, 2017. Because I was the first assistant, while I did not get the more prestigious underground parking space, I had an assigned parking space in the open-air lot on one side of the federal building. After the tragic bombing of the Oklahoma federal building, a building eerily similar in construction and appearance to the Hawai'i federal building, only federal employees were allowed to park in these spaces. But no fence surrounds the parking area. Anyone can gain access directly to any vehicle on the lot. After a long day of work and after attending the arraignment of the Kealohas, their first appearance in court as criminal defendants, as I walked to my white two-door Mazda 2 to drive home, I saw bees. Hundreds of them. They were swarming all over my front passenger-side wheel and some were inside my car, as I had left my windows slightly ajar to let out the heat of the day. I'm not afraid of bees, having grown up in Vermont and having often been called upon by my parents to knock beehives off tree limbs or from under our house's eaves. This had led to many, many bee stings—to which I am not allergic, but still, being stung is no fun. And this wasn't just a few bees flying around; it was a colony. I had never, ever before seen a bee in the parking lot, much less a colony. But there they were. On my car. In my car. Over my car. Not my neighbor's nice Lexus parked a few feet away, but on my little Mazda. And on this day of days.

The beekeeper who came to collect the bees told me that the hive, which she believed was located in a rotted-out section of a tree not too far away, must have gotten flooded in the recent rains, forcing the queen to move out right onto the underside of my front passenger side wheel. After she calmed them down with smoke, she scooped up the queen and placed her inside her portable beehive. As she explained, once the queen was inside all the other bees would follow. She had all the bees scooped up in short order, and I was able to drive home without a single stinger in me. It was a strange event to say the least, and again with the timing, the day the Kealohas were arraigned. I quickly put the thought out of my mind that this was some sort of hex, reminding myself of my wife's comment that as long as I was doing my job, as long as I was seeking justice, and doing the right thing, we were protected. I knew we were. ❖

CHAPTER 26

Justice Served: A Time of Reckoning

After months and months of delay due to the COVID-19 pandemic, which had all but closed federal courthouses throughout the country, the Kealohas came before Judge Seabright for sentencing on November 30, 2020. Katherine was to be first, to be followed by Louis. More than a year and a half had passed since they were found guilty. Katherine had been in jail since her conviction, while Louis was free on bond.

During that time a lot had happened—some for the better, some for the worse. On September 13, 2019, the civil verdict against Florence and Gerard was overturned by a state judge and dismissed. This was based upon the now proven fact that Katherine had repeatedly lied on the witness stand during that trial. On the other hand, my boss, Peter Wolff, who had served as the federal defender for the District of Hawai'i for twenty-four years, was informed by the Ninth Circuit Court of Appeals that he would *not* be retained for an additional four-year term. There were many reasons given, privately, for his non-reappointment. None, in my opinion, were justified. Disappointingly, some of the reasons raised were complaints made by powerful people who were still aligned with the Kealohas, while others were made by people who were simply threatened by the prestige our office, and particularly I, had gained due to our representation of Gerard. I surmised from comments made to me that these individuals and members of the district court preferred a more "compliant" office.

Had we gone too far in our zealous representation of Gerard after his case had been dismissed? Was our collaboration with the FBI and with Wheat somehow "unethical" for a public defender? My answer is no. These allegations were the exact same ones that had been made against Lawson by Louis's attorney in his letter to the dean of the University of

Hawaiʻi law school in 2019. Allegations that had been thoroughly dismissed as preposterous. Certainly, we knew from the numerous private and public comments made and letters we had received over the years that the public did not share these sentiments. Moreover, given that we legally represented Gerard as a client as a victim of a crime, even after his charges had been dismissed, the accusation was misplaced and, quite frankly, unfounded. When pressed to state what rule of the ethics code we had violated, which would be a very damning allegation if true, the Ninth Circuit judges who made this accusation refused to answer.

My other clients were overwhelmingly supportive and saw no conflict with my having helped the government prosecute the Kealohas even while I defended them against this same government. Many times, during dinner out with my wife, random people had come up to us to thank me for what my office and I had done in bringing the Kealohas to justice. Often these people were either law enforcement agents or family members of law enforcement officers. They wanted me to know that even though they were pro–law enforcement, no one liked corrupt cops. One memorable moment occurred at a University of Hawaiʻi basketball game. As I walked up the aisle, a gentleman who was also a season ticket holder like myself, whom I only knew from attending the games, stuck out his hand as I passed by. He was a large man with a full beard and a hand the size of a bear's paw. The only thing I knew about him was that he was a retired police officer, I think a major. But he knew who I was. I shook his hand and he quickly pulled me towards himself. We were nose to nose. I was a bit concerned, as I had no idea which side of the fence he was on. All he said was, "Get the motherfucker!"

To be fair, after Peter Wolff had served as head of the office for twenty-four years, there were several former employees who were unhappy with him, as well as with my supervision of the office over the years. Their discontent, combined with the various other political agendas in play, were cited as reasons to justify his non-retention. I did not apply for his position. It didn't seem right, nor did I expect to be appointed given the accusation made against me by Ninth Circuit judges that I had somehow been unethical in my zealous representation of Gerard. When one such former employee was appointed as the new head of the office, I chose to leave. Peter Wolff and I both retired on October 31, 2020. I had been a federal public defender, in Philadelphia and Hawaiʻi, since 1987, over thirty-three years. Enough was enough. By the time the Kealohas were sentenced, I was no longer Gerard's attorney.

Seating in Judge Seabright's courtroom for the sentencing hearings was limited due to precautions necessitated by the pandemic. Social distancing had to be enforced within the courtroom, which meant that seats had to be left empty between people. I had been specifically invited to attend but at the last minute was informed there would be *no* seat reserved for me in the courtroom. I was told I could sit in another courtroom and watch on a closed-circuit monitor if I wished. I wanted to see the drama and reaction of all the players in the courtroom. I wanted to be present at the end. And Gerard, who was experiencing last-minute anxiety about the sentencings, wanted me at his side in court. But if I couldn't sit with Gerard, and if I could only see the person speaking on the monitor, there was no reason for me to attend the sentencing hearings. Instead, I chose to listen to the hearings from the comfort of my home.

Federal sentencing guidelines determine a very specific sentencing range, in months, that a judge is required to consider when imposing a sentence in federal court. These calculations are sometimes very complicated, and a court may vary upward or downward from these guidelines if there are compelling reasons to do so. Judge Seabright, in this case, had already informed the Kealohas prior to sentencing that he was likely to sentence them above the recommended sentencing guideline range. But how far above was anyone's guess. Katherine was facing, at the high end of her guideline range, 121 months plus a consecutive two years mandated by law for her conviction on the identity theft charges. Louis was looking at 63 months on the high end of his sentencing range.

Katherine was up first. Katherine's new attorney, Gary Singh, tried his best to offer mitigating evidence on her behalf, but given all she had done it was not an easy task. I did not envy his position. I had been there many times myself. Singh argued that, while not directly asserting it excused her criminal behavior, Katherine had been under the influence of prescription pain pills for years that had clouded her judgement. It was about all he could say.

In the days just prior to sentencing, Katherine had submitted a five-page letter to the court. In it she supposedly expressed her acceptance of responsibility. Her letter began by saying that "[i]t has taken the fear, loneliness, despair, conflict, daily cruelty and pain of prison to completely break me down, in order to build the courage to speak the truth about my life." She then apologized, in general, to "anyone" she might have harmed. But not once in the five-page letter did she offer any apology directly to Gerard or Florence or even mention them by name. Katherine also proclaimed that she alone was guilty and that the others who were convicted at trial with her, including Louis, were innocent and "should go home." As she said, "All three of them are good family men, who do not deserve to go to prison." She continued, "I took advantage of their friendships and of our relationships, and their only mistakes were in trusting me and associating with me…. I accept full responsibility for my widespread destruction that I've caused…. I wish I could explain it or even understand it, but I can't. The only thing I know for certain is that I alone am responsible for all of the damage and destruction." She then forgave, without specifying who she was talking about, all those who "did not speak the truth."

While some might wish to view her statements as virtuous, a form of martyrdom, to most of us it appeared to be yet another attempt by Katherine to invalidate the jury's verdict, a verdict that had been reached after several weeks of trial testimony. Katherine was declaring that the jury had gotten it wrong because people had lied on the stand. It was the type of acceptance letter that, in a normal case, would have done far more damage than good, as it demonstrated no real contrition for her criminal wrongdoing at all. But Judge Seabright did not need Katherine's letter to justify the sentence he wanted to impose; he had enough other ammunition not to give her letter a second thought.

Katherine, to my surprise, also chose to stand up in court and allocute. Allocution is the right of every defendant to directly speak to the sentencing judge before sentence is imposed. For the first time, she somewhat apologized to Gerard and Florence for her actions. I say "somewhat" because most of her apology consisted of her asking Gerard to someday find it in "*his* heart" to "forgive *her*." To me, this demonstrated that, yet again, Katherine could not help thinking only of herself at this important moment in her life.

The prosecution's remarks were brief. The government did not need to rehash everything that they had already proved during the trial to Judge Seabright. Consistent with the plea agreements they had reached with Katherine, the government did not ask for an upward variance but rather just the high end of the sentencing guideline range: 121 months plus the two-year consecutive sentence mandated by the identity theft charges.

It was now Gerard's turn to make a statement to the court as a victim. Gerard was too anxious to speak, so Eric Seitz, Gerard's civil attorney who was representing Gerard in his civil case against the Kealohas and the City and County of Honolulu, read Gerard's statement to the court. It was short but pointed, blaming Katherine for the pain and suffering he and his mother had endured for many years. Gerard wrote, "It wasn't bad enough that you stole from my mother—your own grandmother—but you also harassed, mocked, and humiliated her... You will be released someday...but you can never erase the pain, grief and tremendous damage you caused us."

Charlotte Malott, Gerard's sister, spoke on behalf of Florence and the entire Puana 'ohana. She too spoke about the pain and shame Katherine had put Florence through, the loss of their family home and specifically the outrageous and insulting claim that Florence was incompetent. "For shame," she said. Charlotte made it clear that all Florence had wanted was an explanation and an apology, which she had never gotten and now never would.

*   *   *

The time for Judge Seabright to impose sentence had arrived. Judge Seabright recounted all the wrongful acts that Katherine was responsible for that would serve to justify the sentence he was about to impose. Judge Seabright spoke for a good thirty-five minutes. He held little back. You could hear in the tone of his voice the anger he felt. I thought going into the sentencing hearing that Judge Seabright would impose a slightly higher sentence than the high end of the guidelines recommended (121 months plus 24 months), but after listening to him lambast Katherine, I felt he really was going to go much higher than I had predicted.

Judge Seabright also made it clear, specifically because Katherine and her lawyers had still not conceded that Katherine was the infamous "Alison Lee Wong," that as far as he was concerned Alison Lee Wong was seated right before him occupying the same seat as Katherine. Judge Seabright found her and Louis's behavior "shocking," saying that it could not have occurred without the Kealohas having HPD at their beck and call. Further, Judge Seabright told Katherine that in her attempt to marginalize Gerard and Florence for the civil case, she had clearly gotten Louis and CIU to do her dirty work. Judge Seabright held that even though the jury had found the Kealohas guilty of obstruction under the conspiracy charge, he had no doubt that they were also guilty of the more serious civil rights violations. He noted that had the jury found her guilty of the civil rights violations, the sentencing guideline range would have been much higher. And it was on this basis that he was justified in imposing a sentence above the guidelines.

Katherine rose to receive her sentence. Judge Seabright imposed 132 months for the conspiracy charges and an additional 24 months for the identity theft, for a total of 156 months in prison, or thirteen years. True to his word, Judge Seabright had varied upwards, but only by eleven months. Many people were disappointed in the sentence, believing it was too lenient given all she had done. Still, thirteen years in prison is a significant sentence, a sentence I wouldn't wish upon anyone. There's no parole in the federal system. An inmate can only earn a little less than two months off a year for good behavior. If Katherine behaved while incarcerated, she would serve about eleven years of her thirteen-year sentence. Being fifty now, Katherine will be at least sixty years old by the time of her release.

Louis was up next. Given that Judge Seabright had varied upward for Katherine, Louis knew he was facing a higher sentence than his guideline range of 63 months at the high end. Louis's lawyer tried to lay most of the blame on Katherine, using the "I am only a man doing what my wife told me to do" argument. But it was hard to swallow, given that Louis ran the twentieth-largest law enforcement department in the country, with over 2,000 officers serving under him. Louis had not written a letter accepting responsibility but, like Katherine, chose to allocute in person. And for the first time Louis attempted to apologize to Gerard. Louis claimed he did what he had to do to "protect his family" because Katherine had convinced him Gerard was a threat. People go to great lengths to protect their family; I understand that. But in this case Louis, in his position as the chief of police, used his authority and officers of his police department to violate his and their oaths of office and the laws they swore to uphold to frame an innocent man. All because Katherine had convinced him Gerard was dangerous and because he had no choice but to follow the wishes of his wife? To me, it appeared by his statement that Louis, even as he stood before the court seeking mercy, still did not understand and accept what he had done. I marveled at the level of hypocrisy that both he and his wife continued to indulge in as they attempted to explain away their actions to the court. Particularly given that they both had spent years arresting, charging and putting people behind bars, many for crimes far less serious than their own.

Judge Seabright outlined the many criminal acts he believed that Louis had engaged in as chief of police. He took great pains, as he had when sentencing Katherine, to make it clear to everyone listening that

Gerard had been framed for a crime he did not commit. That Louis had used his powerful law enforcement position and its resources to falsely arrest and charge Gerard for his own personal ends. Make no mistake, Judge Seabright repeated several times, Gerard had not stolen the mailbox. He was an innocent man. And while Judge Seabright conceded that it appeared that it was Katherine who set everything in motion, Louis was "right by her side, cheering her on, using [his] position" to frame Gerard. "The breadth of this criminal conduct is astounding," Judge Seabright told Louis; "this truly is a case where the truth seems to be stranger than fiction."

Judge Seabright reiterated that, as far as he was concerned, the trial evidence had clearly proven that criminal civil rights violation had also been proven, and he was going to impose a higher sentence than the sentencing guideline range recommended. Louis rose to receive his sentence. Judge Seabright varied upward from the high end of the sentencing range of 63 months to 84 months. Seven years in prison for the former chief of police, now thoroughly disgraced. Because of the pandemic, Judge Seabright allowed Louis to surrender himself in April of 2021, which was later continued to June, so that Louis could be fully vaccinated before entering prison.

Again, many believed the sentence was too lenient. But as I saw it, a seven-year sentence for a man in his early sixties was a long time. And it would not be an easy sentence to serve, not only because Louis was a police officer, but because he had been the chief of police. There would be many inmates in prison who would not take too kindly to him. I felt the sentence was sufficient under the circumstances. To this day, I have no reason to believe Louis knew anything about the original scheme to frame Gerard, though I certainly believe Katherine and Bobby Nguyen were involved from the start. But once Louis learned of what was happening, he was all in. If anyone had a responsibility to stop the abuse of power that was unleashed upon Gerard, it was Louis. Not only did he do nothing to prevent it; he'd jumped right in with both feet.

Gerard told me he too had thought the sentences would be harsher, but he was satisfied and relieved it was over. As he told me, maybe now he could move on with his life and focus on more positive things. While the sentencing hearings for Derek Hahn and Bobby Nguyen were to come the next day, Gerard was no longer anxious. I could hear him let out several deep breaths as we spoke and could sense the tension in his body being released. Good. Good for Gerard. Good for the entire Puana family.

After the Kealohas were sentenced, Wheat, through his office, issued a four-page Department of Justice national press release detailing the nature of their crimes and the sentences imposed. The press release stated:

> The evidence at trial established that the Kealohas used their considerable power, including commandeering the Honolulu Police Department's elite Criminal Intelligence Unit, to frame Gerard with stealing their mailbox. To accomplish this, the conspirators prepped the mailbox to be "stolen," selectively edited grainy surveillance video to conceal their preparatory acts, falsely identified Gerard as the culprit captured by the video, falsified police reports, withheld and destroyed evidence, and repeatedly lied about their activity to investigators, the federal grand jury, and the District Court for the District of Hawai'i.

San Diego United States attorney Robert Brewer was quoted in the press release as saying:

> Today, after years of manipulating the levers of justice to shroud their own crimes, justice was delivered to two corrupt public officials. This was a flagrant and stunning abuse of power that victimized an entire community by undermining public confidence in its leaders and their rule of law. If not for the initial dogged investigation by former First Assistant Federal Defender Alexander Silvert, who brought this matter to the attention of federal authorities, followed by the incredible work by FBI agents and prosecutors Michael Wheat, Joseph Orabona, Janaki Chopra and Colin McDonald, the Kealohas would still be manipulating justice.

The next day Derek Hahn and Bobby Nguyen were sentenced. Hahn had ordered Silva to falsify his reports, directed Bobby to attend Katherine's civil deposition for no apparent official reason, hidden videotape evidence and utilized the resources and manpower of CIU to conduct unwarranted twenty-four-hour surveillance on Gerard. Hahn was sentenced to 42 months in prison, a sentence within his sentencing guideline range. Judge Seabright said while Hahn had, at least, not lied to anyone under oath, his "fingerprints" were all over this case. Although he did not allocute, I was told Hahn had the courtesy and fortitude to turn and face Gerard and his sister, Charlotte, when they spoke to him as victims of his crimes. I respected that.

Bobby was the final defendant sentenced. He showed no contrition and also did not allocute. According to people who were in the courtroom, he never once looked at Gerard and said nothing that would explain his conduct. The mitigation offered up by his attorney was simply that he was just a lowly police officer, a "footman" who had only followed the orders of his superiors. Bobby's attorney argued that not only did Bobby have to follow orders from the Kealohas while on duty; he had to follow "orders" from his wife, Katherine's niece, while off-duty at home. This argument did not sit well with Judge Seabright. In response, Judge Seabright listed the numerous times Bobby had lied under oath. He lied to the grand jury. He lied to the Ethics Commission. He lied to the postal inspector. He lied to the FBI. Judge Seabright said that the sheer number of times Bobby lied, and the ease with which he did it, showed his arrogance. Arrogance that no one would question what he said. Bobby not only had lied with ease, Judge Seabright said, but he fully embraced the lie to help frame Gerard. According to Judge Seabright, rather than being a mere "footman," Bobby was the "Joe Friday that made things happen," and this set Bobby apart from both Niall Silva and Derek Hahn. Although Judge Seabright did not vary upward, he gave Bobby more prison time than Hahn, sentencing Bobby to 54 months, more than four years in prison.

The last two defendants to be sentenced in the case, Niall Silva and Jesse Ebersole, appeared before Judge Seabright on February 3, 2021. Both had pleaded guilty to lying under oath and to the FBI. Silva had admitted that his entire testimony in Gerard's trial was false, as were the two HPD reports he prepared that had been admitted into evidence as Government Exhibit #7. He also admitted he repeatedly lied to the FBI until they confronted him with undisputed evidence that he was not telling the truth, whereupon he finally owned up. He was, however, the first HPD officer to admit there was a conspiracy and to cooperate. Due to his cooperation and testimony during the Kealoha trial, the government filed a motion seeking a downward variance from his sentencing guideline range and asked for probation, citing the importance of his cooperation and his four years on pretrial release without incident.

The day before his sentencing hearing, I was asked by the press if Silva should receive a jail sentence despite his cooperation. Without any hesitation I said yes. Silva had taken an oath, as a police officer, to tell the truth at Gerard's trial and had blatantly and repeatedly violated that oath. If not for the mistrial, Gerard could have been convicted. If Gerard had been convicted, would the United States Attorney's Office have referred the case to the FBI? No. Would the FBI have ever investigated the Kealohas? No. Would Silva have gotten away with his lies under oath? Yes. He did not come forward on his own. He waited until he was trapped and cornered before finding his way to the truth. Yes, I said, he needed to go to jail. I did not make this remark casually. But it is the bedrock of our criminal justice system that people tell the truth on the witness stand at a jury trial. Silva had not, and he was an officer of the law.

I have been threatened by prosecutors on a number of occasions that if my client or one of our witnesses lied under oath, they would be charged and would be put in jail. The same must hold true for law enforcement officers who lie under oath. There cannot be a double standard. The justice system fails if people lie on the stand with impunity, particularly law enforcement officers. It is in the interests of both the defense and the prosecution for witnesses to tell the truth, and, if they don't and the lie is important enough, they must be brought to justice so that others will not follow their example. Here a message had to be sent to HPD that lying under oath was not acceptable and would be met with severe consequences. And that required, in my opinion, that Silva go to jail.

Judge Seabright agreed. The government and Silva's attorney argued in support of a sentence of probation. They recognized that Silva was in a difficult position and was just following orders. Judge Seabright, however, took issue with this argument, stating, "It doesn't work in a war crime tribunal, and it doesn't work here." He noted that Silva had "lied, and he lied, and he lied, and he lied, and he lied," adding, "[t]he message that you can lie as you did for as long as you did, obstruct the truth-seeking function for as long as you did, and then at a late stage come clean and get no jail time is the wrong message. I think it's a dangerous one." Silva was ordered to serve nine months in prison.

Ebersole was the last defendant in the Kealoha saga to be sentenced. He had lied to the grand jury on Katherine's behalf, denying he had had an affair with her. The FBI had traced monies spent by Katherine on their affair to funds she had stolen from Gerard and the Taitos. Ebersole's attorney argued that while Ebersole had lied on behalf of Katherine to cover up their affair, he was ignorant of the crimes Katherine had committed.

In his defense, Ebersole's attorney stated, "Hurricane Katherine swept through this court and through this state and wreaked havoc on not just Mr. Ebersole and the community, but quite a number of people." As a result of his conviction, his attorney pointed out, Ebersole had also lost his twenty-seven-year career with the fire department and was now working as a special projects coordinator for a homeless services center. Judge Seabright was understanding, saying, "Mrs. Kealoha was a master of manipulation. That was evidenced from everything I've seen, and she manipulated you." Ebersole received a two-year probationary sentence.

The sound of the gavel resonated throughout the courtroom as Judge Seabright exited. And that was it. Justice had been served. Gerard's long nightmare was finally over. Maybe Florence could rest in peace.

In the early morning hours of February 13, 2020, Florence had joined her husband. She did not live to know the sentences that had been imposed. I asked Gerard to read a short message from me at her funeral. It was my final goodbye to a great lady of Hawai'i.

"Although I knew Florence for only a short time, her strength and spirit were undeniable. When I first met her when she was 93, her eyes

Gerard and Florence Puana

had burned brightly as she reached out to grab my hand to welcome me into her daughter's home. Her voice was soft, but firm. She did not waiver in her faith or in her courage to speak her truth. Even then, she wished no one ill will. That was not her way. I am so grateful that, in my own small way, I could help her let others know what really happened to her and Gerard. I am saddened to this day that we could not save the family home she and her husband built, but I am glad Florence was able to see her own vindication—even if she, as she would say, needed no such thing. We all did, and I'm glad I was a part of it. I know the Puana family will stay strong and true to itself."

*   *   *

What has been called "the most important public corruption trial the state has ever seen" had come to an end. I had lived and breathed this case for more than seven and a half years, from July 2, 2013, to February 3, 2021. When Gerard first sat in my office and proclaimed not only that he was innocent but also that he was being framed by two of the most powerful and influential law enforcement people in Hawai'i, I could never have imagined, never in a million years, that his case would lead to the exposing and unraveling of the largest public corruption scandal in Hawai'i history. And to think it all started with the theft of a little white mailbox. ❖

Epilogue

While Katherine has been in prison since her conviction in June of 2019, Louis Kealoha, Bobby Nguyen, Derek Hahn and Niall Silva all surrendered to begin to serve their sentences in June of 2021. Bobby and Derek have appealed their convictions to the Ninth Circuit Court of Appeals.

But this is not the end of the mailbox conspiracy saga. The trial of Katherine's brother, Rudy Puana, for allegedly writing illegal opioid prescriptions is still pending. In yet another surprising development, the government claims it has a photo of Katherine doing a line of cocaine on Louis's desk at HPD to win a bet with her brother. Wheat continues to bring witnesses before the federal grand jury, and it's expected that further indictments will be forthcoming against prominent figures in Honolulu City and County government. These possible indictments most likely relate to the still outstanding target letters against former prosecutor Keith Kaneshiro, corporation counsel chief Donna Leong and others for obstruction of justice allegations and questions regarding the propriety of the $250,000 buyout given to Louis for his early retirement. Former City and County managing director Roy Amemiya, who sits right below the mayor in the hierarchy of city government, received a "letter" from Wheat in June of 2021 indicating he is now the target of Wheat's ongoing criminal investigation. And should either Kaneshiro, Leong or Amemiya decide to cooperate with federal authorities and provide information on other wrongdoing within Honolulu City and County government, the ramifications for Hawai'i state politics could be impacted for many years to come. It appears that the door into public corruption that Gerard Puana's case kicked open is far from being closed.

A few weeks prior to Louis's surrendering to serve his sentence, Gerard's civil attorney, Eric Seitz, took Louis's deposition in Gerard's pending civil rights lawsuit against HPD and the City and County of Honolulu. In a surprising and unexpected development, Louis did a 180 and testified, under oath, that no crime was ever committed by him or his wife against Gerard and they hadn't framed him. Despite being confronted with his signed plea agreement and sworn testimony before Judge Seabright in which he admitted to having framed Gerard and lying under oath at Gerard's trial, Louis maintained that none of it was true. Louis even further denied that he had testified during Gerard's trial that Gerard was the person in the videotape who stole the mailbox. When confronted with a transcript of his testimony where he expressly stated it was Gerard in the videotape surveillance footage, Louis simply responded that he didn't remember saying that. It is yet to be determined how this will play out in the civil trial and/or whether Louis will face new perjury charges. Louis's sentence was lighter than it otherwise might have been because he had signed the plea agreement and accepted responsibility for his crimes before Judge Seabright. It now appears that after having been given this benefit and having already been sentenced, Louis feels free to return to his claim of absolute innocence with impunity.

In a welcome sign of change, the Honolulu Police Commission has become more aggressive in upholding its responsibilities, with the appointment of two new commissioners with legal backgrounds, one a retired state judge and the other a former state attorney general. They have pushed for more transparency and accountability and seem to be willing to ask the tough questions. HPD chief Susan Ballard chose to resign when the Police Commission's 2021 performance evaluation found her lacking in several key areas. Ballard claimed she had little choice, since it appeared she had lost the confidence of the Police Commission and the mayor. HPD continues to be in a state of disarray, with divided loyalties, and has clearly not yet recovered from the Kealoha scandal. Given Ballard's resignation, the Police Commission now has the responsibility of appointing a new police chief a little more than two years after Louis's resignation. Newly elected mayor Blangiardi, along with the city council, have both publicly declared they want a say in the selection of the next chief, even though the authority to appoint another new chief rests solely with the Police Commission.

Many believe the Kealohas and their police officer co-defendants were simply a few bad apples who made individually bad decisions and have likened them to the Keystone Cops. This has become an ongoing theme repeatedly echoed by government and HPD officials whenever they have the opportunity. Unfortunately, many people are beginning to believe this to be true. But nothing could be further from the truth. Their actions, however inept, threatened the very core of Honolulu's law enforcement system. These were some of the highest members of Honolulu's law enforcement community, who used their authority and the heavy hand of law enforcement to frame an innocent man. This included a large portion of an entire unit within the police department, the CIU. And no one checked them. Not the Police Commission. Not the Ethics Commission. Not the Office of Disciplinary Counsel. And not the Honolulu Office of the Prosecuting Attorney. Those few individuals who did take notice lost their jobs. It was only through federal intervention that justice ultimately prevailed. Gerard was lucky. But others who have been falsely accused, convicted and sentenced to years in jail have not been so fortunate.

Law enforcement agencies are inherently undemocratic in structure and philosophy. It's only the checks and balances by government oversight agencies and the courts that ensure law enforcement serves justice in a fair, impartial and unbiased manner. When these institutions fail, people like the Kealohas flourish.

It's uncertain whether the City will learn from and embrace the opportunity to effect meaningful change that Gerard's case presents. The opportunity exists, but there are tremendous institutional forces resistant to change. Even now, in the face of recent HPD shootings of several unarmed civilians, HPD and SHOPO are standing their ground against meaningful reform. And the Ethics Commission quietly dismissed all of their investigations into the Kealohas that Totto and DeCaires had initiated, without making any findings and without any introspection as to how the Kealohas had been able to successfully subvert their process. Gerard himself is still waiting for his full measure of justice. He has sued the City and the Kealohas for compensation for the illegal acts committed against him, but the City has refused to settle his civil lawsuit and his case appears to be headed to trial. Whatever the legal reasons may be for not settling his case, I am disheartened over the simple lack of compassion and humanity being demonstrated by the City. No one should have to endure what Gerard went through. It appears that legal gamesmanship is winning out over doing what's right. I, for one, remain hopeful that, in the end, the City will do right by Gerard, right by the Puana 'ohana and right by the entire Hawai'i community so the healing can begin. I am also hopeful that meaningful and lasting reforms will be implemented to ensure that this type of criminal conduct is routed out and prevented before anyone else is subjected to the criminal abuse Gerard endured. It's a tall order but entirely attainable if we remain committed to the fundamental principle of justice for all. ❖

Chronology

2009	Florence Puana obtains reverse mortgage based upon advice of Katherine Kealoha, her granddaughter. Condo purchased from a portion of the funds for Gerard Puana.
6/29/11	Gerard Puana arrested for unauthorized entry into a dwelling (his neighbor's patio) due to argument over parking space.
9/10/12	Letter sent from Florence Puana to Katherine Kealoha regarding status of reverse mortgage after Florence discovers loan not paid off.
9/15/12	Katherine Kealoha sends two letters (including "Rue the Day" letter) to Florence Puana.
3/7/13	Florence and Gerard Puana file civil lawsuit against Katherine Kealoha.
3/13/13	Gerard's request for a DANC plea is rejected by state judge; he is sentenced to forty-seven days in jail, credit for time served, and five years of probation.
6/12/13	State court accepts DANC plea from Gerard, nullifying conviction status.
6/19/13	First day of Katherine Kealoha's deposition in civil case.
6/21/13	11:28 p.m.: Mailbox in front of Katherine and Louis Kealoha's Kāhala residence "stolen."
6/22/13	8:59 a.m.: CIU officer Silva claims he retrieved hard drive from Kealoha residence.
6/22/13	1:28 p.m.: Katherine Kealoha calls 911 to report theft.
6/22/13	1:35 p.m.: HPD officers Rosskopf and Jurison respond to 911 call and process crime scene.

6/25/13	CID homicide detectives Akagi and McCormick assigned to investigate mailbox theft.
6/27/13 –6/29/13	Gerard photographs and writes down license plate numbers of cars he believes are conducting surveillance of him and his residence.
6/27/13	Gerard calls 911 to report his residence is under surveillance. HPD officer Gibo responds.
6/28/13	Gerard and his brother-in-law, Rick Hartsell, involved in car chase with HPD officers when Gerard believes his home is under surveillance.
6/28/13	Detective Akagi interviews Carrie Arakaki at her home regarding Gerard's possible use of her car to steal mailbox.
6/29/13	5:00 p.m.: Katherine Kealoha identifies Gerard as the person in the videotape surveillance footage.
6/29/13	5:10 p.m.: Gerard arrested in church parking lot by District 6 CRU officers. Gerard is charged with the state crime of felony theft and detained at HPD headquarters.
6/29/13	6:29 p.m.: Carrie Arakaki given polygraph examination.
7/1/13	Gerard is charged with the federal crime of destruction of a mailbox and released on bond in federal court. State charges are dismissed. Office of the Federal Defender is appointed to represent Gerard.
7/2/13	Detective Akagi completes and files his CID closing report.
9/13	Florence Puana sells her home.
9/19/13	A deputy prosecutor, on orders from Katherine, asks state court to rescind DANC plea and re-enter felony conviction against Gerard Puana. This request is denied on November 19, 2013.
11/25/13	Florence Puana's deposition is taken to preserve her testimony for trial should she be unable to testify.
9/24/14	Louis Kealoha holds press conference and claims he turned mailbox investigation over to deputy chief McCauley on the evening of June 21, 2013.

12/1/14	Katherine Kealoha files petition in state probate court to have a conservator appointed to oversee Florence Puana's estate, claiming Florence Puana was incompetent and under the improper influence of Gerard Puana.
12/2/14	Gerard Puana federal criminal trial begins with jury selection.
12/3/14	Trial postponed due to illness of lead prosecutor AUSA Osborne.
12/4/14	AUSA Tong appears as lead trial attorney. Opening statements made. Retired CIU officer Niall Silva testifies. Louis Kealoha testifies and causes a mistrial while on direct examination. Court dismisses case without prejudice and sets new trial date of April 28, 2015.
12/12/14	Meeting with AUSAs Osborne and Tong.
12/16/14	Judge signs government motion to dismiss federal charges against Gerard Puana with prejudice. FBI asked to investigate.
1/14/15	Meeting with FBI.
2/12/15	Jury rules in favor of Katherine Kealoha in civil trial. Katherine Kealoha is awarded over $600,000 in damages.
7/23/15	First meeting with special prosecutor Wheat. Gerard takes and passes polygraph examination.
9/15/15	First grand jury empaneled by special prosecutor Michael Wheat to investigate our claims that Gerard Puana was an innocent man framed by the Kealohas for a crime he did not commit.
5/19/16	US Marshal seen driving City and County prosecutor Keith Kaneshiro and HPD deputy chief McCauley into federal building through the basement parking structure for their first appearance in the grand jury.
6/15/16	Chuck Totto, executive director of the City and County Ethics Commission, who was investigating the Kealohas on ethics violations, resigns under pressure.
6/22/16	Katherine Kealoha writes a letter to her boss, Keith

	Kaneshiro, claiming criminal case against Gerard Puana botched by inept federal prosecutors.
8/31/16	Retired CIU officer Silva receives target letter from special prosecutor Wheat.
9/22/16	Gerard Puana testifies before the grand jury.
12/15/16	Silva pleads guilty to conspiracy to obstruct justice. Admits his entire trial testimony was false.
12/18/16	Chief Louis Kealoha receives target letter. Goes on leave with pay.
1/6/17	Louis Kealoha retires and, in addition to being allowed to retire in good standing, allowing him to receive his full pension, is also given an additional $250,000 payoff.
1/13/17	FBI, armed with search warrants, raid the offices of the City and County prosecutor and the municipal building where HPD backup servers are stored.
10/19/17	Kealohas indicted and arraigned in federal court on multiple counts of civil rights violations and conspiracy to obstruct justice, along with CIU officers Derek Hahn, Bobby Nguyen, Daniel Sellers and Gordon Shiraishi. Kealohas also charged with bank fraud and identity theft charges.
10/25/17	Police Commission names Susan Ballard as new HPD police chief. Ballard is the first woman appointed as chief in the history of the department.
1/5/18	Ransen Taito pleads guilty to obstructing justice for lying to the grand jury at Katherine Kealoha's request regarding monies illegally taken by Katherine from his and his sister's trust accounts.
7/9/18	Jesse Ebersole, a Big Island firefighter, is charged with lying to the grand jury about his affair with Katherine Kealoha. FBI believes funds used by Katherine Kealoha to pay for various hotels and trips with Ebersole came from monies she had stolen from Gerard and Florence Puana and the Taitos.
9/17/18	Katherine Kealoha resigns.

2/7/19   Katherine Kealoha indicted for a third time, along with her brother, Dr. Rudy Puana, on drug charges stemming from his alleged improper writing of opioid prescriptions.

2/11/19   CIU officer Daniel Sellers pleads guilty to lesser charges and agrees to cooperate.

2/12/19   State attorney general Clare Connors files a petition with the Hawaiʻi Supreme Court to remove Keith Kaneshiro from office.

3/7/19   Keith Kaneshiro places himself on leave with pay. Petition to the Hawaiʻi Supreme Court is withdrawn.

3/25/19   Louis Kealoha's attorney, Rustam Barbee, writes letter to the University of Hawaiʻi Richardson School of Law demanding that professor and Hawaii News Now legal expert Ken Lawson be silenced or fired for commenting on the guilt of the Kealohas prior to their trial.

5/13/19   The trial of the Kealohas begins with jury selection at Neal S. Blaisdell Center.

5/31/19   Alexander Silvert testifies for the prosecution at the trial of the Kealohas.

6/20/19   Trial testimony comes to a conclusion. Closing arguments to be held in the coming days.

6/27/19   Verdict returned. All defendants found guilty except for Gordon Shiraishi, who is found not guilty.

6/28/19   Katherine Kealoha is remanded into custody by the court due to her long-term obstructionist behavior.

8/24/19   Florence Puana celebrates her 100th birthday.

9/13/19   Civil verdict in favor of Katherine Kealoha and against Florence and Gerard Puana reversed and vacated due to fraud upon the court by Katherine Kealoha.

10/22/19   Louis and Katherine Kealoha plead guilty to the remaining bank fraud charges. Both also admit that they had conspired to frame Gerard. In addition, Katherine Kealoha pleads guilty to identity theft and to obstructing police investigations into her brother's alleged improper opioid prescriptions.

12/10/19	Peter Wolff, the federal public defender, is told he will not be retained by the Ninth Circuit for another four-year term after serving for over twenty-four years.
2/13/20	Florence Puana passes away.
10/31/20	Peter Wolff's term comes to an end. Alexander Silvert opts to retire on the same day.
11/30/20	Katherine Kealoha sentenced to thirteen years in prison. Louis Kealoha sentenced to seven years in prison.
12/1/20	Derek Hahn sentenced to four years in prison. Bobby Nguyen sentenced to four and a half years in prison.
1//21	All charges against Ransen Taito dismissed by the court at the request of special prosecutor Wheat.
2/3/21	Niall Silva sentenced to nine months in prison. Jesse Ebersole sentenced to probation.
5/21	Louis Kealoha is deposed in Gerard's civil case and denies all wrongdoing despite having pled guilty and admitting under oath that he had conspired to frame Gerard for the mailbox theft.
6/1/21	Louis Kealoha, Derek Hahn and Bobby Nguyen surrender to begin serving their prison sentences.
6/21	Former City managing director Roy Amemiya receives a "target letter" from Wheat.
9/21	The federal grand jury continues to hear evidence, and Wheat's investigation continues.

Acknowledgments

Writing this book has been an adventure and a tremendous learning experience. I've always believed you're never too old to learn new things, but that doesn't mean it's easy. In the course of writing and editing, and editing, and editing this book I've learned so much and have come to thoroughly enjoy the process. I had no idea writing could be so enjoyable and that a sentence could be rewritten and restructured in so many different ways. But at some point, you gotta stop.

First and foremost, I have to thank my wife, Diana. None of this would have been possible without her love and support. She literally lived this story as much as I did from the moment Gerard Puana was charged with federal crimes in July of 2013 to the end. She was with me every step of the way, as each event described in the book happened in real time. My wife, also a writer in her own right, lovingly edited this story as I struggled at times to put it all down on paper. She smoothed out many of the rough edges, and sometimes she had to use a sledge-hammer to do it. And we're still happily married!

I also have to thank my agent and editor, Roger Jellinek. Since I'm a first-time author and didn't have a clue what I was getting myself into or what I was doing other than knowing that I had a story to tell, he patiently walked me through the editing and publishing process. His painstaking edits and suggestions were incredibly insightful and helpful. Interestingly, although we had never met in person—or even over Zoom during the creation of this book, as this was written entirely during the COVID-19 pandemic—I feel I know him well and that we have been friends for years.

And to my son Che, who had to endure, for years, his father talking and retelling everything that happened in the case to anyone and every-one who would listen. At times he would simply raise his hand to quiet me, saying he could tell the story better and, more importantly, faster than me. And he could, and he did.

A very special thanks goes out to my friends Marilyn Carlsmith, Michael Hirst and Max Mizono. All read early drafts of the book and made extremely helpful suggestions. But most importantly, their enthusiasm and encouragement really spurred me on to keep working on the book, knowing that they thought I was headed in the right direction.

To Adam Choka, Kate Wright and Brian Wise, whose investigations were the backbone of everything we uncovered. Their complete dedication to the job at hand and their unwavering desire to fight injustice were something to behold and helped strengthen my own resolve. True professionals in every sense of the word. And to Lynelle Oshita, my administrative assistant, for her attention to detail in making sure our court pleadings were timely, accurate and professional.

To my entire FPD office, particularly Peter Wolff, who backed me up every step of the way while those in power believed we had no real evidence that some of the highest-ranking members of Hawai'i's law enforcement community were conspiring to frame Gerard. I am grateful for everyone's patience as they listened to my musings about the case day after day, year after year.

And to my neighbors and friends Helen and her late husband Art, who supported me by coming to court on the first day of trial even though we had only met a few months earlier. As non-lawyers, their opinion of what happened in court confirmed my own thoughts of how things had gone. They soon became founding members of the "cone of silence," as I revealed secrets about the case that no one else yet knew.

To Lynn Kawano, Nick Grube, Rick Daysog, Manolo Morales, Ken Lawson and Jennifer Sinco Kelleher, who, as members of the press, came to embrace Gerard's story and helped to turn public opinion in his favor. They have no idea how much their dogged reporting helped Gerard make it through his ordeal and how supportive it was of my own efforts to get his truth known when those in power were doing everything they could to marginalize and cover up what happened.

To Michael Wheat and his entire prosecution team for their dedication and commitment to unearthing the truth, no matter where it led them.

And, most importantly, I want to thank Gerard and the entire Puana family, particularly his mother, Florence. Gerard's determination and steadfastness to have the truth come out no matter what the odds gave this story life and breath. His resolve to expose the truth, even when no one believed him and in the face of possible incarceration, was an inspiration to us all. He is truly "my bro," as he would say.

Last but not least, I simply have to thank Uber, my not-so-miniature sixteen-year-old long-haired dachshund. He kept me company at all hours of the day and night as I typed away, never knowing or caring what I was doing so long as he was with me, always wagging his tail or wanting a belly rub. He'll be getting extra treats. ❖

Index

About the Author

Alexander Silvert was raised in New York City and Vermont. After graduating from UCLA and driving a cab in New York for a year, and taking a further year of political science at New York University, he switched to Boston College Law School. Upon graduating from law school in 1984, he worked as a state and federal public defender in Philadelphia before moving to Honolulu in 1989 with his wife and three-week-old son to work at the Hawai'i Federal Public Defender office. He served as the first assistant FPD from 1992 to his retirement in October 2020. During his tenure he handled numerous high-publicity cases, including representing two defendants in potential federal death penalty cases. In 2000 the author was named Federal Defender of the Year by the National Association of Federal Defenders. Silvert currently provides legal consultation services to defense attorneys in federal criminal cases.

In July 2013, the author began his representation of Gerard Puana, who was charged with destruction of a mailbox owned by Honolulu chief of police Louis Kealoha and his wife, Katherine Kealoha, third-ranked Honolulu city prosecutor. The case continued for over seven years, with the author starting as defender and ending as the key instigator of the federal prosecution of the Kealohas and their accomplices in what turned out to be the greatest public corruption case in Hawai'i's history. ❖